AF352190

Writing everything in a book is like leaving
a sword in a child's hand.

Clemente Alessandrino, *Stromateis**

*quotation in Jorge Luis Borges, *Other Inquisitions*, 1960

Scrivere in un libro tutte le cose è lasciare
una spada in mano a un bambino.

Clemente Alessandrino, *Stromateis**

*citazione in Jorge Luis Borges, *Altre inquisizioni*, 1960

NEƎN

EDITED BY MILTOS MANETAS   A CURA DI MILTOS MANETAS

CHARTA

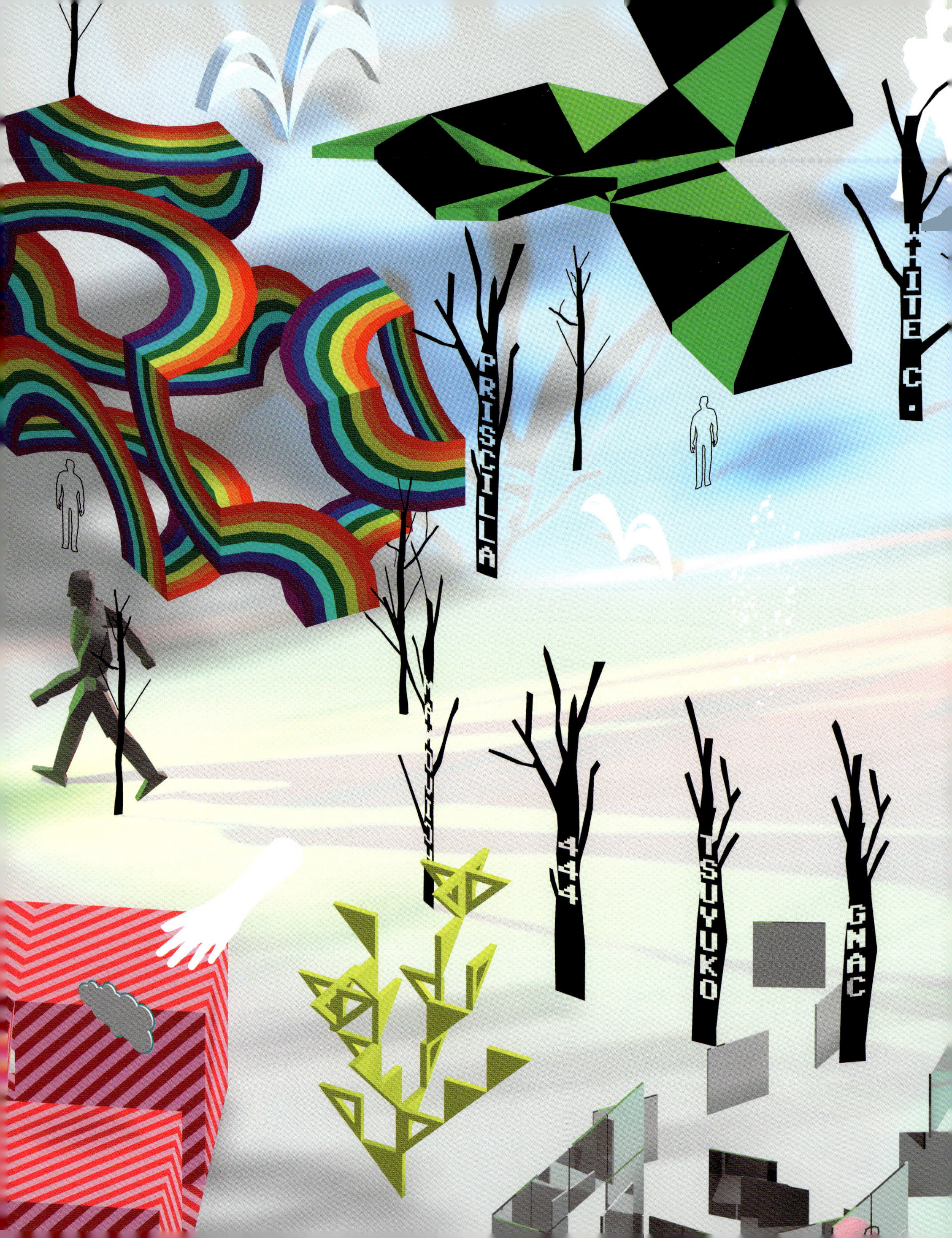
PRISCILLA
ITE C.
444
TSUYUKO
GMAC

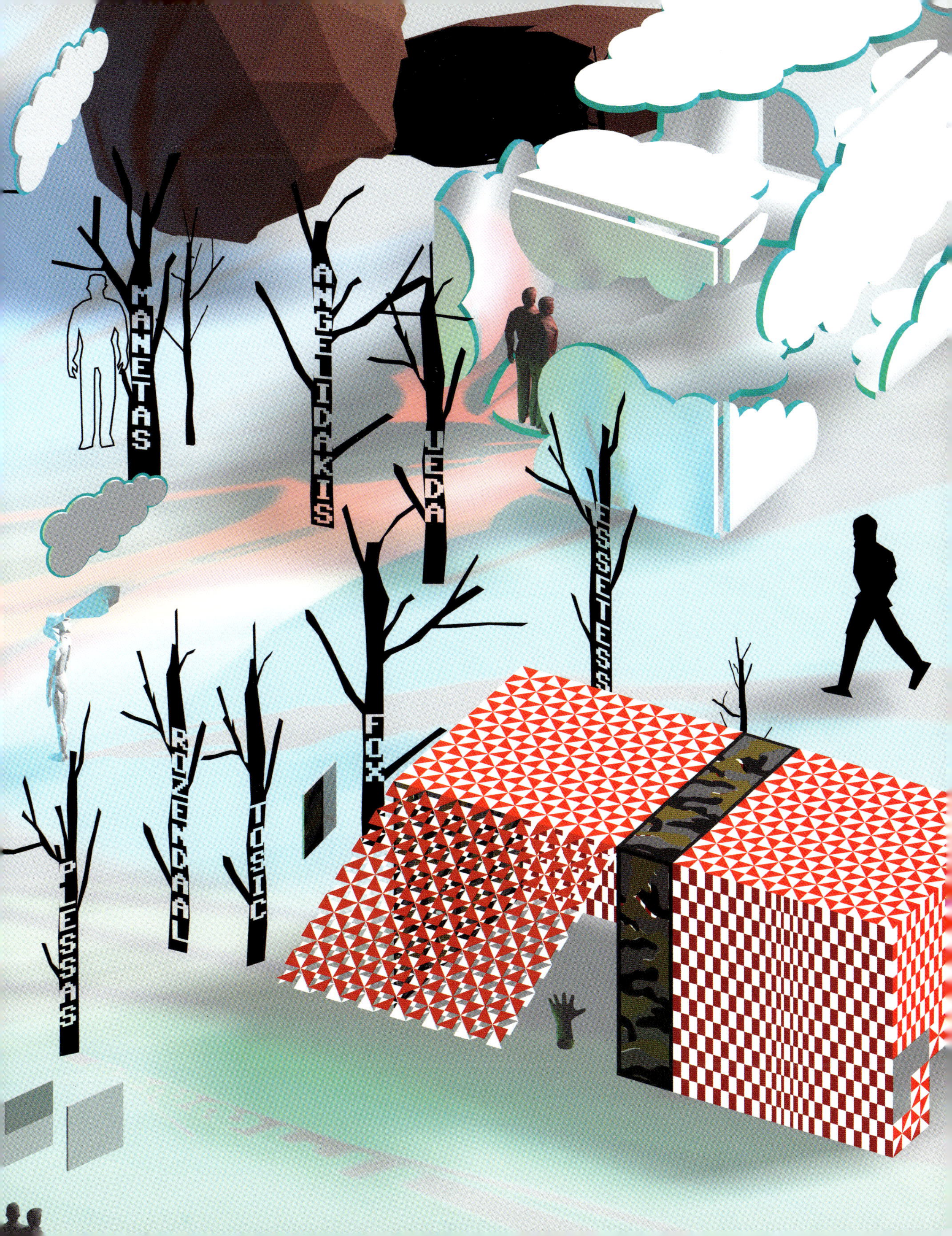
MANETAS
ANGELIDAKIS
UEDA
ESSETESS
FOX
RIZEKDAAL
UOSIC
PLESSAS

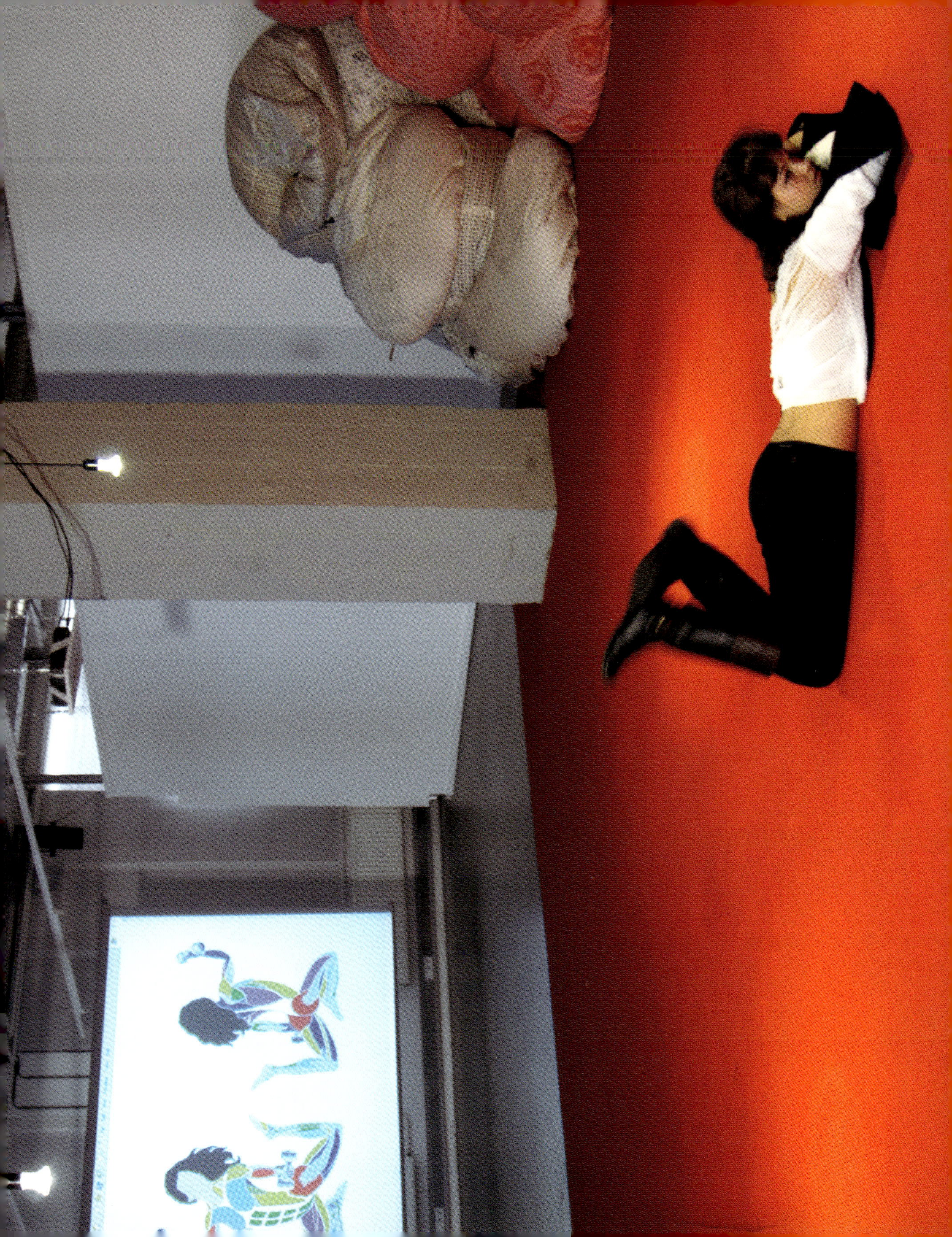

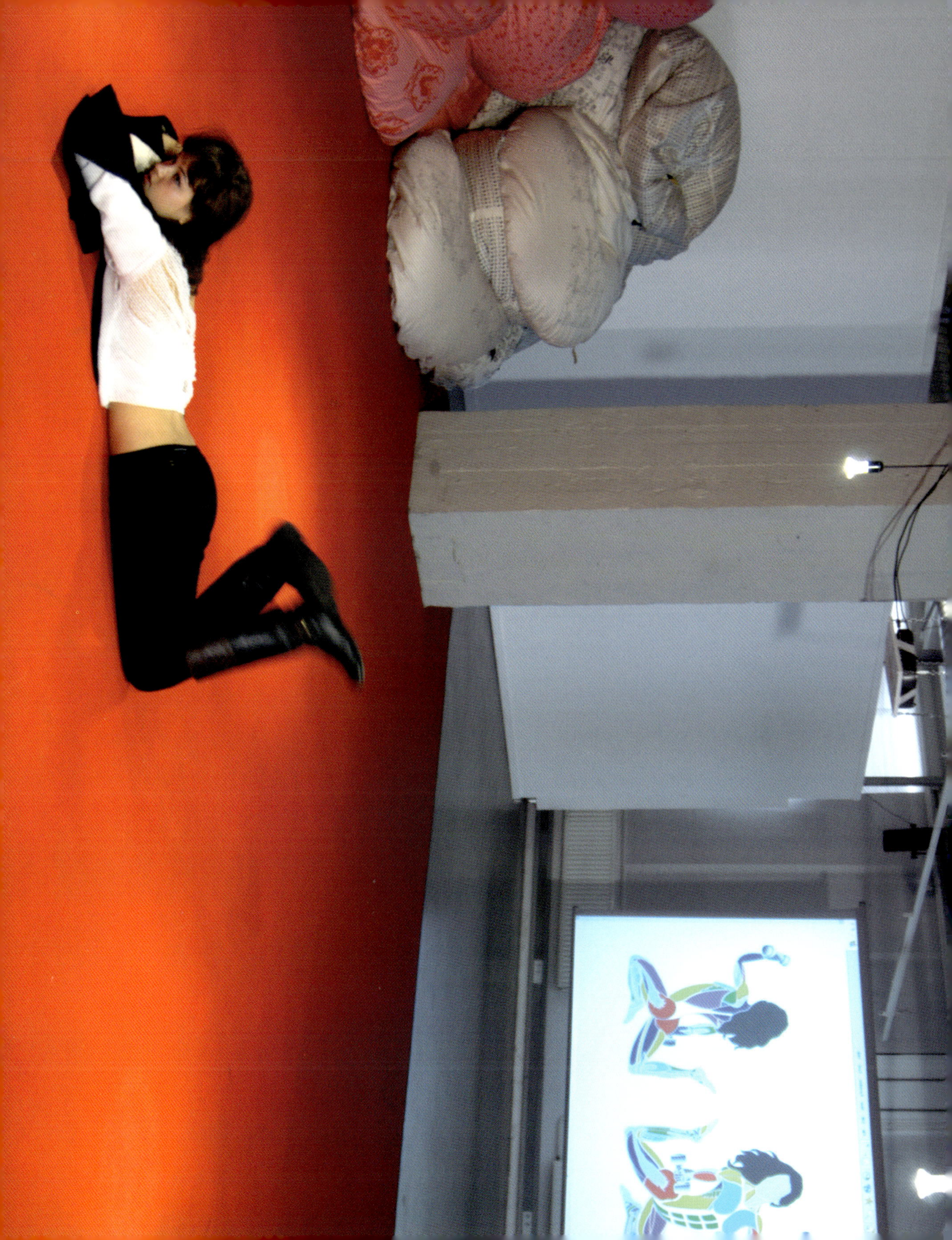

. . . in the space of MU, in

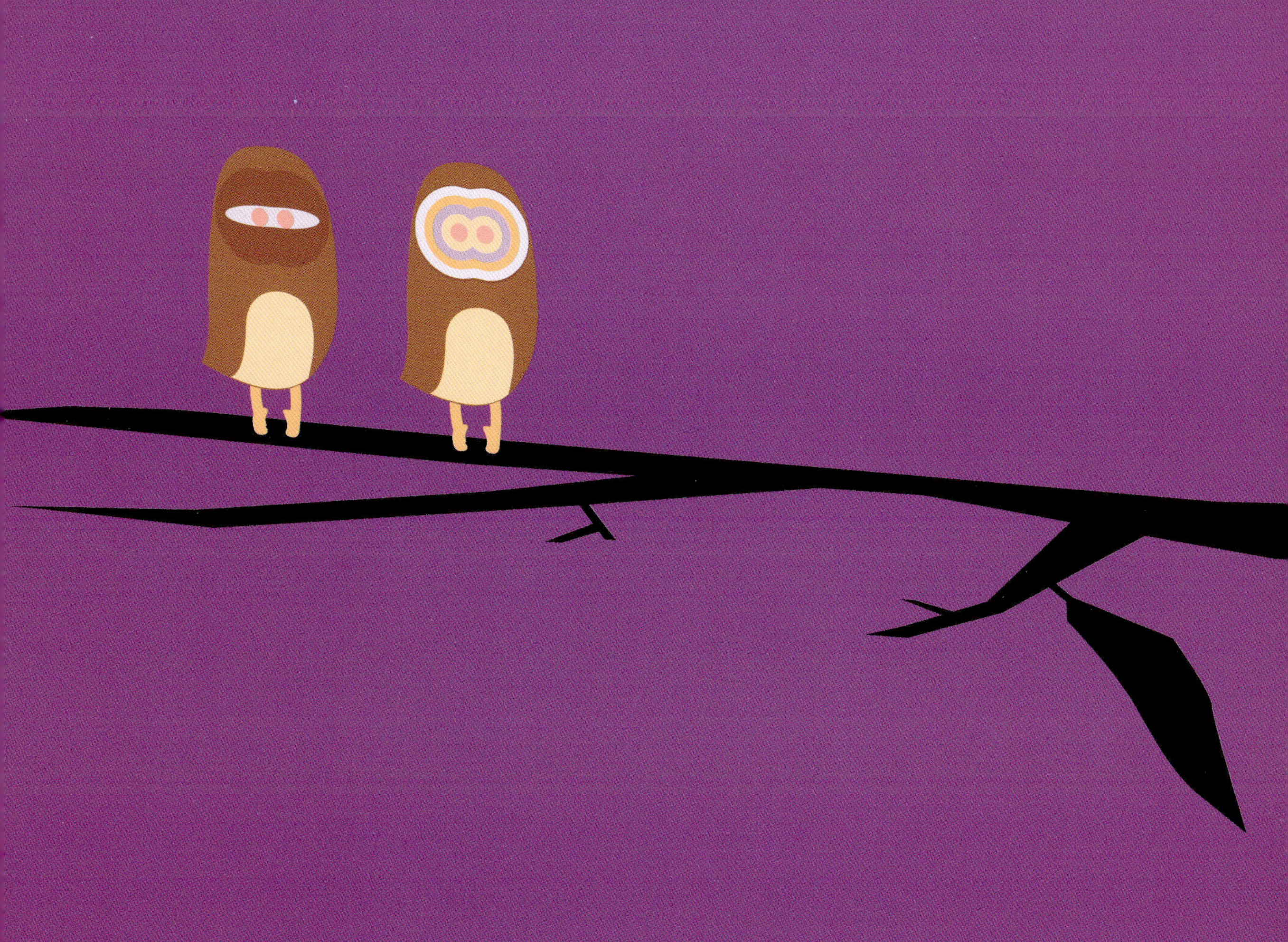

ndhoven, after NeenToday

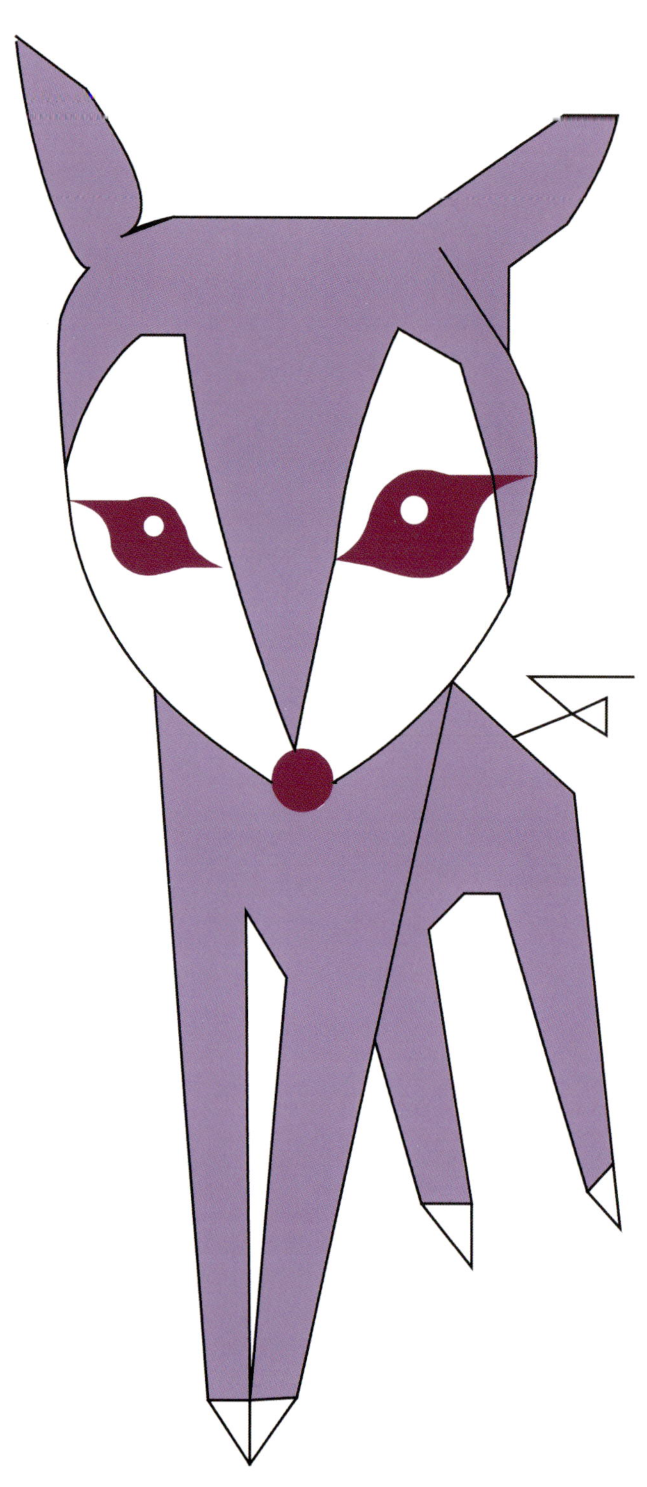

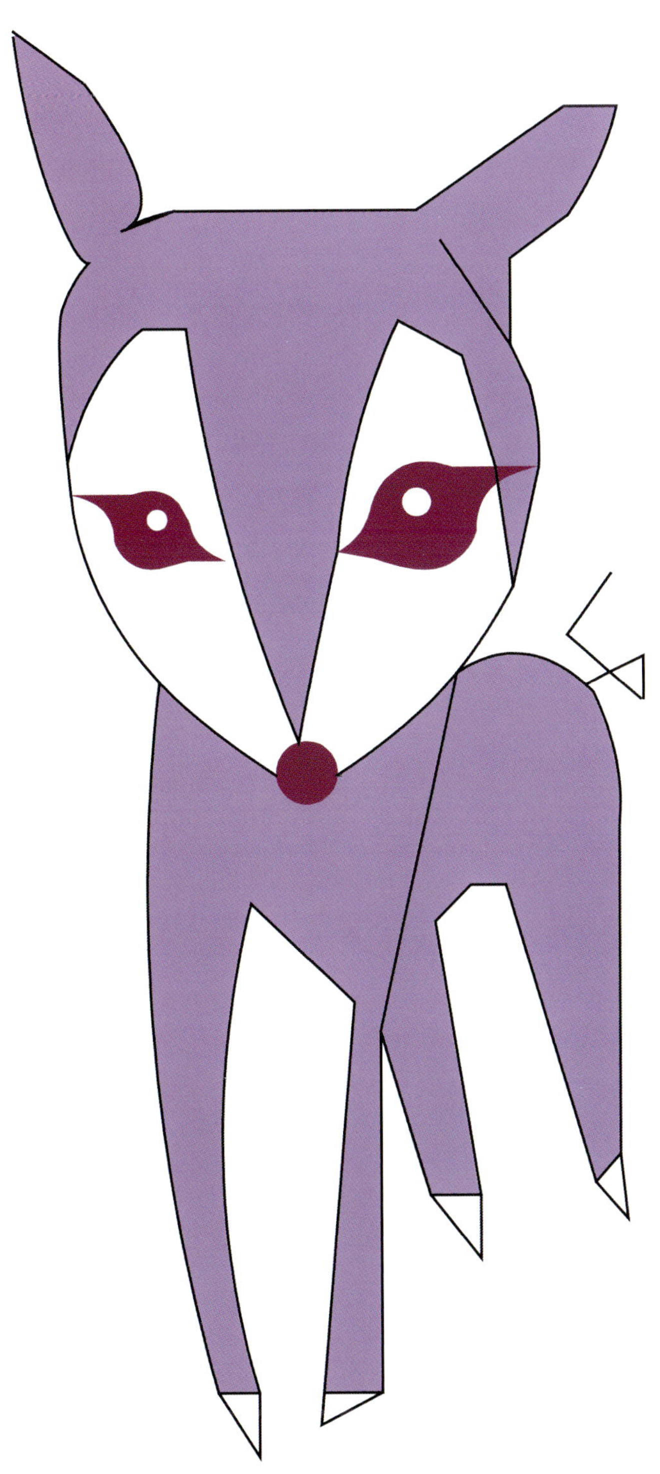

THIS BOOK

This book is not a Neen book. Alas, Neen is not what it looks like
when you see it in pictures; neither can it be described by words.
Risking appearing mystical, I would say that the whole of Neen is larger
than the sum of its parts. That's also because Neen started from the
word itself—it was only a sound without sense when we bought it from
the Lexicon company, it was just a feeling really, and later it met some
of its expressions in the works and the activity of the people who are
included in this volume.
Most of these works are animations and Web sites, but Neen
can also be found in industrial design and fashion, in music and poetry,
or in certain contemporary life coincidences such as looking at your
watch and noticing that it's 4:44 am. Even some people's style
can be Neen (such as: "This person is very Neen!").

THE ANIMATED WORLD

Last century's concepts of cyberspace, contemporary art,
fashion, and style slipped together with us into our present and they
are now the same they were before, but still a bit different.
This universe is animated in a different way than the one before 2000,
and Neen is definitely an element of this newly Animated World.

THE NEEN ELEMENT

This book describes the first steps of Neen, how it all started with
a presentation at the Gagosian Gallery in New York, how a group
of foreigners who found themselves playing together with some native
guys in Los Angeles discovered the first sides of Neen, and how these
people and their friends began showing these findings by using art
galleries and the museums around the world as temporary
Neen hotels.

Miltos Manetas, Milan, March 2006

QUESTO LIBRO

Questo libro non è un libro Neen: purtroppo Neen non è quello che
sembra quando lo vedi nelle immagini e non può essere nemmeno
descritto a parole.
A rischio di sembrare mistico, direi che Neen, nel suo insieme,
è maggiore della somma delle sue parti.
Anche perché Neen è partito dalla parola stessa: era solo un suono
senza senso quando lo abbiamo comprato dall'azienda Lexicon,
di fatto era solo una sensazione che in seguito ha incontrato alcune
delle proprie espressioni nei lavori e nell'attività delle persone
comprese in questo volume.
La maggior parte di questi lavori sono animazioni e siti Web, ma Neen
si può trovare anche nell'industrial design e nella moda, nella musica
e nella poesia o in certe coincidenze della vita contemporanea, come
quando guardi l'orologio e ti rendi conto che sono le 4:44 del mattino.
Anche lo stile di alcune persone può essere Neen
(del tipo: "questo tizio è molto Neen!")

IL MONDO ANIMATO

I concetti del secolo scorso di cyberspazio, arte contemporanea,
moda e stile sono scivolati insieme a noi nel nostro presente
e, oggi, sono al tempo stesso gli stessi di prima e leggermente diversi.
Questo universo è animato in modo diverso da quello precedente al
2000 e Neen è decisamente un elemento di questo nuovo Mondo
Animato.

L'ELEMENTO NEEN

Questo libro descrive i primi passi di Neen, come tutto sia iniziato con
una presentazione alla Gagosian Gallery di New York, come un gruppo
di stranieri che si sono trovati a giocare insieme a dei ragazzi
losangelini abbiano scoperto le prime facce di Neen e come queste
persone e i loro amici abbiano iniziato a esporre i risultati ai quali
erano giunti, usando le gallerie d'arte e i musei di tutto il mondo
come temporanei hotel Neen.

Miltos Manetas, Milano, marzo 2006

May 31, 2000
Gagosian Gallery, Chelsea, New York

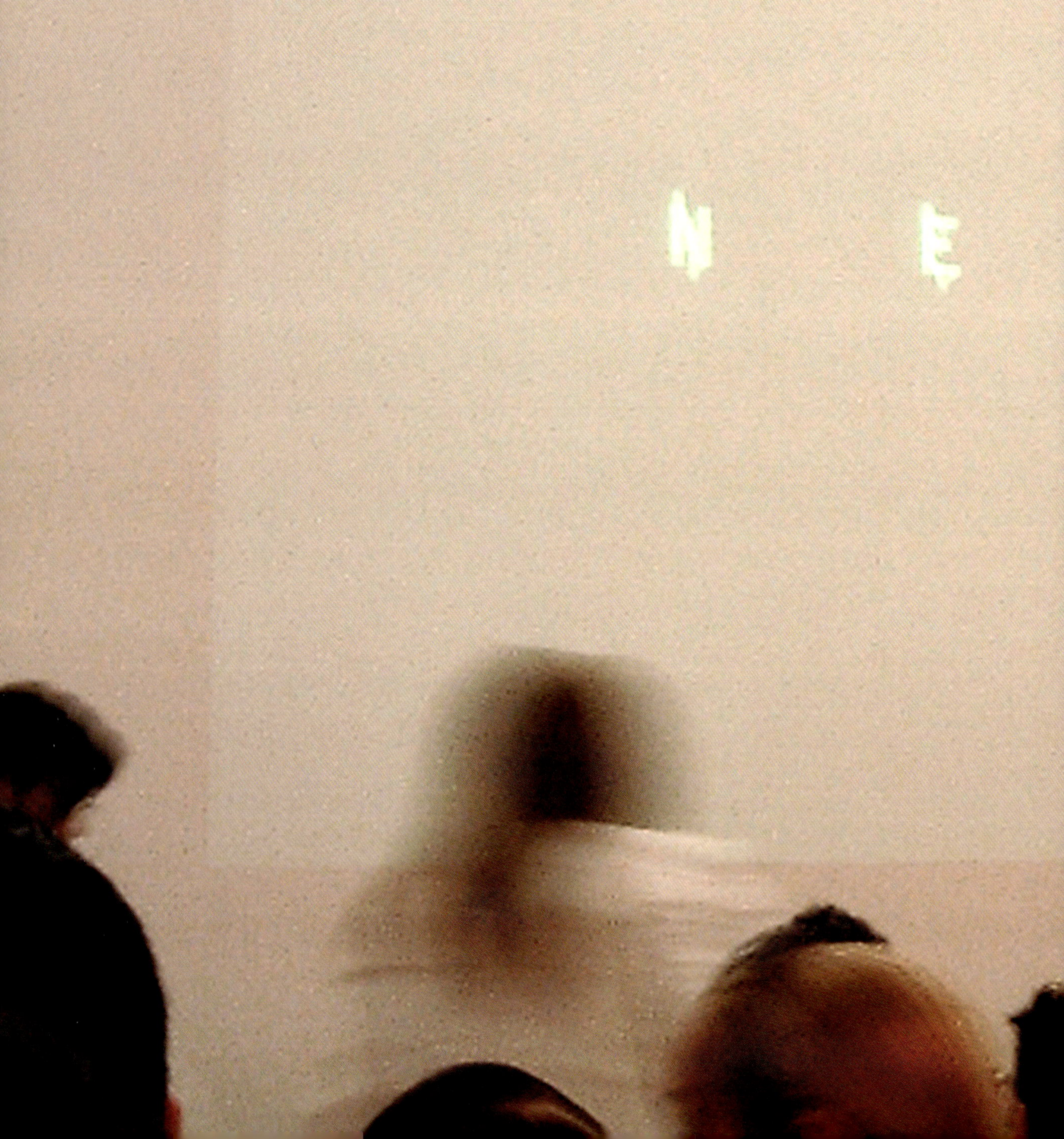

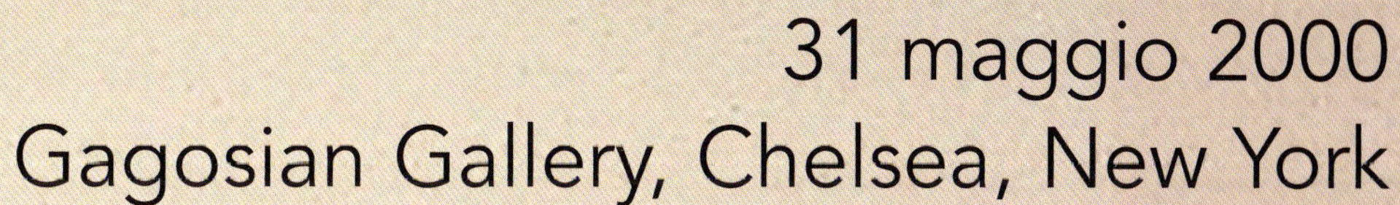

31 maggio 2000
Gagosian Gallery, Chelsea, New York

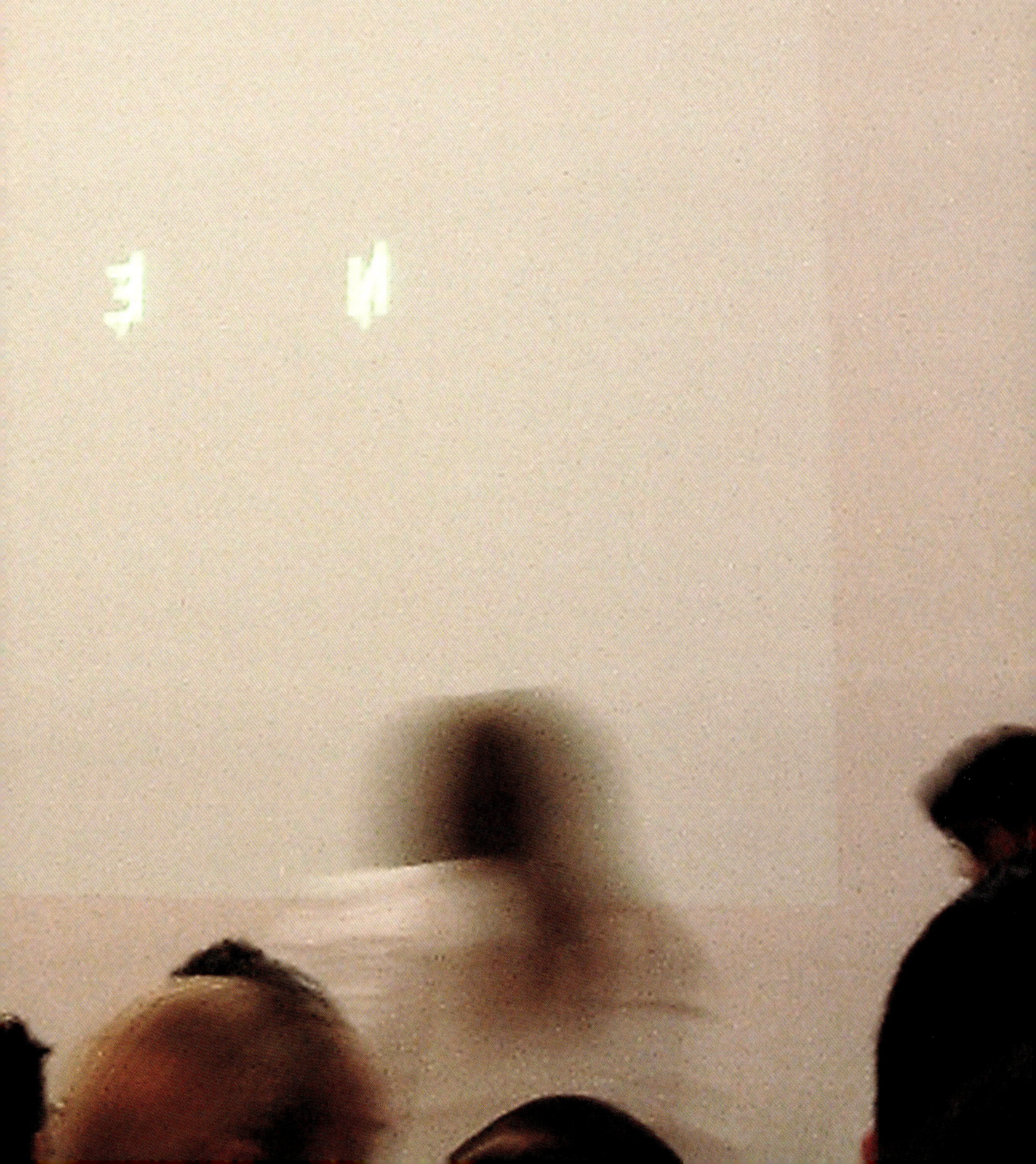

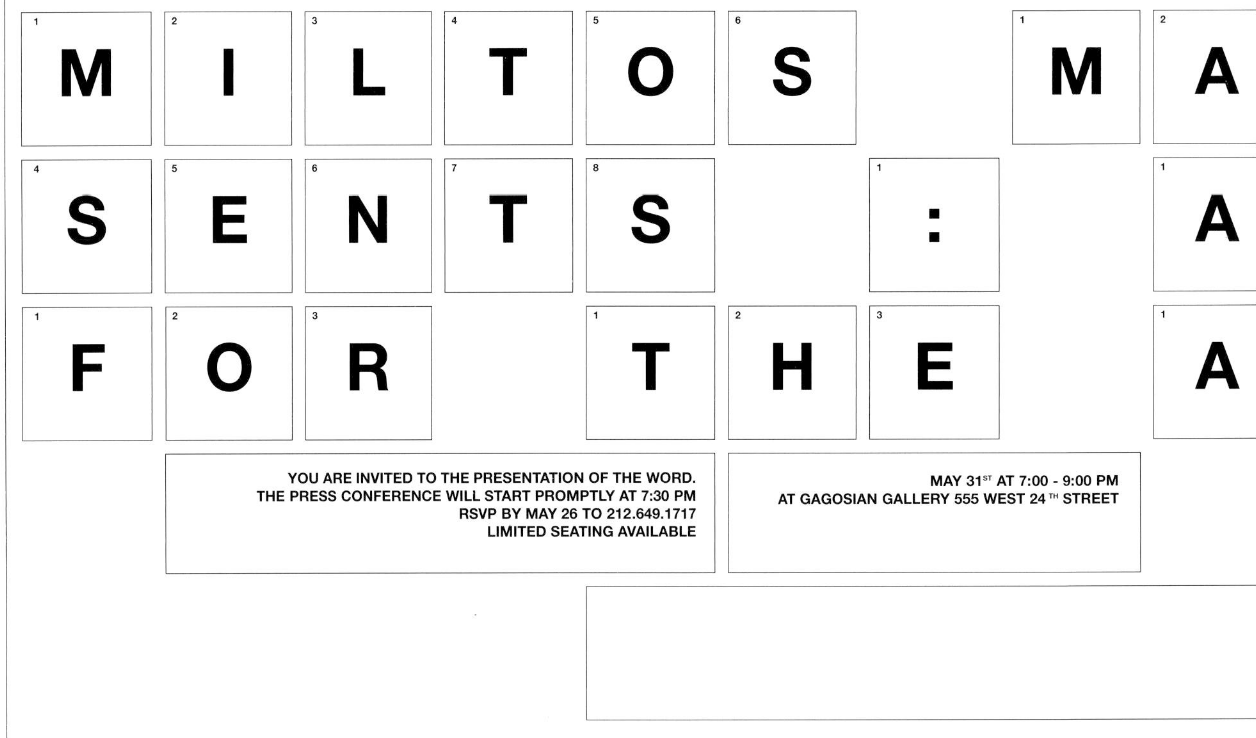

Invitation designed by Richard Pandiscio

Neen came into existence in May 2000

May 31, 2000 – 7 pm

Gagosian Gallery, Chelsea, New York City

A conference with: Yvonne Force - producer, Art Production Fund; Miltos Manetas - artist;
David Placek - President of Lexicon Branding; J.C. Herz - writer and giornalist, author of *Joystick Nation*;
Peter Lunenfeld - writer, author of *The Digital Dialectic* and *Snap to Grid*; Steven Pinker - MIT Professor,
Department of Brain and Cognitive Sciences, author of *Words and Rules*, *The Language Instinct,*
and *How the Mind Works*; Joseph Kosuth - artist.

Music: Gnac

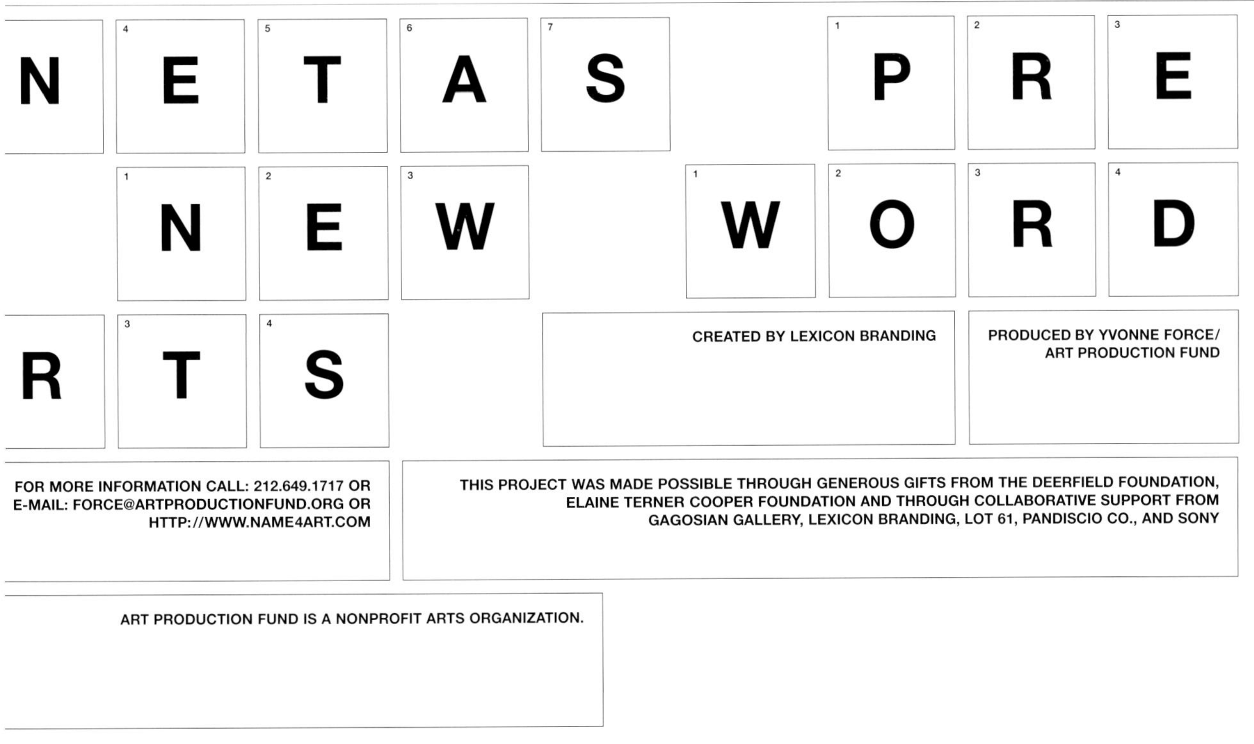

Invito progettato da Richard Pandiscio

Neen è nato nel maggio del 2000

31 maggio 2000 - h 19.00

Gagosian Gallery, Chelsea, New York City

Una conferenza con: Yvonne Force - produttrice, Art Production Fund; Miltos Manetas - artista;
David Placek - presidente della società Lexicon Branding; J.C. Herz - scrittore e giornalista,
autore di *Il popolo del joystick*; Peter Lunenfeld - scrittore, autore di *The Digital Dialectic* e *Snap to Grid*;
Steven Pinker - professore presso il Dipartimento di Scienze Cognitive del MIT, Boston, autore di
Words and Rules, *L'istinto del linguaggio* e *Come funziona la mente*; Joseph Kosuth - artista.

Musica: Gnac

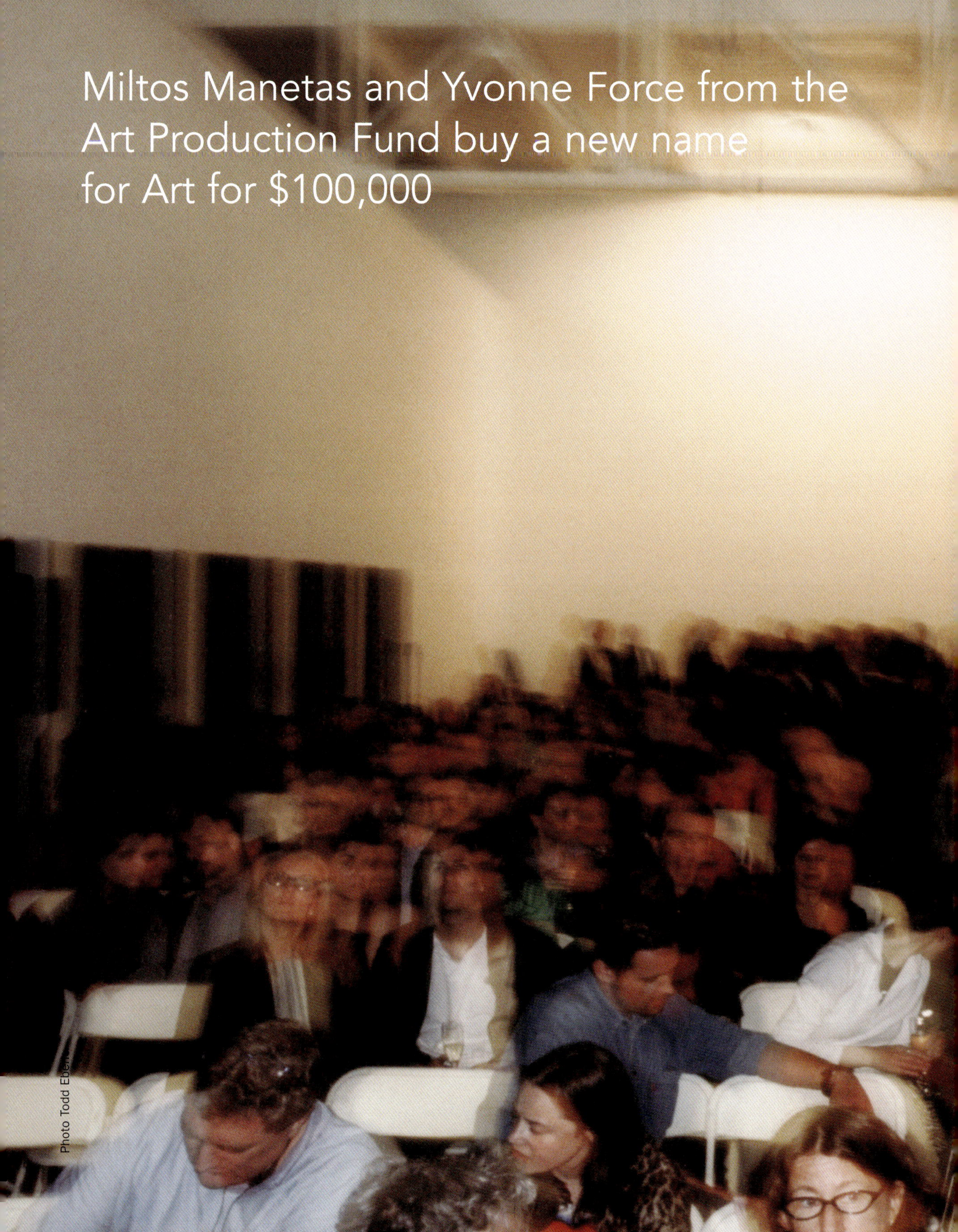
Miltos Manetas and Yvonne Force from the
Art Production Fund buy a new name
for Art for $100,000
Photo Todd Eben

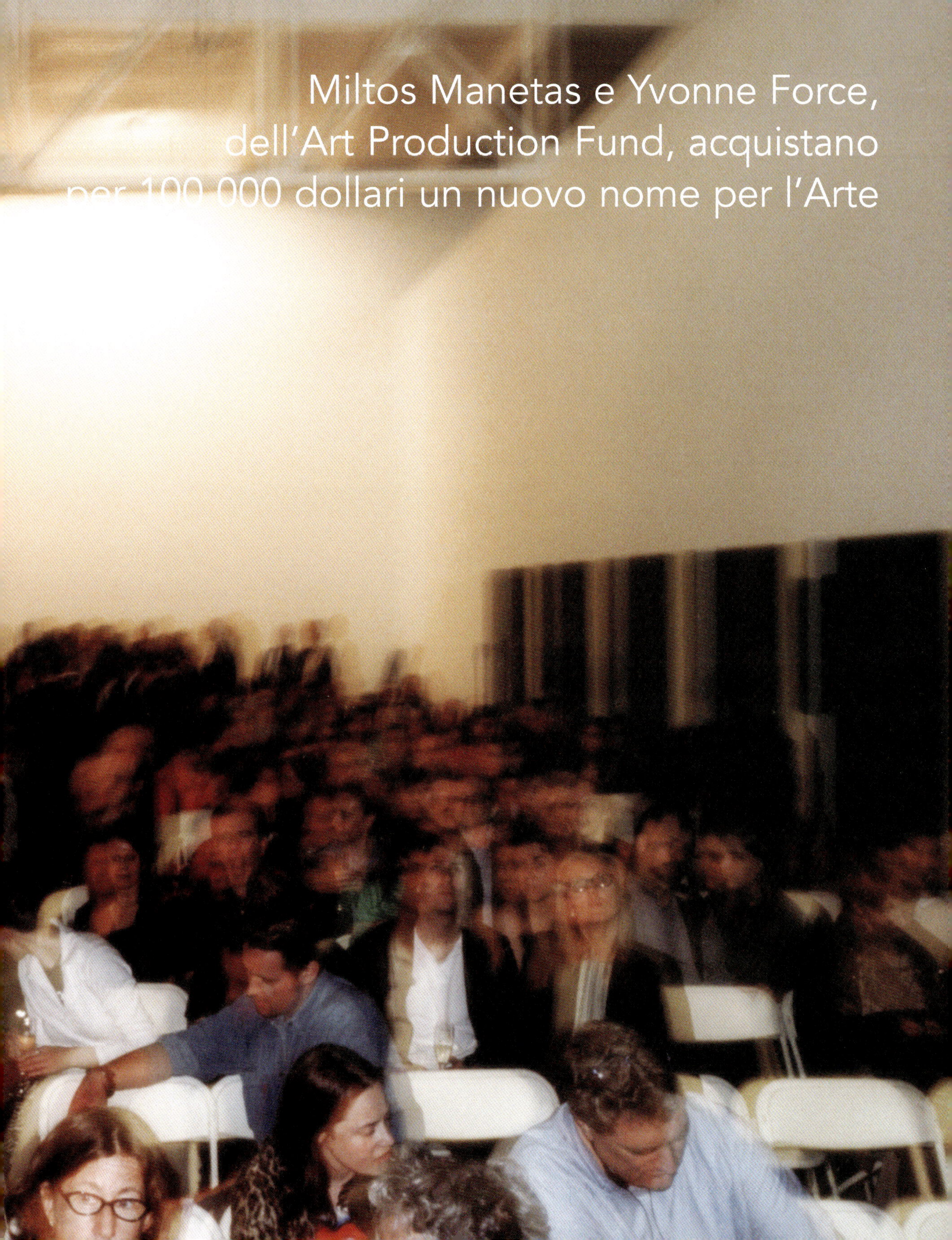

Miltos Manetas e Yvonne Force,
dell'Art Production Fund, acquistano
per 100.000 dollari un nuovo nome per l'Arte

May 31, 2000, video with the intervention of Joseph Kosuth at the Gagosian Gallery conference

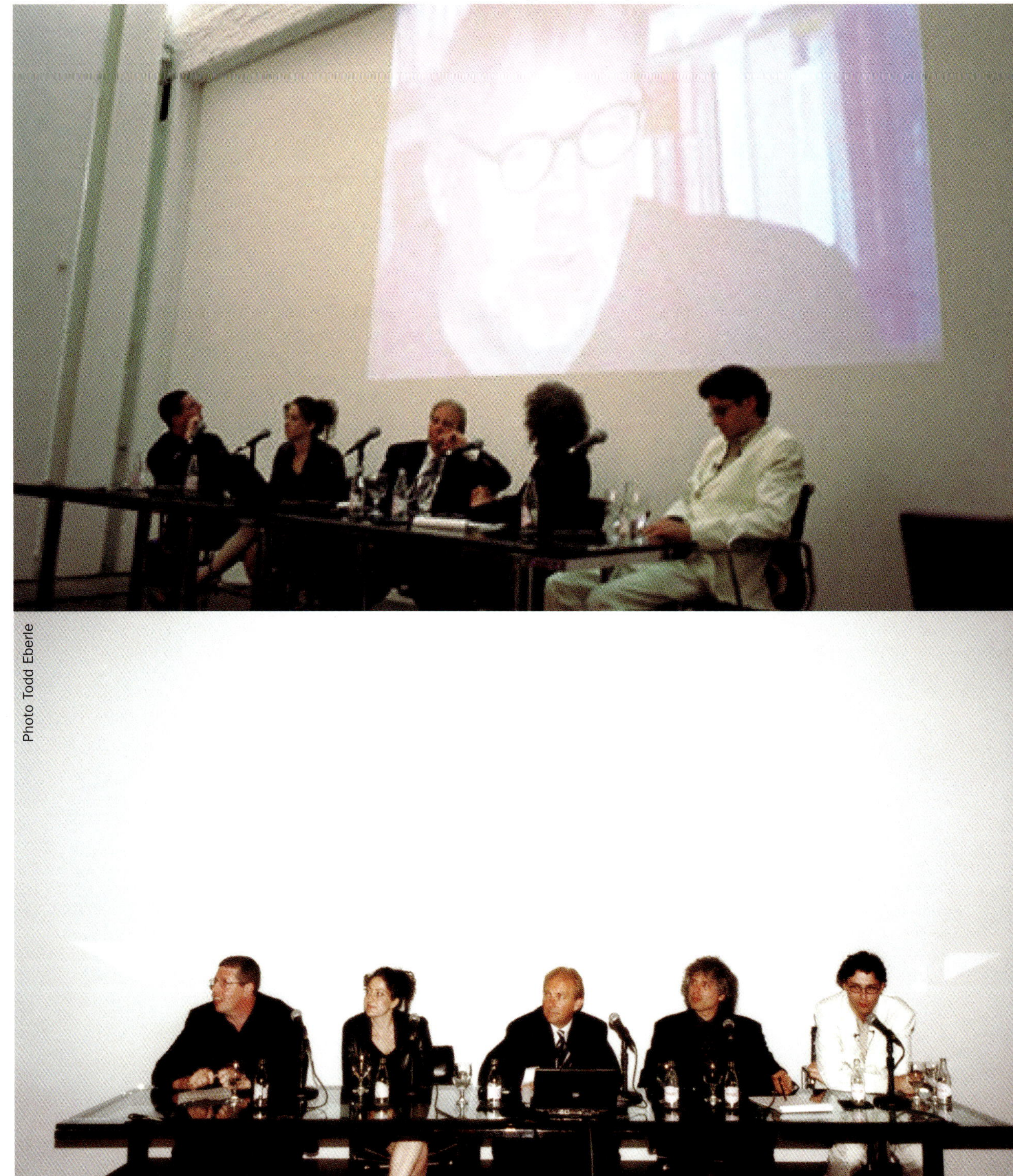

from left to right: Peter Lunenfeld, J.C. Herz, David Placek, Steven Pinker, and Miltos Manetas.
Each panelist was invited to talk for exactly five minutes

31 maggio 2000, video con intervento di Joseph Kosuth alla conferenza presso la Gagosian Gallery

da sinistra a destra: Miltos Manetas, Steven Pinker, David Placek, J.C. Herz e Peter Lunenfeld.
Ciascuno di loro è stato invitato a parlare esattamente per cinque minuti

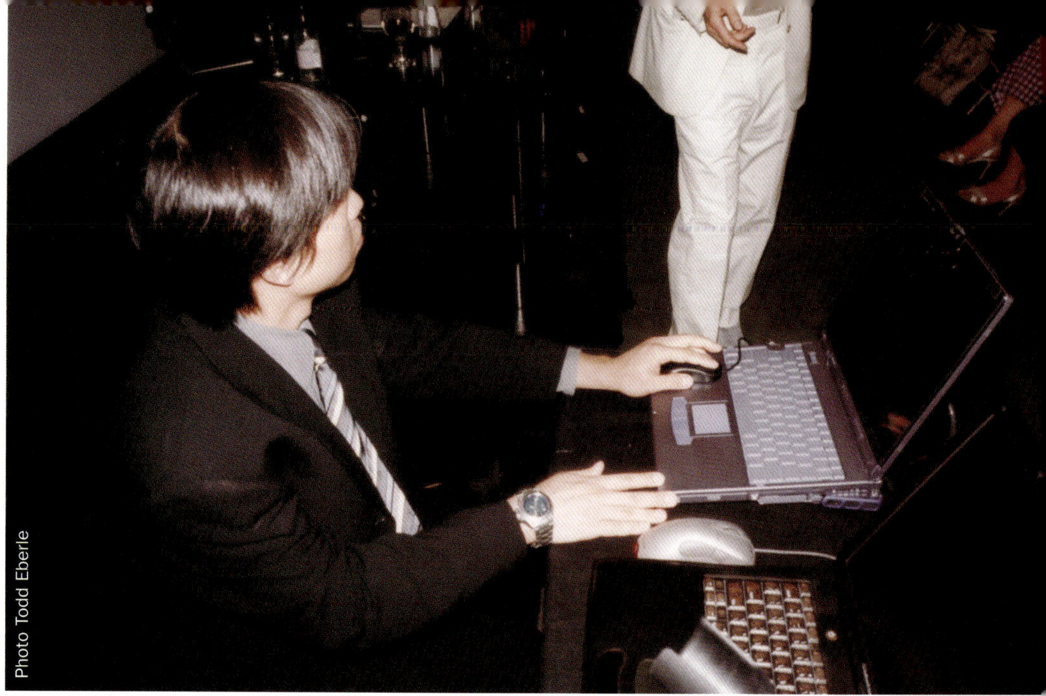

Miltos Manetas shows different animations, images, etc. that suggest a mental frame for the new word. At this point and for the rest of Mr. Manetas' presentation, the screen of the projection turned green, for some obscure technical reason! The next day, the projection company, embarrassed, returned $8,000 to Ms. Force. It was as if the machines were sending a signal and their message was that Neen should represent not only human creativity, but also the creativity of the intelligent machines.

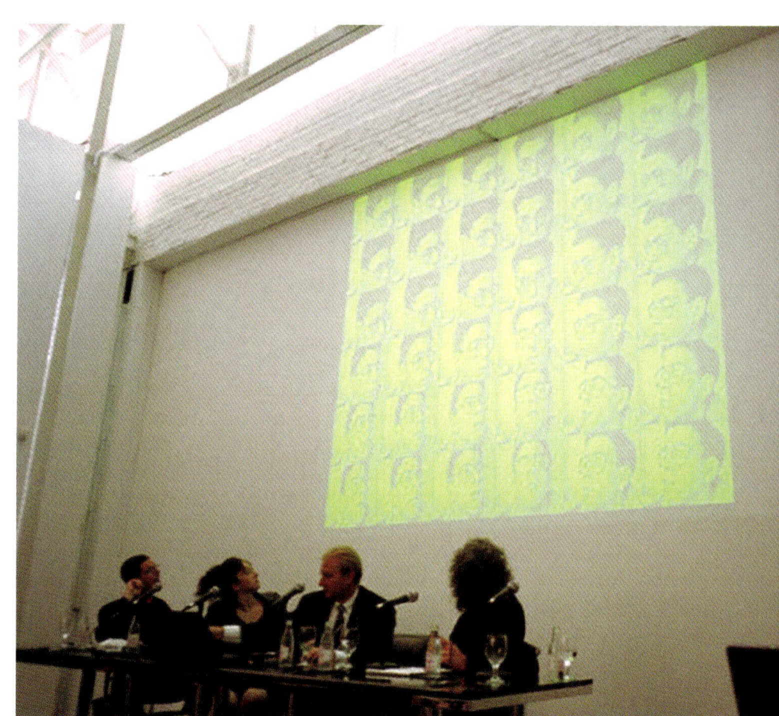

After the presentations and Miltos Manetas' demo, Mr. Sushi Matsuda, who was invited to the event to represent Sony, gave his Vaio laptop the command to present the new name. "Ladies and Gentlemen. May I have your attention please? The new name for contemporary art is 'Neen.' Shall I repeat? N-E-E-N. I hope that you like it. It is made by a computer program. Have a nice evening."

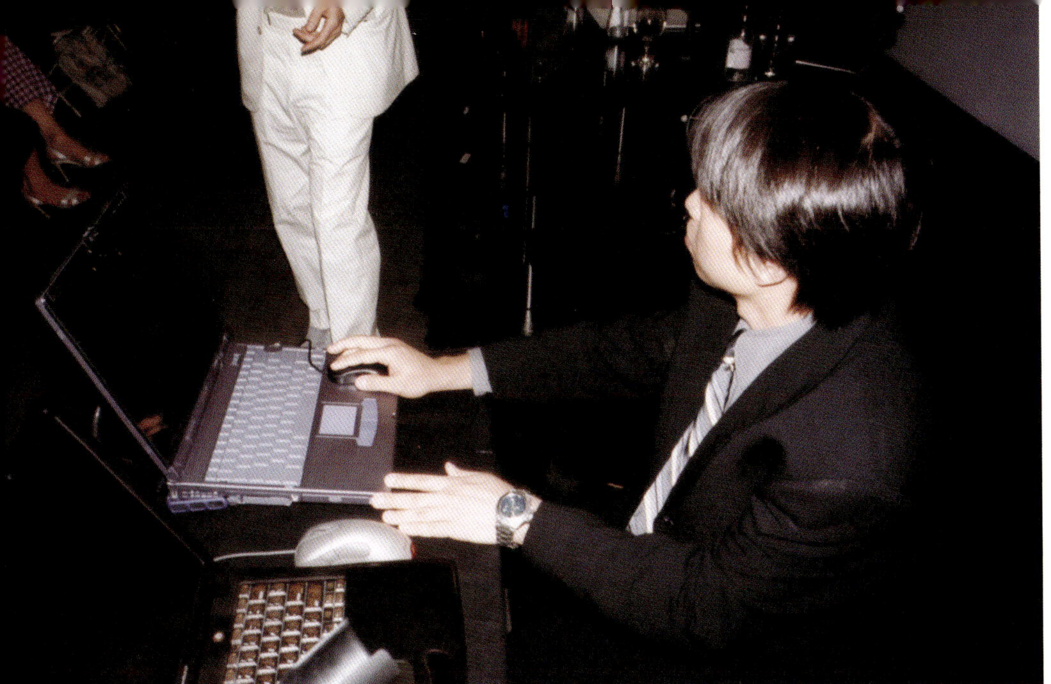

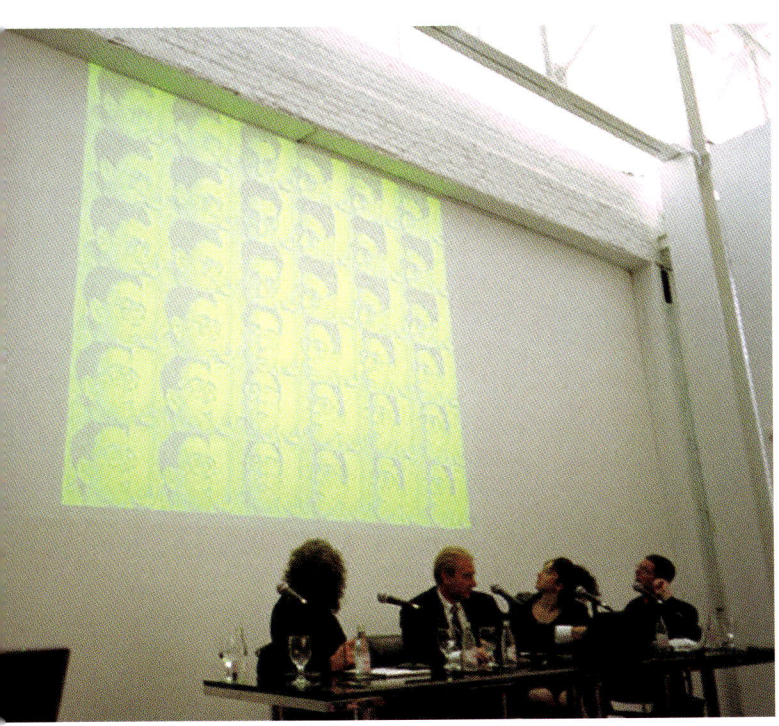

Miltos Manetas mostra diverse animazioni e immagini che suggeriscono il contesto mentale per la nuova parola. A questo punto, e per il resto della presentazione di Manetas, lo schermo della proiezione (per qualche oscura ragione tecnica) diventa verde! L'indomani, la società incaricata dell'impianto di proiezione, imbarazzata, restituirà alla signora Force l'assegno da 8000 dollari.
Era come se le macchine stessero inviando un segnale, e il loro messaggio era che Neen avrebbe dovuto rappresentare non solo la creatività umana, ma anche quella delle macchine intelligenti.

Dopo le presentazioni e il demo di Miltos Manetas, Sushi Matsuda – invitato all'evento in rappresentanza della Sony – sta dando al suo portatile Vaio l'ordine di presentare il nuovo nome: "Signore e signori, posso avere la vostra attenzione prego? Il nuovo nome per l'arte contemporanea è Neen. Ripeto: N-E-E-N. Spero che lo gradiate. È stato creato da un programma per computer. Vi auguro una piacevole serata".

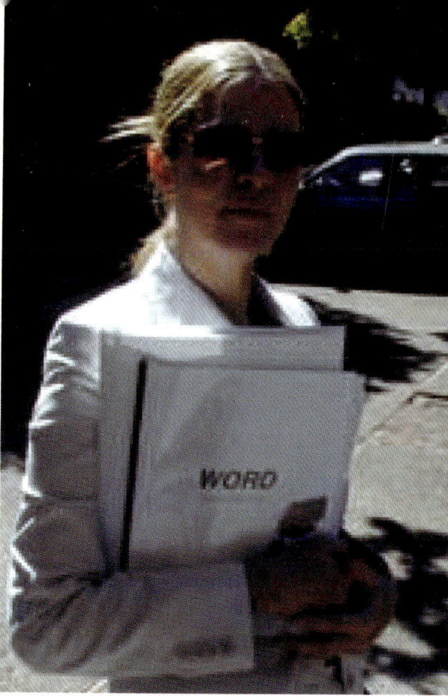

Yvonne Force in Sausalito, California,
at Lexicon's office, January 2000

LEXICON'S PROJECT ARCHIVE

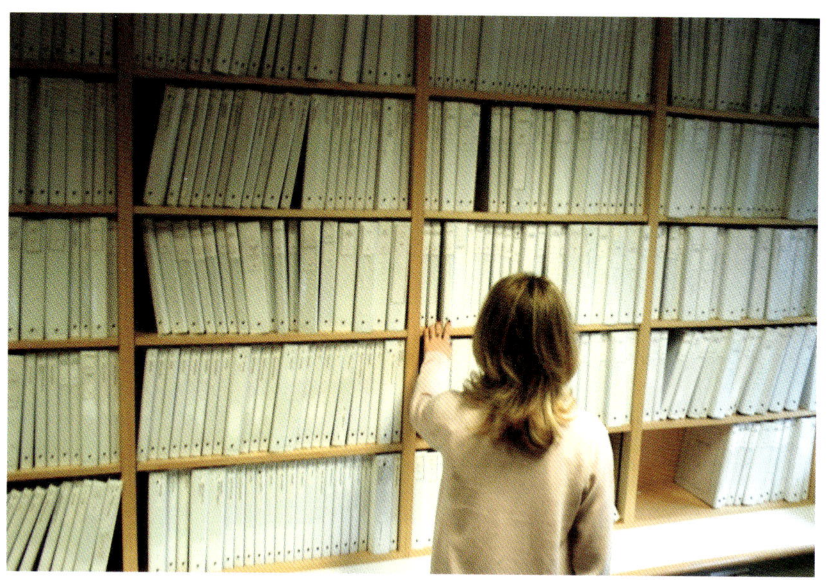

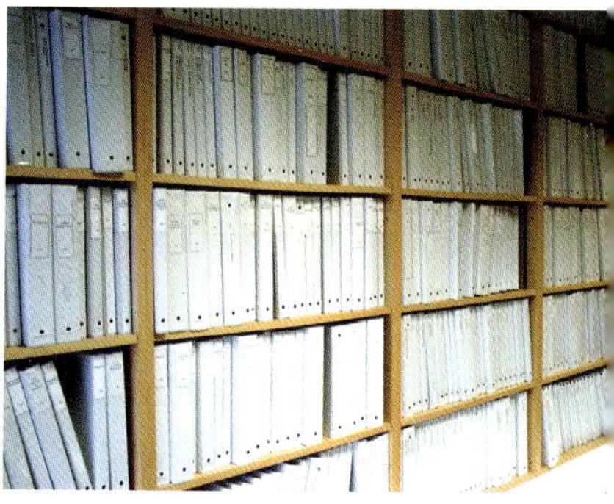

We want to name
something we don't really know,
but we know it exists.
A new feeling.
(instructions to Lexicon)

Lexicon Branding Inc. was founded in 1982 and is based in Sausalito, California. Lexicon is responsible
for creating memorable names such as PowerBook, Pentium, BlackBerry, OnStar, and Dasani.
Lexicon is the patriarch of the nascent naming business. President David Placek worked his way up and out of
advertising proper to found the company in 1982, gambling on the need for such a niche.
In fourteen years, Lexicon has named more than 1,300 companies, products, and services.
Over the years, the company's business has boomed along with the rest of the industry.
Last year alone, with a staff of fifteen, Lexicon dished out more than 130 names.

Alex Frankel, "Name-o-rama," *Wired*, no. 5.06, June 1997

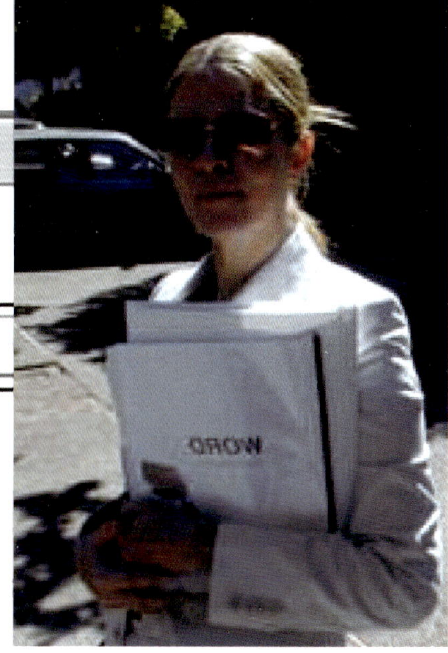

Yvonne Force negli uffici Lexicon a Sausalito,
California, gennaio 2000

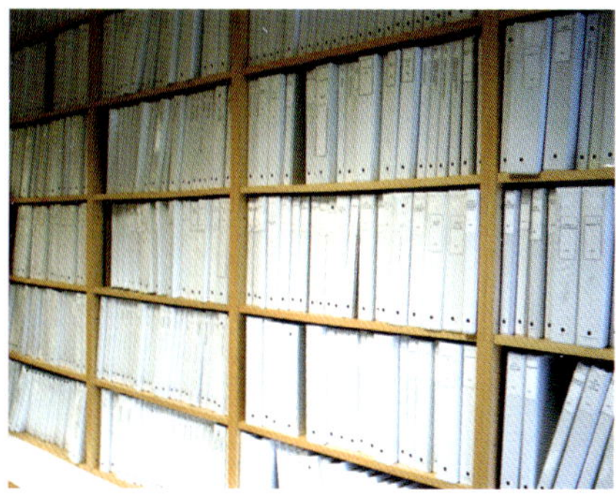

Vogliamo dare un nome a
qualcosa che non conosciamo
veramente ma che sappiamo
esistere. Un nuovo sentimento.
(istruzioni alla Lexicon)

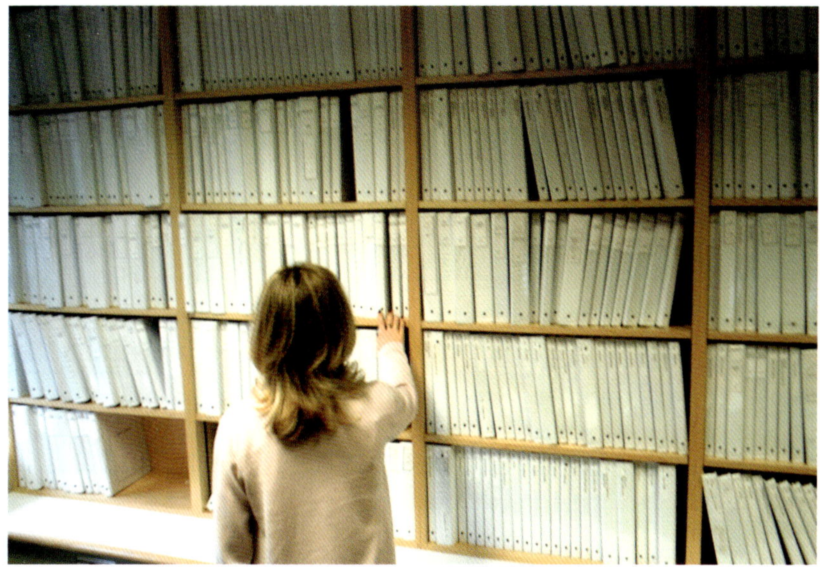

La società Lexicon Branding Inc. è stata fondata nel 1982 e ha la propria base a Sausalito, California.
Lexicon è responsabile della creazione di nomi memorabili quali PowerBook, Pentium, Blackberry, OnStar e Dasani.
Lexicon è il patriarca del nascente commercio dei nomi. Il presidente David Placek si è fatto strada in ambito
pubblicitario, fino a fondare l'azienda nel 1982, scommettendo sull'esigenza di una tale nicchia. In quattordici
anni, Lexicon ha dato un nome a più di 1300 aziende, prodotti e servizi. Nel corso degli anni, il business
dell'azienda è esploso insieme al resto dell'industria. Solo l'anno scorso, con un personale di quindici persone,
Lexicon ha sfornato più di 130 nomi.

Alex Frankel, "Name-o-rama", *Wired*, n. 5.06, giugno 1997

ELECTRONIC

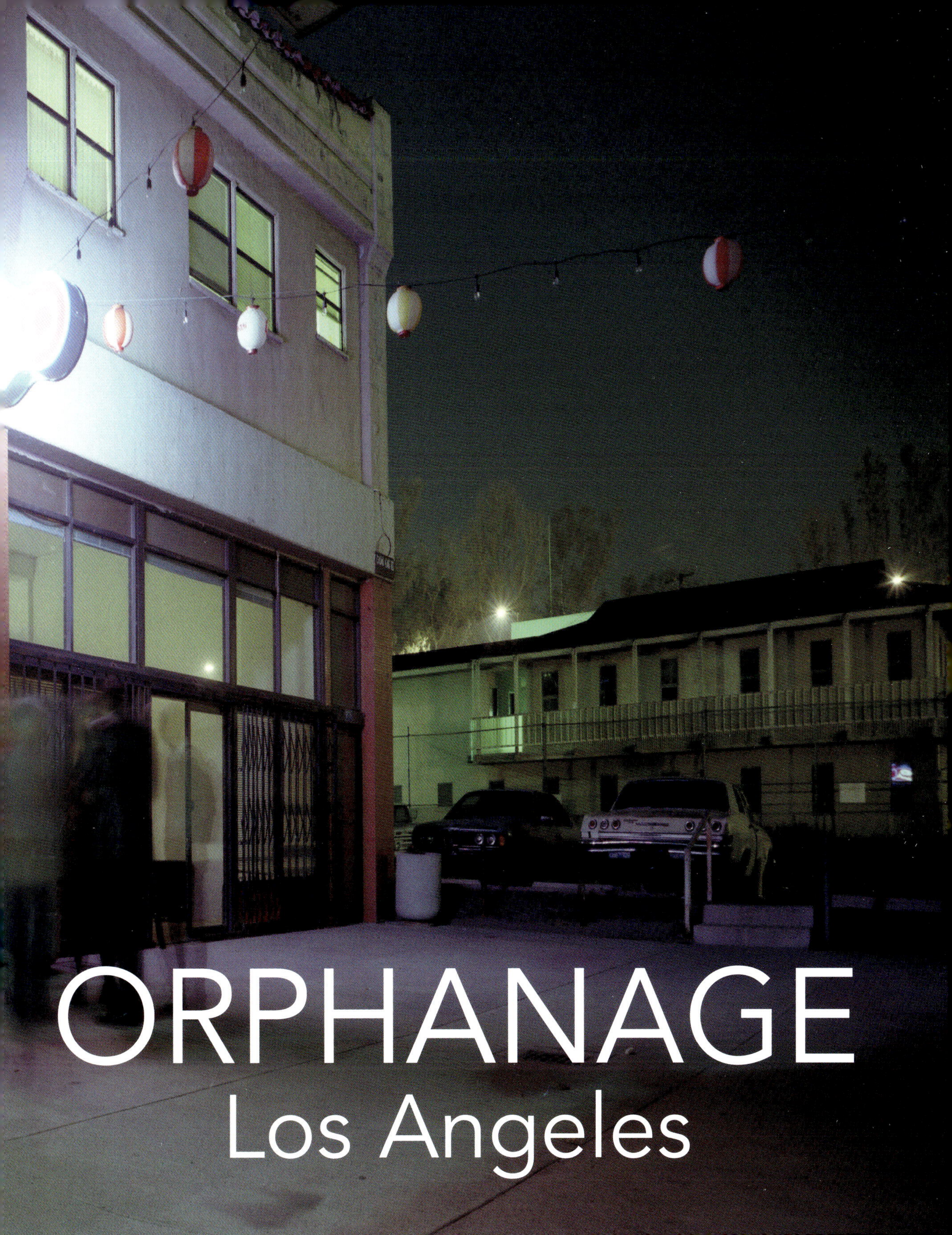
ORPHANAGE
Los Angeles

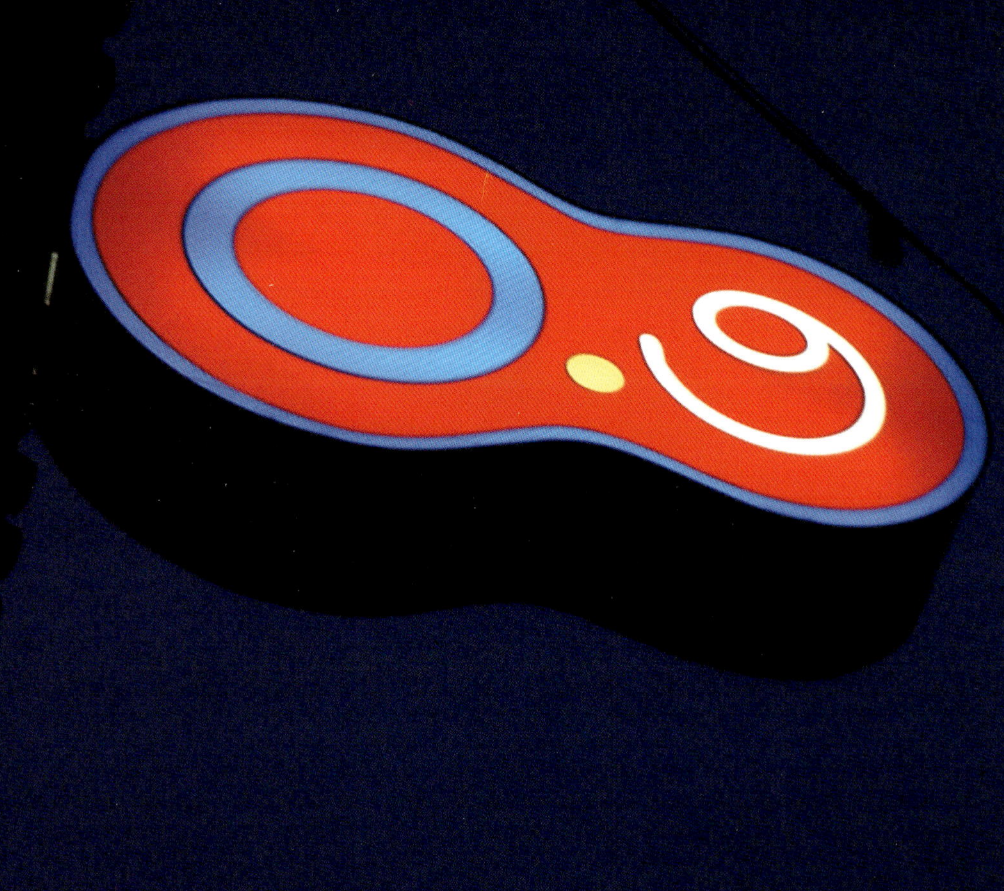

ElectronicOrphanage sign designed by Takaya Goto and sponsored by Art Production Fund

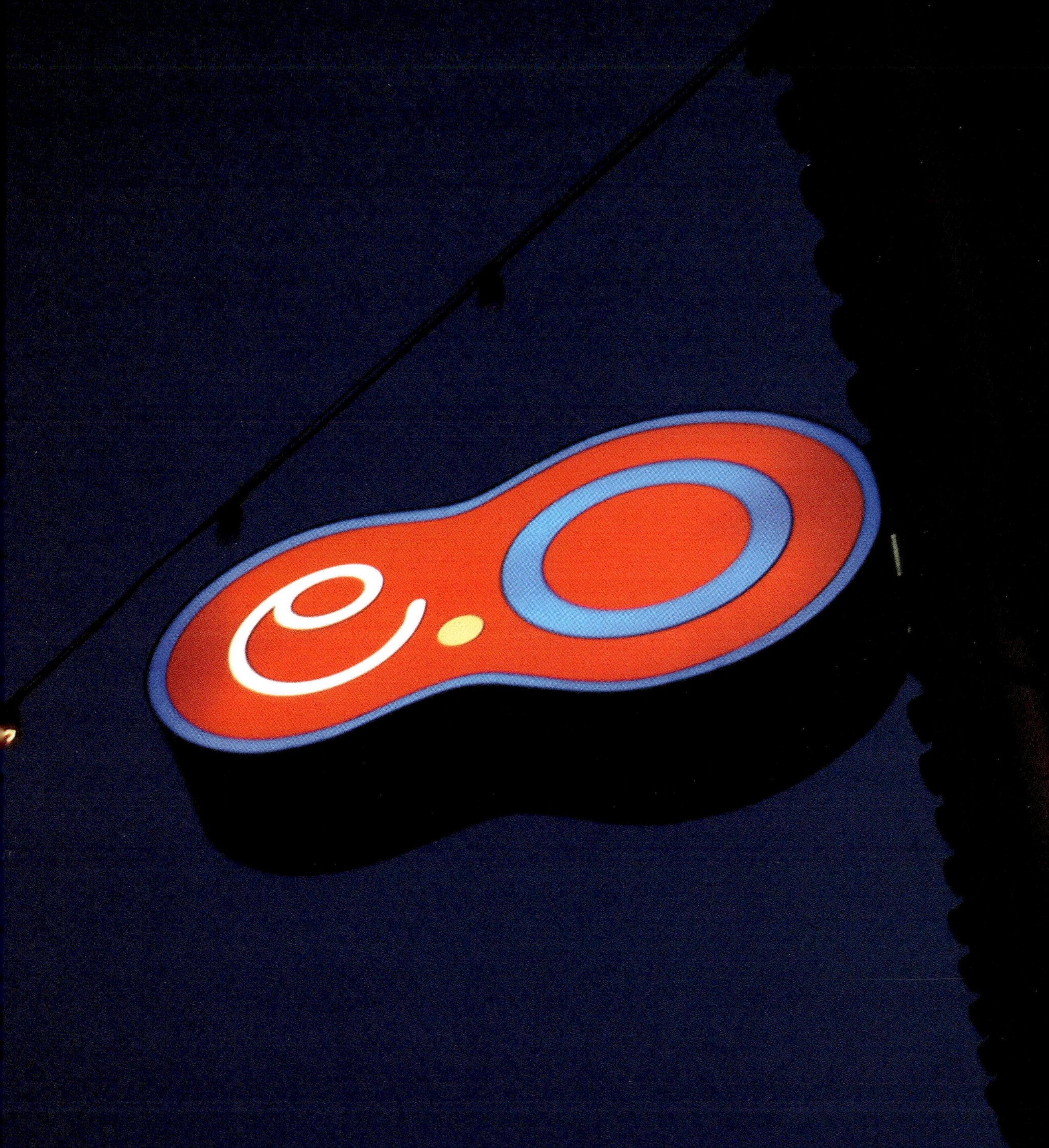

Marchio ElectronicOrphanage disegnato da Takaya Goto e sponsorizzato da Art Production Fund

Miltos and I became partners and moved to Los Angeles where it's easy to build a new culture and situation just like a simulation in a virtual world. We found a space in Chinatown on a street called Chung King Road. The space was called ElectronicOrphanage (E.O.) and the activity of it was a non-profit lounge, where cool people could come and brainstorm about new media theory or just have fun hanging around in a virtual world together with people who are on the other side of the real world. A person who later became my favorite film director, Barbet Schroeder, was one of the many interesting characters who came by. We thought about cute moments of Internet and technology as a part of lifestyle and as a possible new form of art. We created Neen situations on and off the Internet. We spent every day thinking what is Neen and what is not, who is Neen and who is not. More and more, intellectuals and smart lost souls joined our movement.
Between Neenstars, we exchange ideas according to our identities. For instance, if one of them makes a graphic that will suit my personality, it becomes my piece, or if I invent a domain name that will go with Angelo's interactive piece, I would give it to him.
It always has to be poetic and have a sharp point of view.

Mai Ueda, *Mai Ueda Times*, 2006

Miltos e io ci mettemmo insieme e ci spostammo a Los Angeles dove è facile proporre una nuova cultura e una nuova situazione, tanto quanto in una simulazione nel mondo virtuale. Aprimmo uno spazio nel quartiere Chinatown, in una strada chiamata Chung King Road. Lo spazio venne chiamato ElectronicOrphanage (E.O.): era uno spazio non profit, dove persone interessanti potevano venire a ragionare insieme sulla teoria dei nuovi media o semplicemente a divertirsi, entrando in un mondo virtuale insieme a gente che si trovava dall'altra parte del mondo reale. Barbet Schroeder, che in seguito sarebbe diventato il mio regista preferito, fu uno dei personaggi più interessanti a frequentare il posto. Pensammo a piacevoli momenti dedicati a Internet e alla tecnologia come parte di uno stile di vita e come una possibile nuova forma d'arte. Creammo situazioni Neen dentro e fuori Internet. Passammo ogni giorno a pensare cosa fosse Neen e cosa no, chi è Neen e chi non lo è. Sempre più intellettuali e brillanti anime perse si unirono al movimento.
Tra Neenstar vi è scambio di idee, in accordo con le proprie identità. Per esempio, se uno realizza una grafica che è adeguata alla mia personalità, questa diventa una mia opera, oppure se io invento il nome di un dominio Internet che si adatta a un pezzo interattivo di Angelo, lo darò a lui.
Deve sempre mantenersi poetico e avere un punto di vista tagliente.

Mai Ueda, *Mai Ueda Times*, 2006

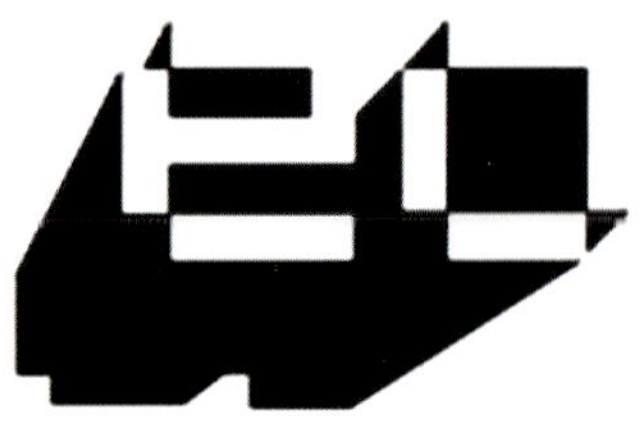

HIRE THEM TO DO NOTHING

The ElectronicOrphanage was used to hiring people. You got paid $8 per hour to do nothing really, just look at computers and the Internet and play video games. You were free to do anything you wanted to, but if you created stuff that looked like contemporary art, or design, you would lose your job. If instead you tried strange visual things with the computer, that was encouraged. So finally, some of the "Orphans" started making what soon became the first Neen pieces, while some other ones started discovering such Neen pieces on the Net and in video games.
The E.O. was part of the Los Angeles Chinatown scene; it was situated at Chung King Road and was surrounded by art galleries. During the openings of these galleries, there would be a projection at the E.O.
The public could look inside from the windows and the open door, but entrance was not allowed.
It was like looking at a giant monitor.
The first show of the E.O. was just a desktop pattern.
Mike Calvert, the first Los Angeles Orphan, took the Evian water label, scanned it, and erased the logo from it.
It was projected at the E.O., the ultimate desktop pattern: Evian's mountain with the computer files laying on it.

Miltos Manetas, electronicorphanage.com, 2002

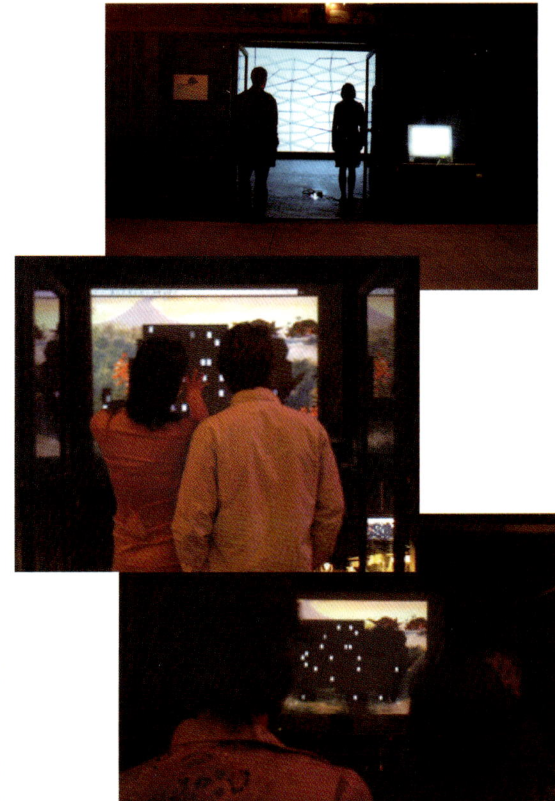

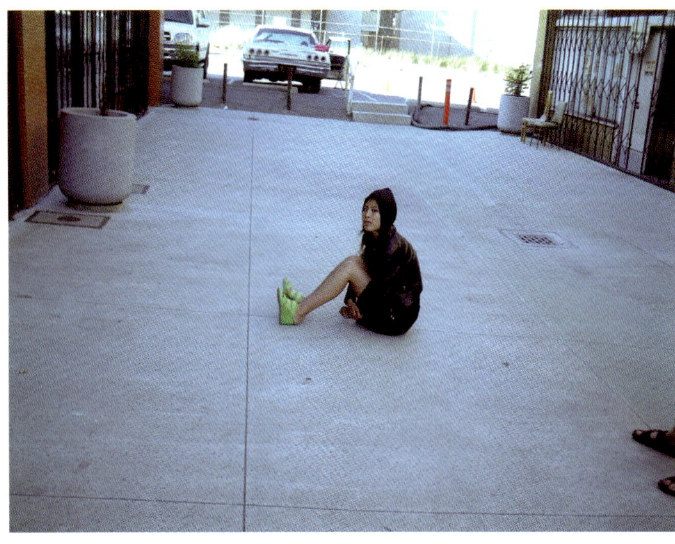

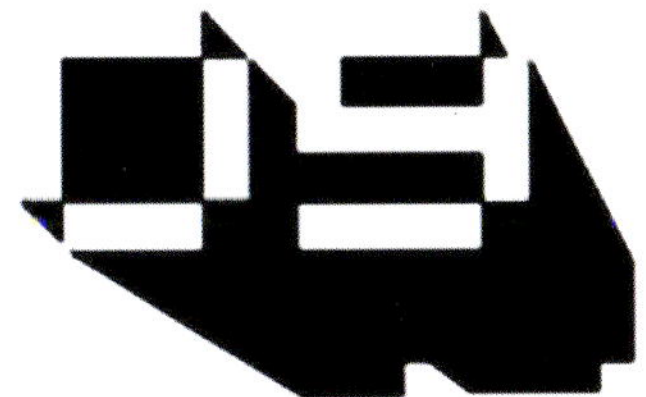

ELECTRONICORPHANAGE, LOS ANGELES, 2001-2003

LI INGAGGIAMO PER NON FARE NIENTE

L'ElectronicOrphanage era solito ingaggiare persone.
Potevi guadagnare otto dollari all'ora per non fare
veramente nulla, se non guardare i computer e Internet
e giocare ai videogiochi. Eri libero di fare qualsiasi cosa ma,
se realizzavi cose che somigliavano all'arte contemporanea,
o al design, perdevi il tuo lavoro. Se invece creavi strane
cose visuali con il computer, questo veniva incoraggiato.
Così, infine, alcuni "orfani" cominciarono a fare cose che
presto sarebbero diventate le prime opere Neen, mentre
altri avevano già cominciato a scoprire opere Neen
su Internet e nei videogiochi.
L'E.O. era parte della scena di Los Angeles Chinatown,
era situato nella Chung King Road ed era circondato
da gallerie d'arte. Durante i vernissage di queste gallerie,
c'era sempre una proiezione all'E.O.
Il pubblico poteva guardare all'interno dalla vetrina
o dalla porta aperta, ma l'entrata non era consentita.
Era come guardare un monitor gigante.
Il primo spettacolo all'E.O. fu semplicemente lo sfondo
del desktop di un computer. Mike Calvert, il primo orfano
di Los Angeles, prese l'etichetta di una bottiglia di Evian
e vi strappò il logo. Proiettato all'E.O. divenne il desktop
più incredibile: la montagna di Evian con i file del computer
in sovrapposizione.

Miltos Manetas, electronicorphanage.com, 2002

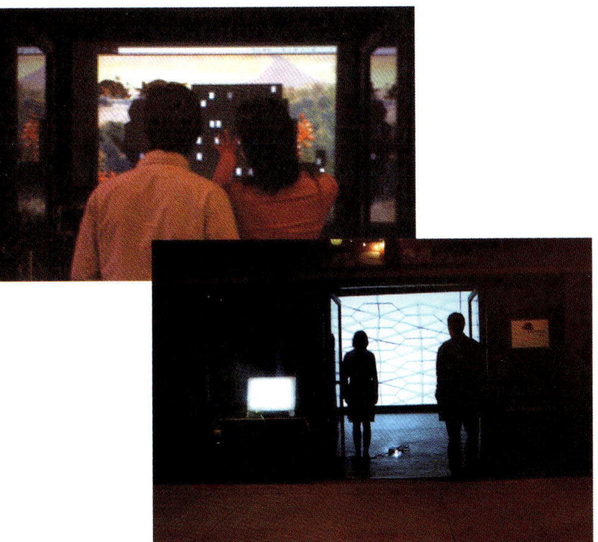

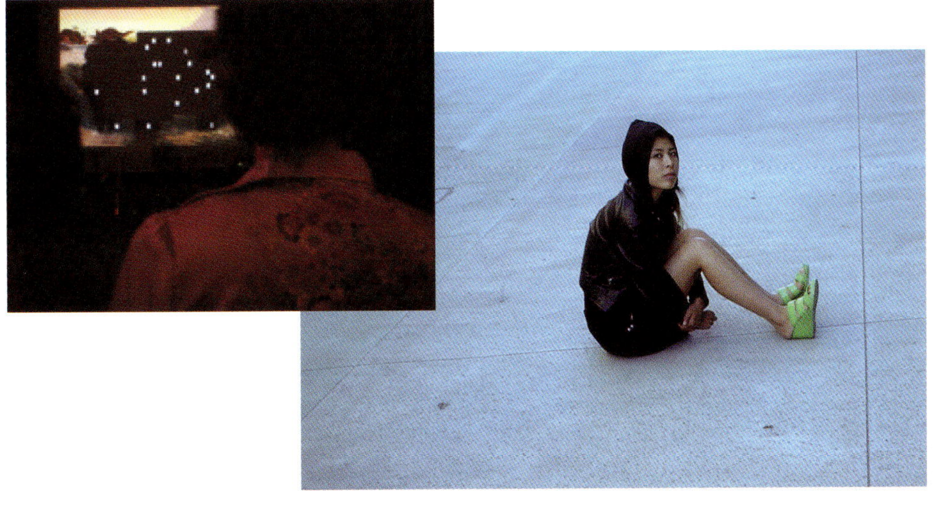

GENERATION FLASH

This generation does not care if its work is called art or design. This generation is no longer interested in the "media critique" which preoccupied media artists of the last two decades; instead, it is engaged in software critique. This generation writes its own software code to create its own cultural systems, instead of using samples of commercial media.
The result is the new modernism of data visualizations, vector nets, pixel-thin grids, and arrows: Bauhaus design in the service of information intelligence. Instead, the Baroque assault of commercial media, Flash generation serves us the modernist aesthetics and rationality of software.
Information intelligence is used as a tool to make sense of reality while programming becomes a tool of empowerment.

Lev Manovich, whitneybiennial.com/theories, 2002

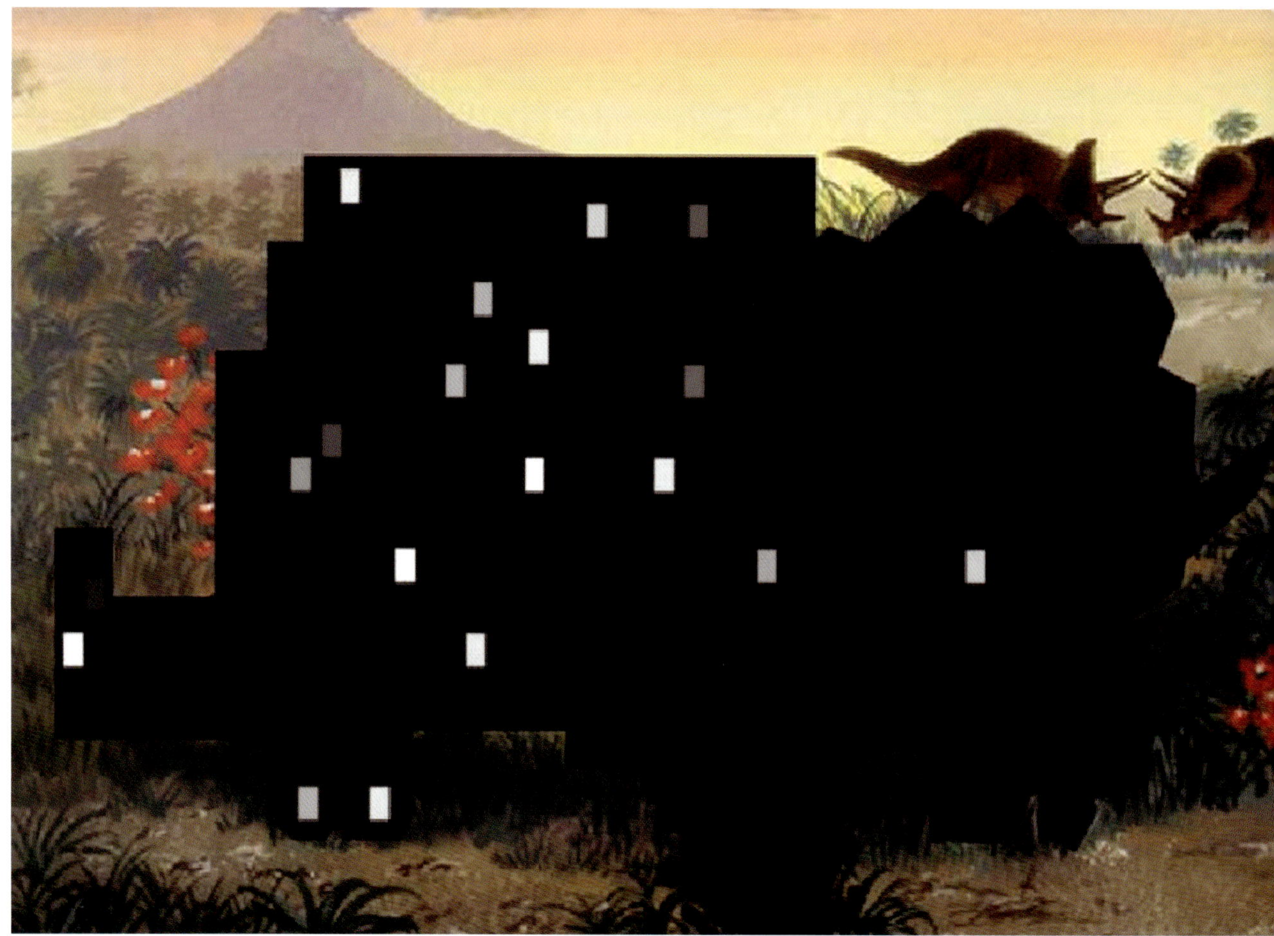

John White C., *Steg*, 2001, animation at the ElectronicOrphanage, May 19, 2001

Questa generazione non si preoccupa se il proprio lavoro viene chiamato arte o design.
Non è più interessata alla "critica dei media" che è stato motivo di preoccupazione per i media artisti delle ultime due decadi; all'opposto, è impegnata nella critica del software.
Questa generazione, invece di utilizzare pezzi provenienti dai media commerciali, scrive il codice del proprio software personale allo scopo di crearsi i propri sistemi culturali.
Il risultato è il nuovo modernismo della visualizzazione di dati, vettori, reti, griglie di pixel e frecce: il design Bauhaus al servizio dell'*information intelligence*.
Invece dell'assalto barocco tipico dei media commerciali, la "generazione Flash" ci fornisce l'estetica modernista e la razionalità del software. L'*information intelligence* è utilizzata come uno strumento per creare senso e realtà, mentre la programmazione diviene uno strumento per acquisire potere.

Lev Manovich, whitneybiennial.com/theories, 2002

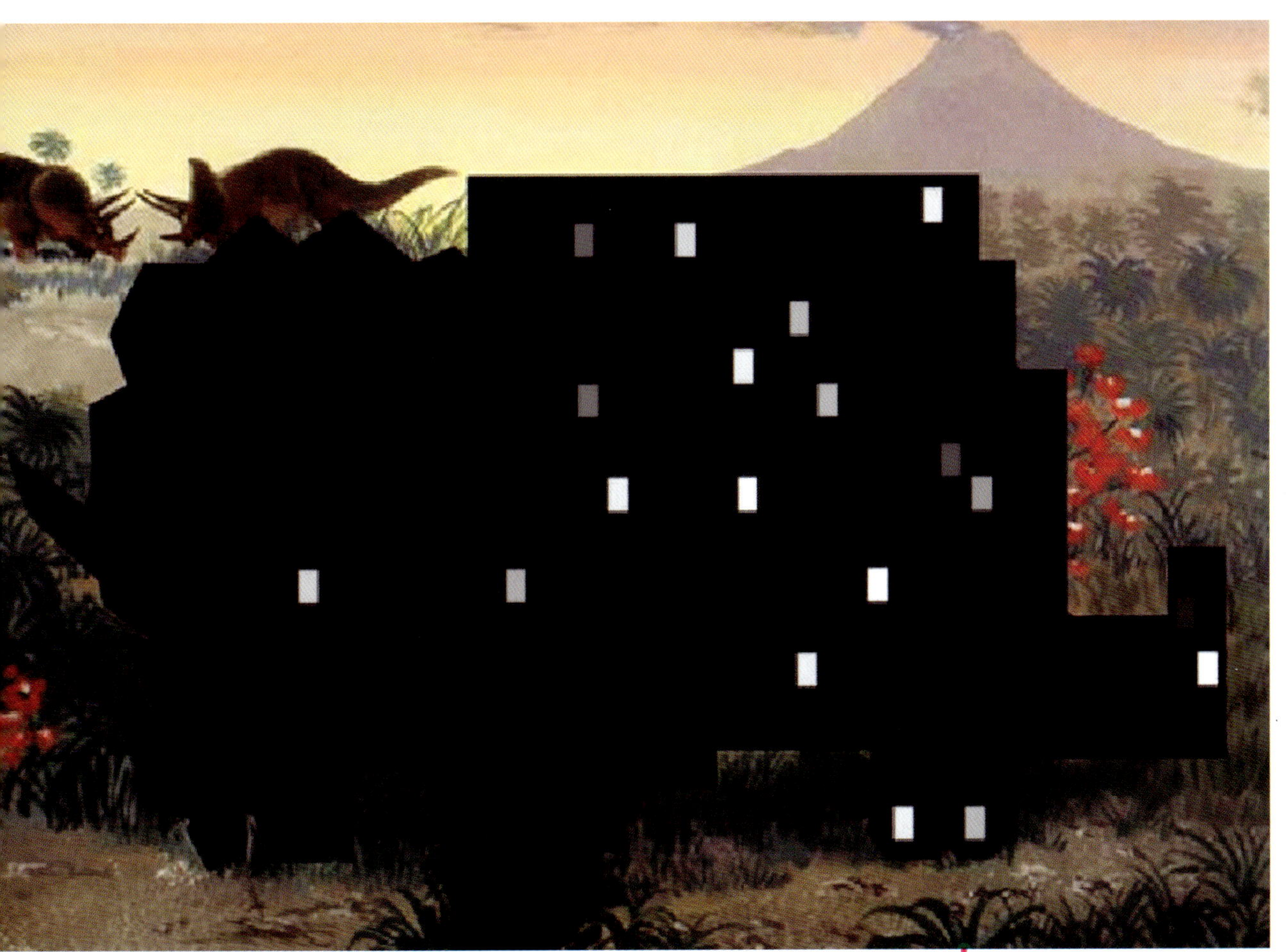

John White C., *Steg*, 2001, animazione all'ElectronicOrphanage, 19 maggio 2001

ElectronicOrphanage is a space designed
like a desktop interface,
a storefront that changes function
with a single click: office by day
and exhibition space by night.
The workstations are configured
as ceiling-mounted columns
on wheels, and when you fold up the seats
and push back the columns,
they form a projection wall in the back of
the space, turning the storefront
into a screen.

Andreas Angelidakis, 2002

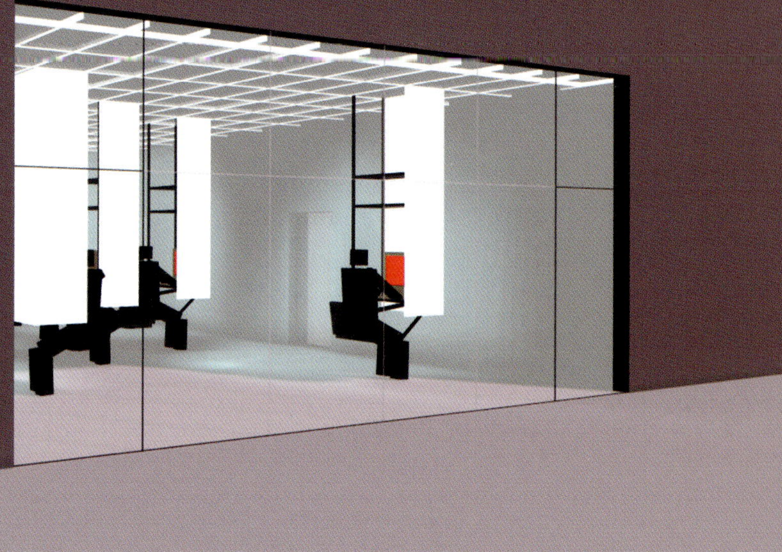

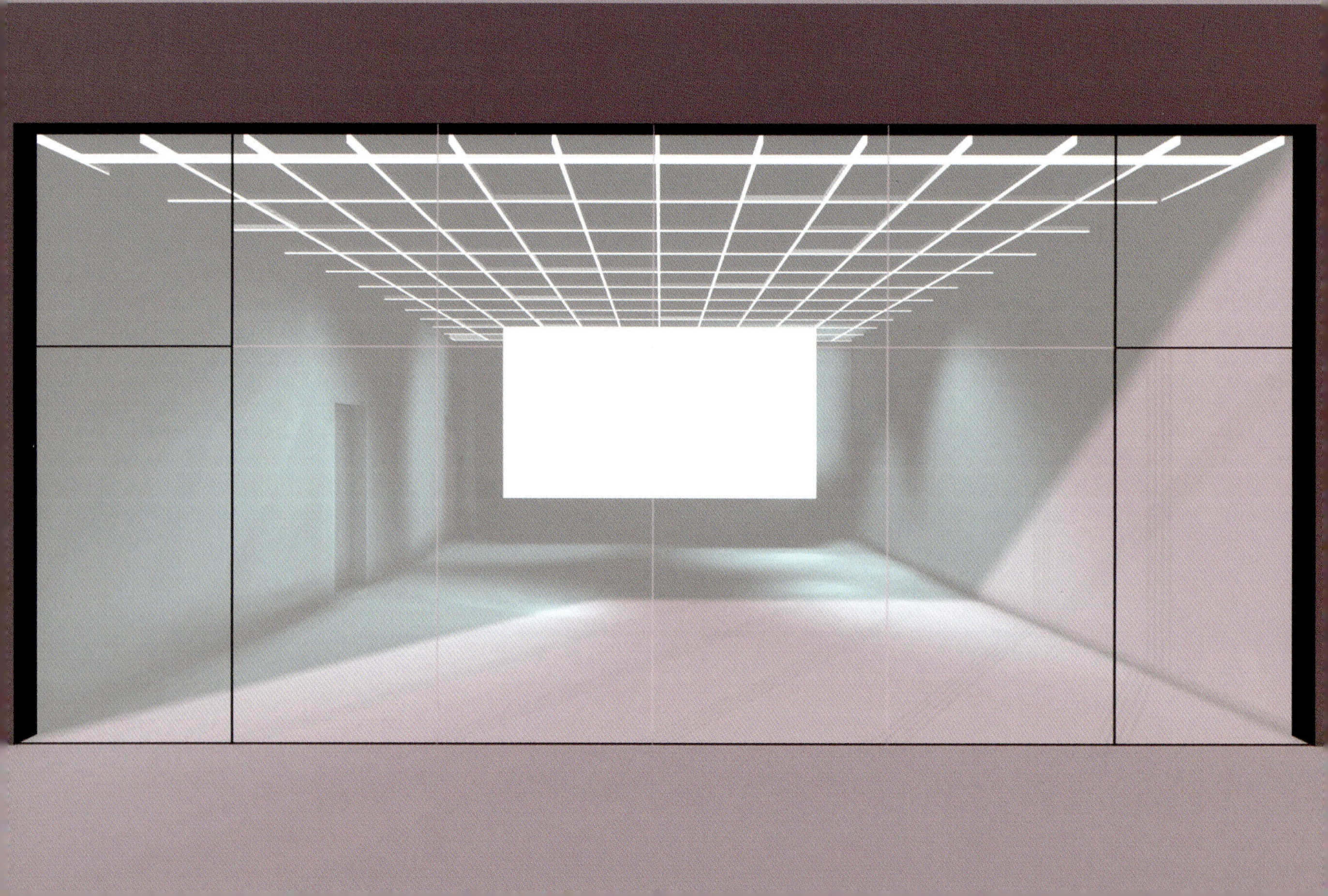

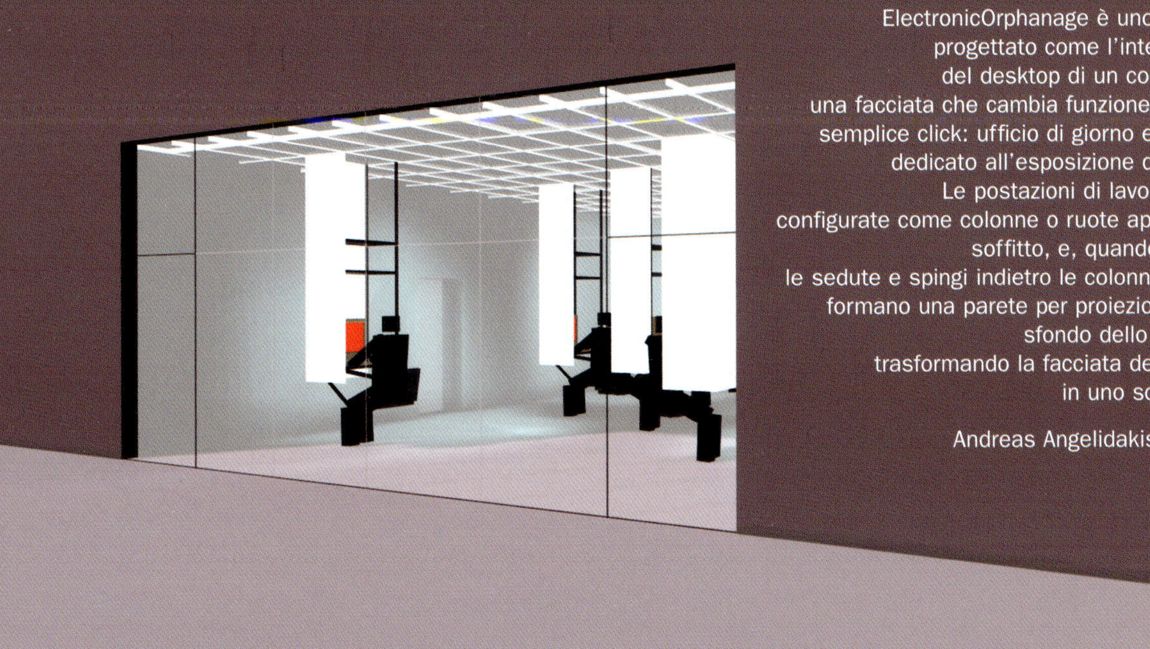

ElectronicOrphanage è uno spazio
progettato come l'interfaccia
del desktop di un computer,
una facciata che cambia funzione con un
semplice click: ufficio di giorno e spazio
dedicato all'esposizione di notte.
Le postazioni di lavoro sono
configurate come colonne o ruote appese al
soffitto, e, quando chiudi
le sedute e spingi indietro le colonne, esse
formano una parete per proiezioni sullo
sfondo dello spazio,
trasformando la facciata del locale
in uno schermo.

Andreas Angelidakis, 2002

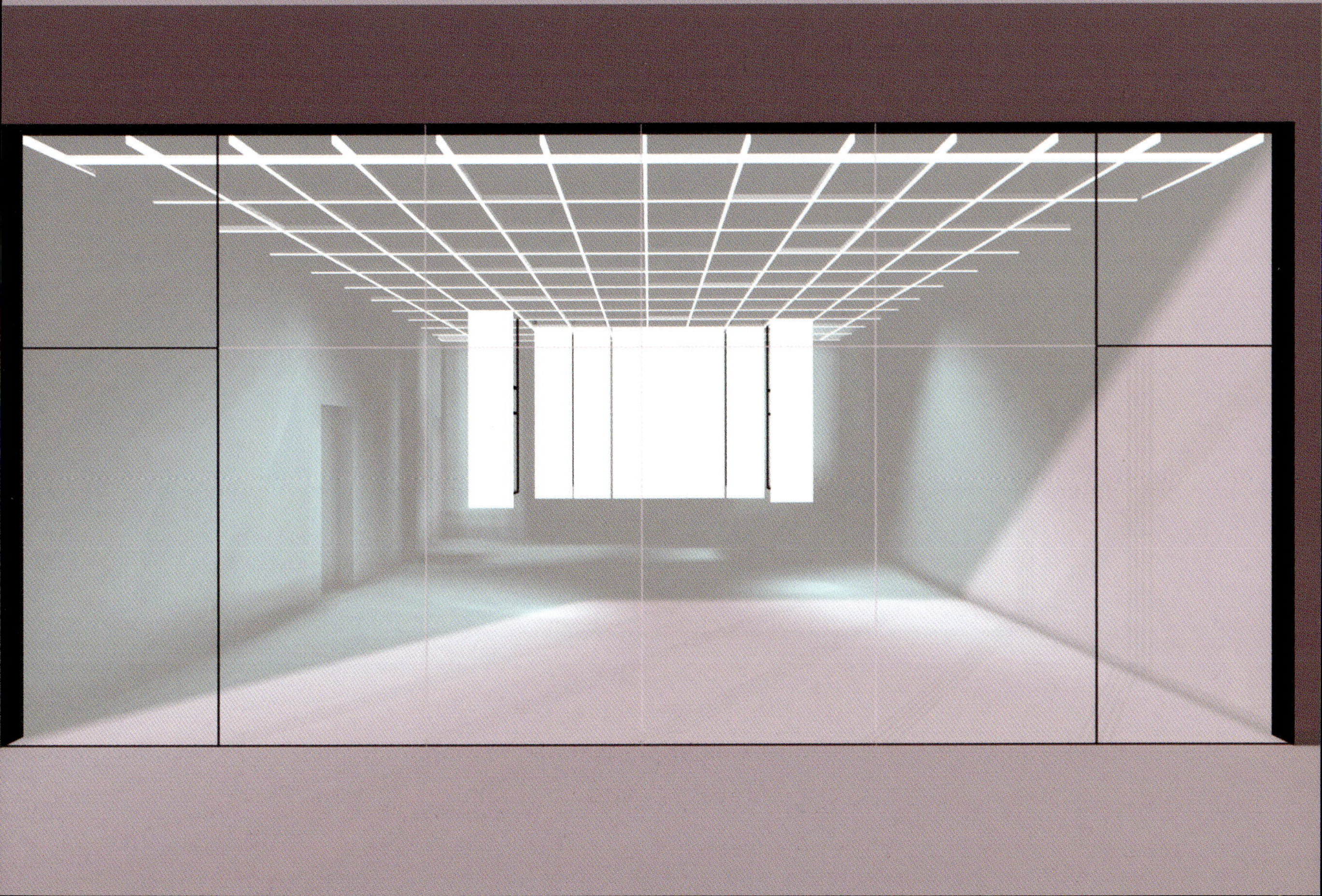

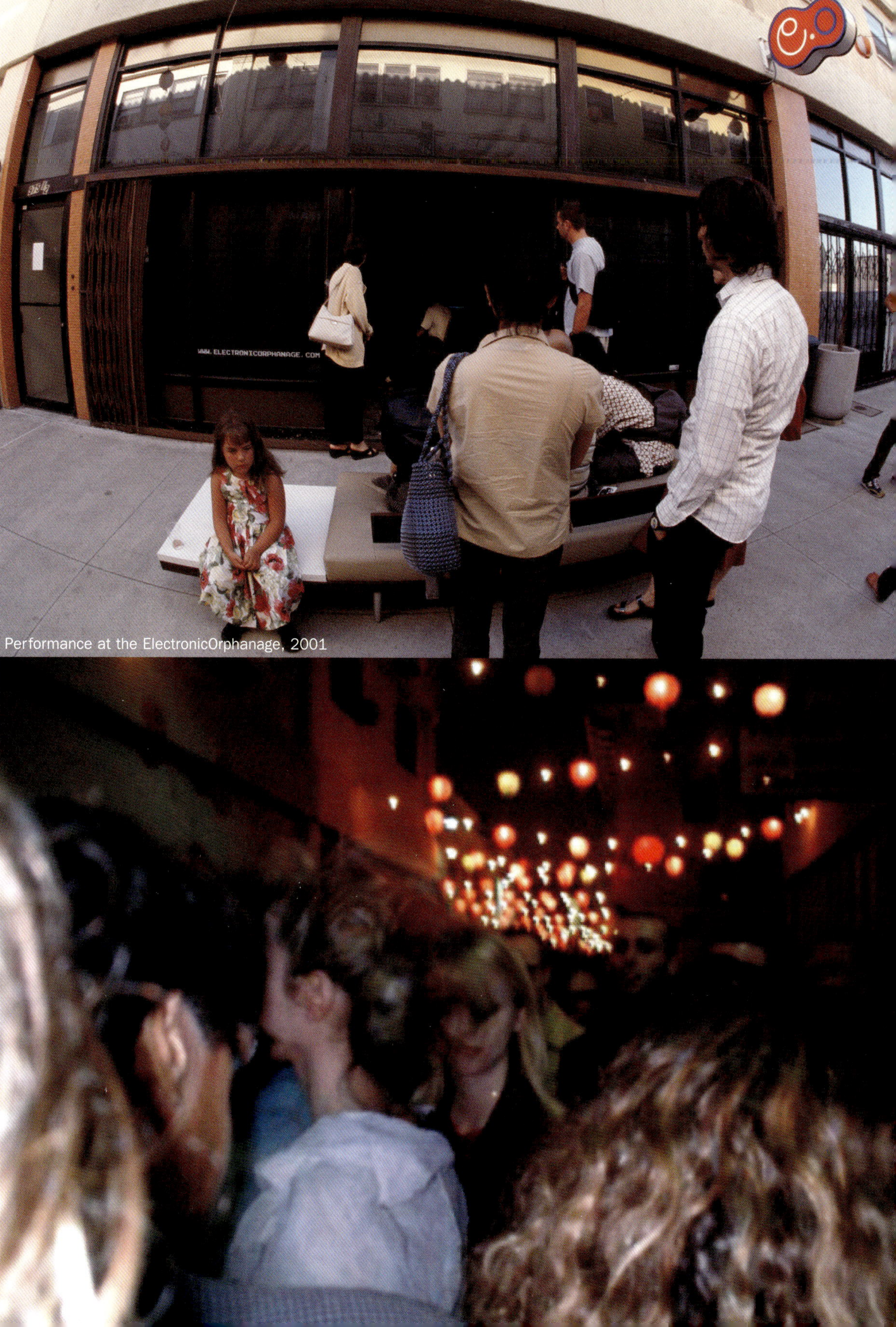

Performance at the ElectronicOrphanage, 2001

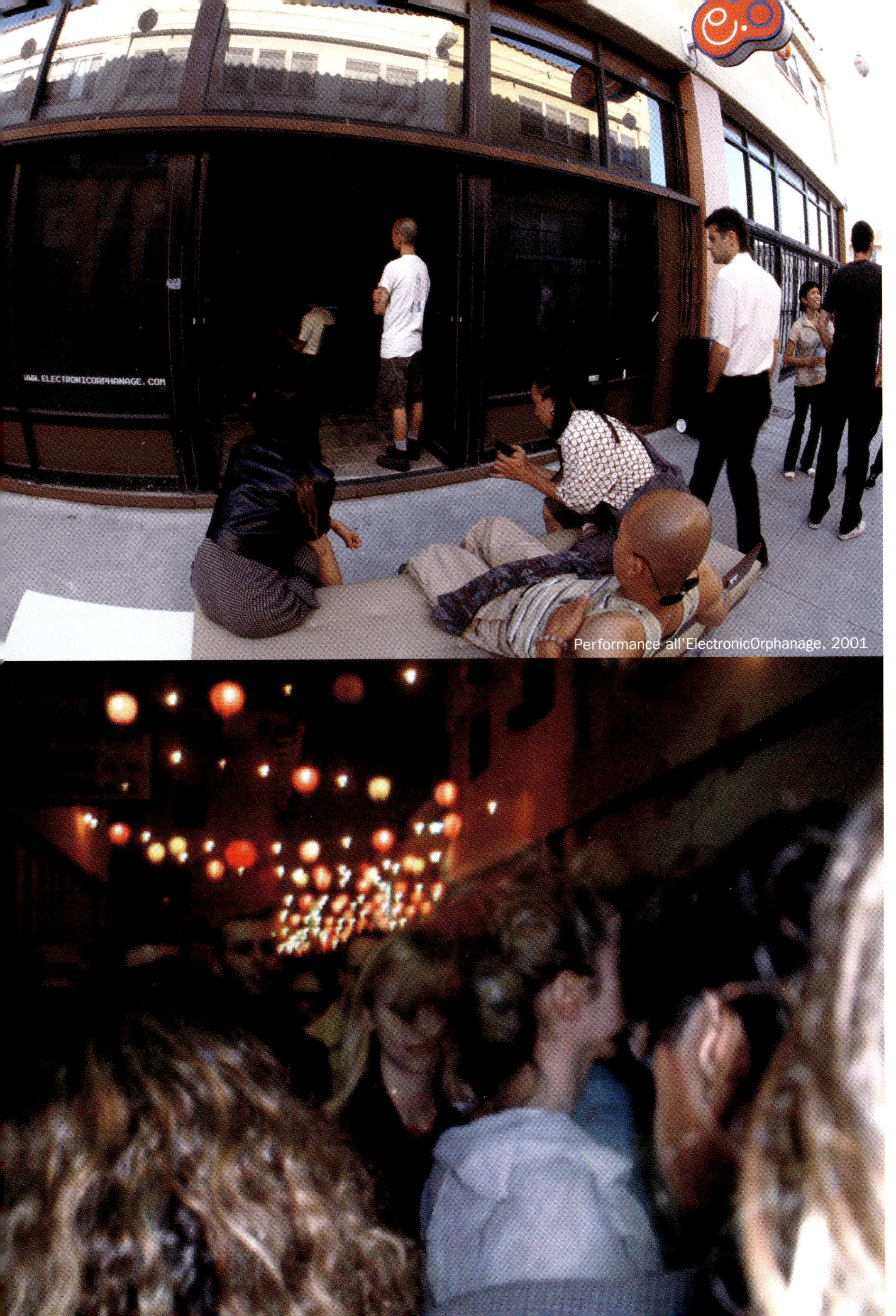
WWW.ELECTRONICORPHANAGE.COM
Performance all'ElectronicOrphanage, 2001

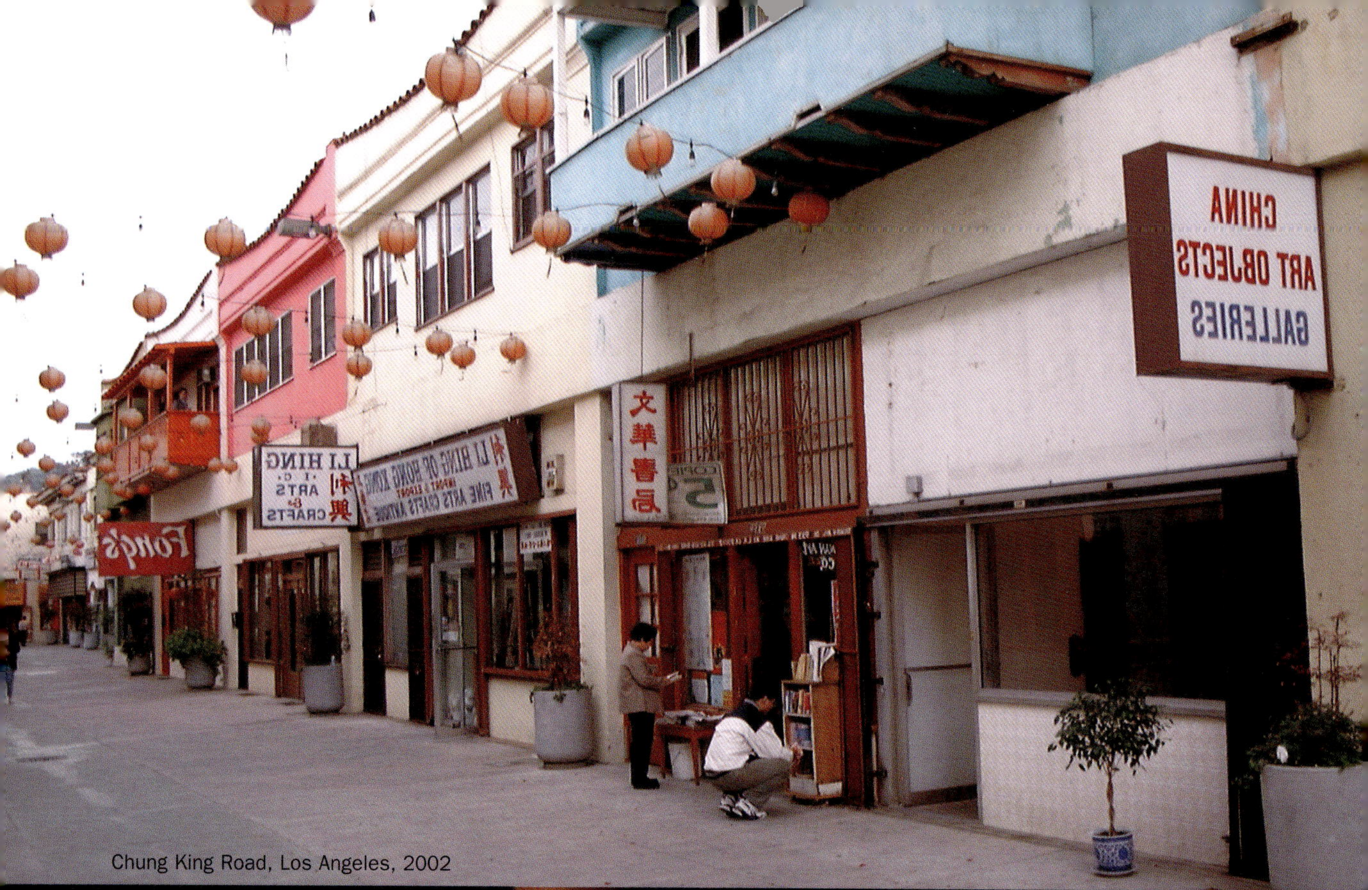

Chung King Road, Los Angeles, 2002

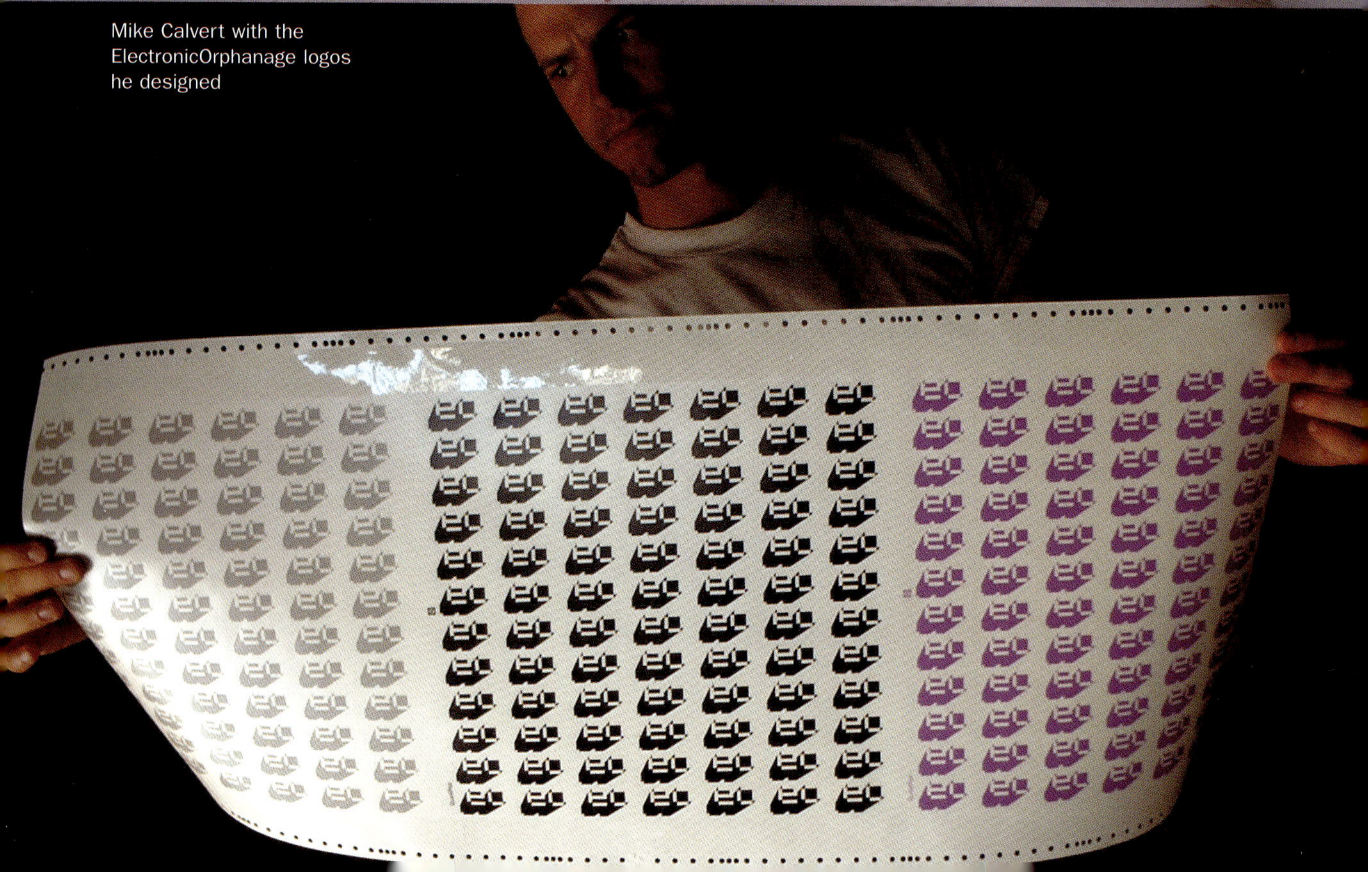

Mike Calvert with the
ElectronicOrphanage logos
he designed

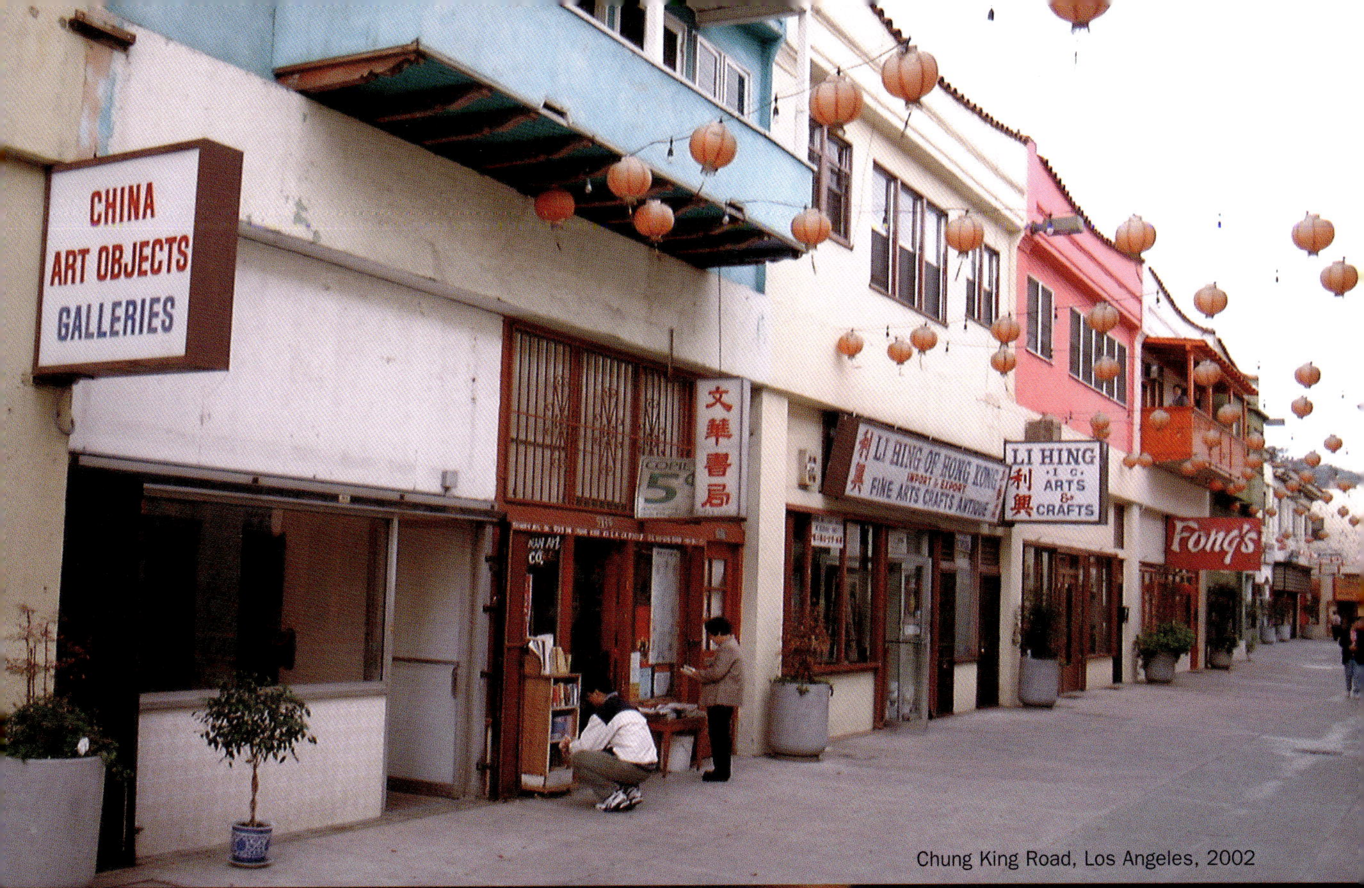

Chung King Road, Los Angeles, 2002

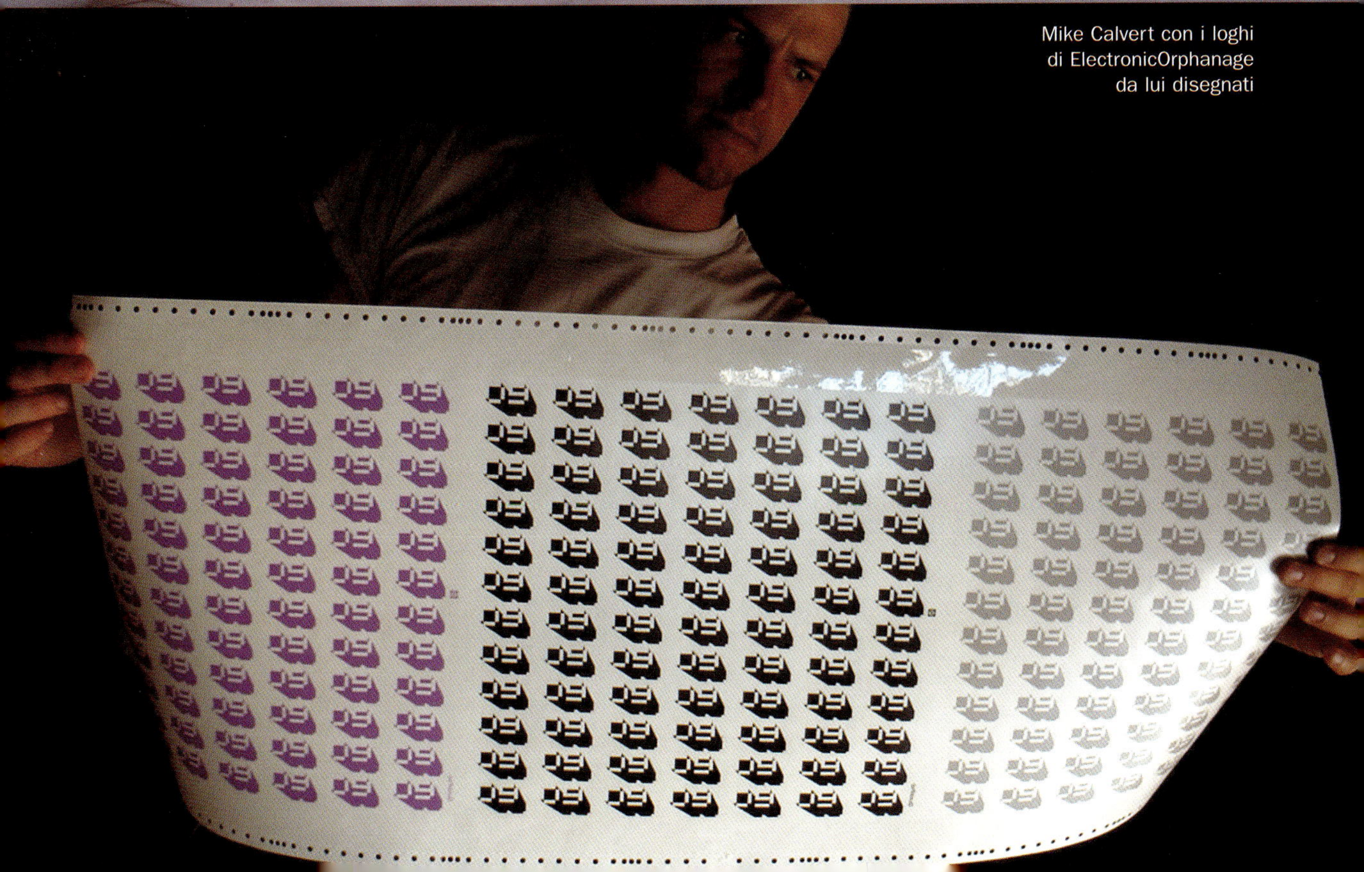

Mike Calvert con i loghi
di ElectronicOrphanage
da lui disegnati

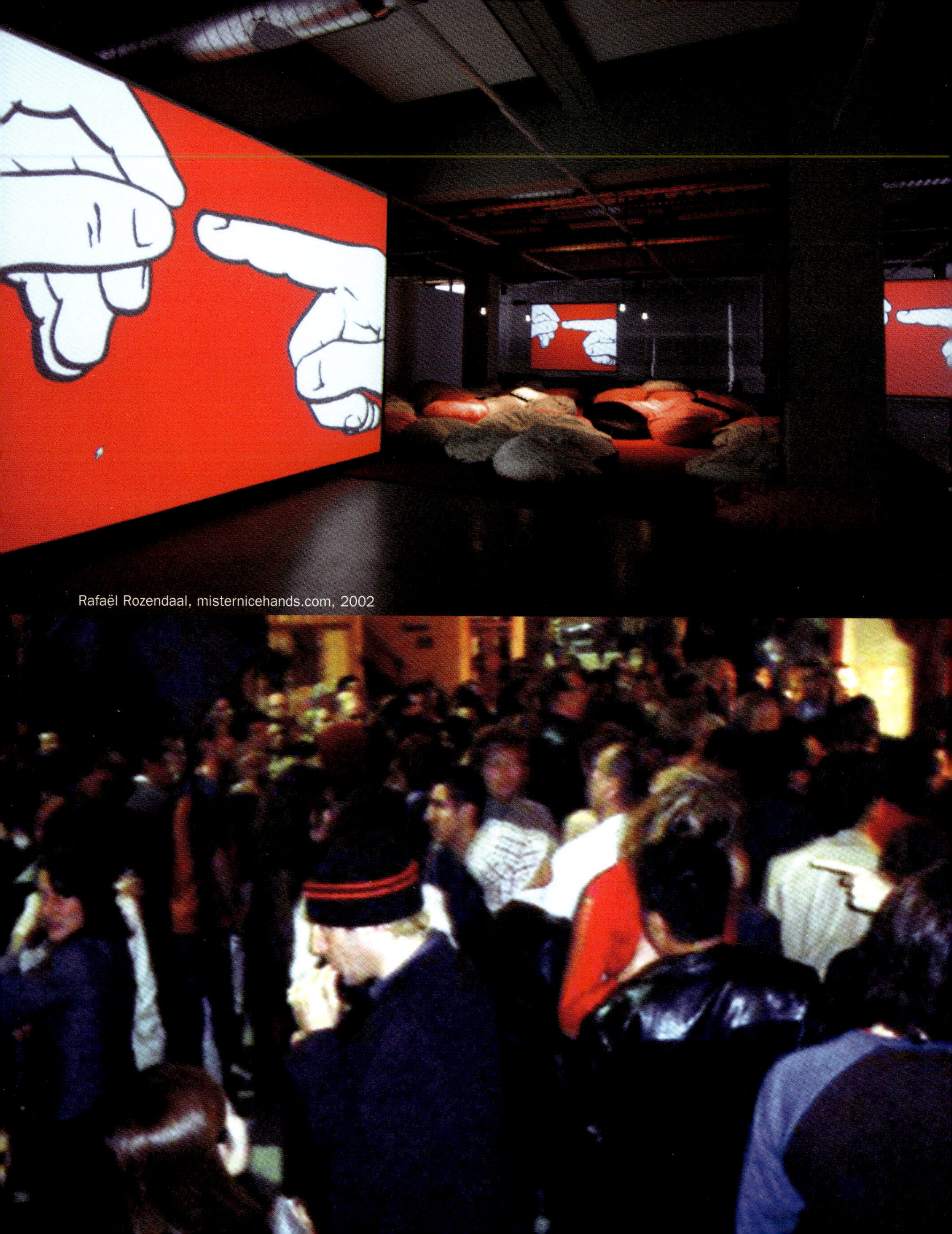

Rafaël Rozendaal, misternicehands.com, 2002

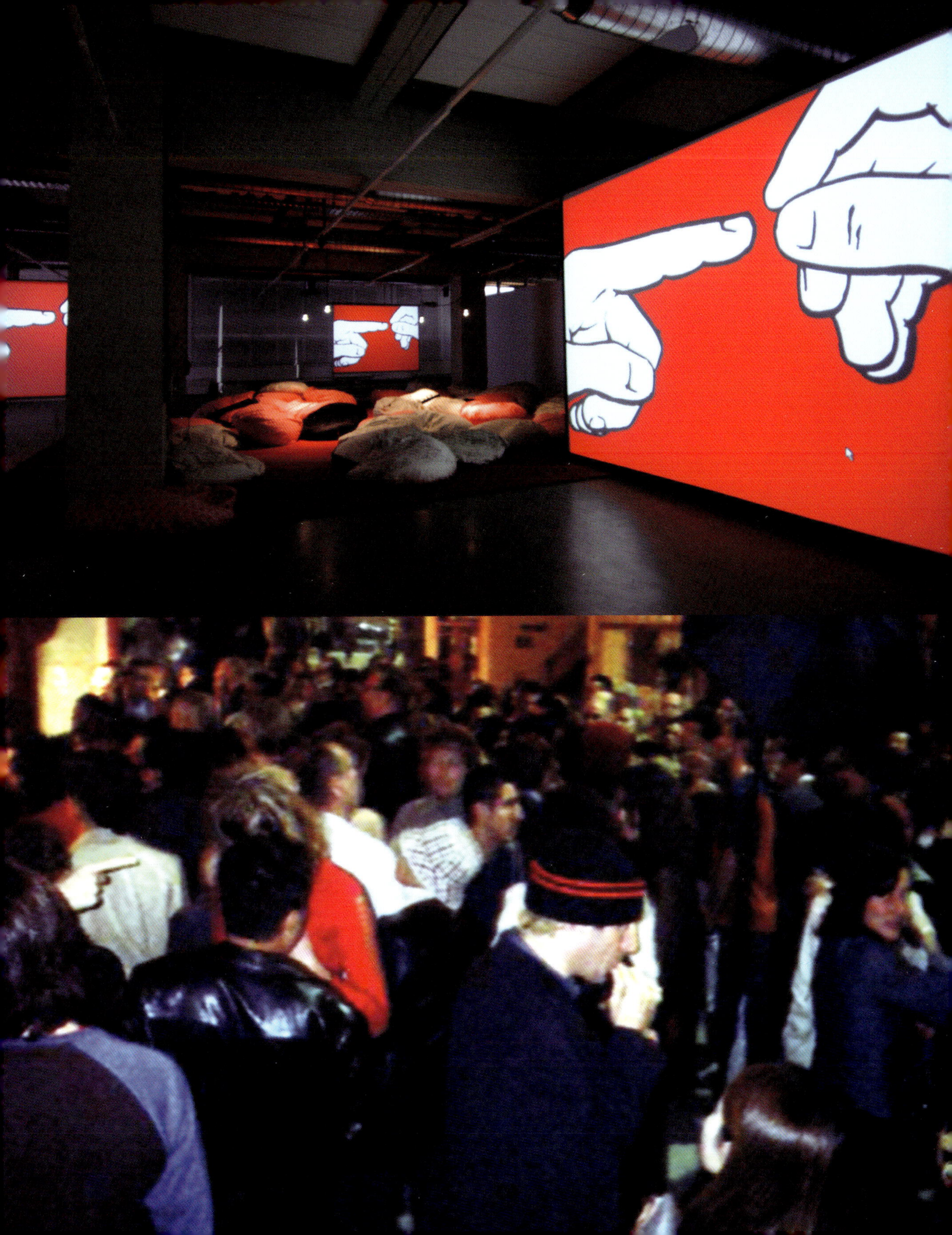

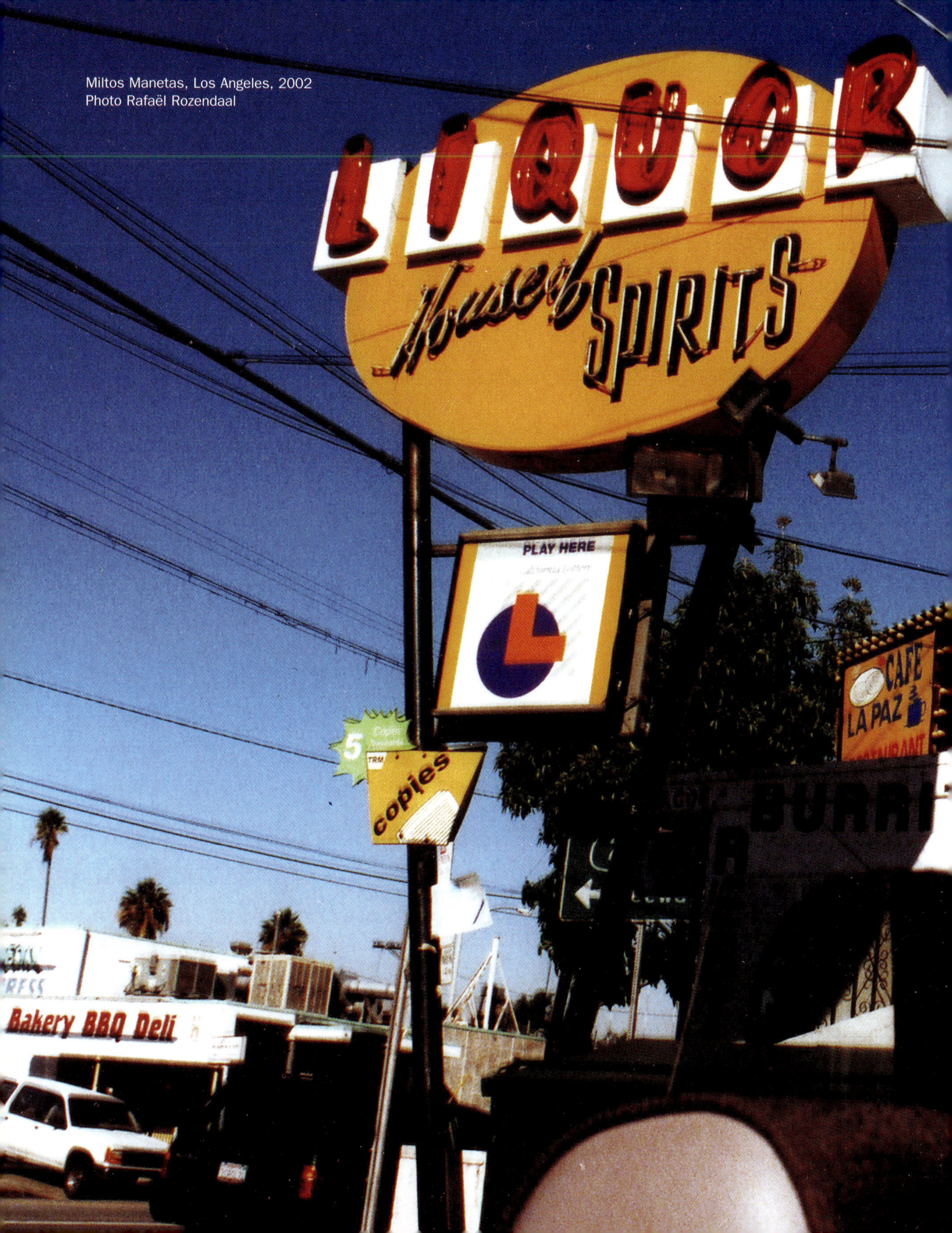

Miltos Manetas, Los Angeles, 2002
Photo Rafaël Rozendaal

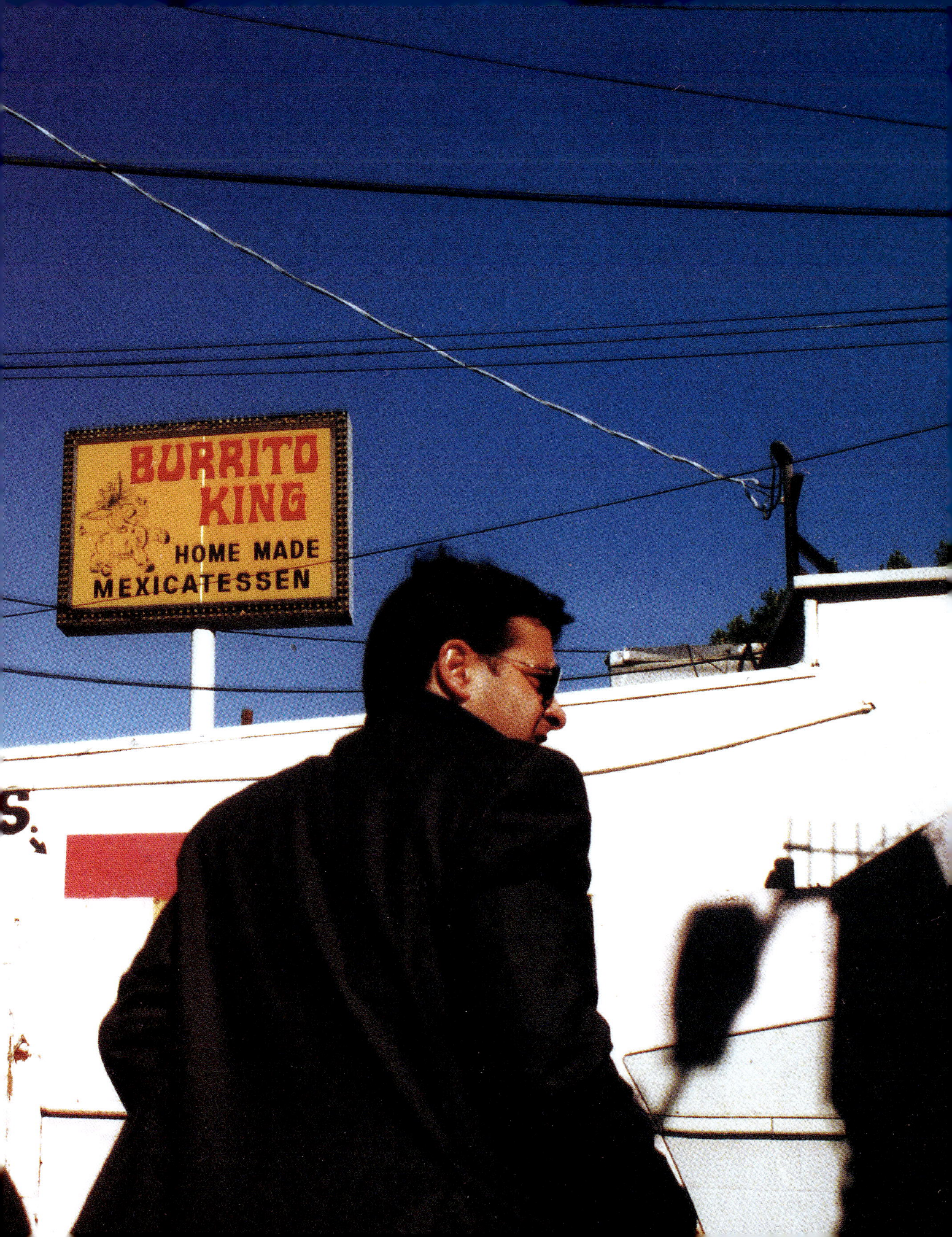
BURRITO
KING
HOME MADE
MEXICATESSEN

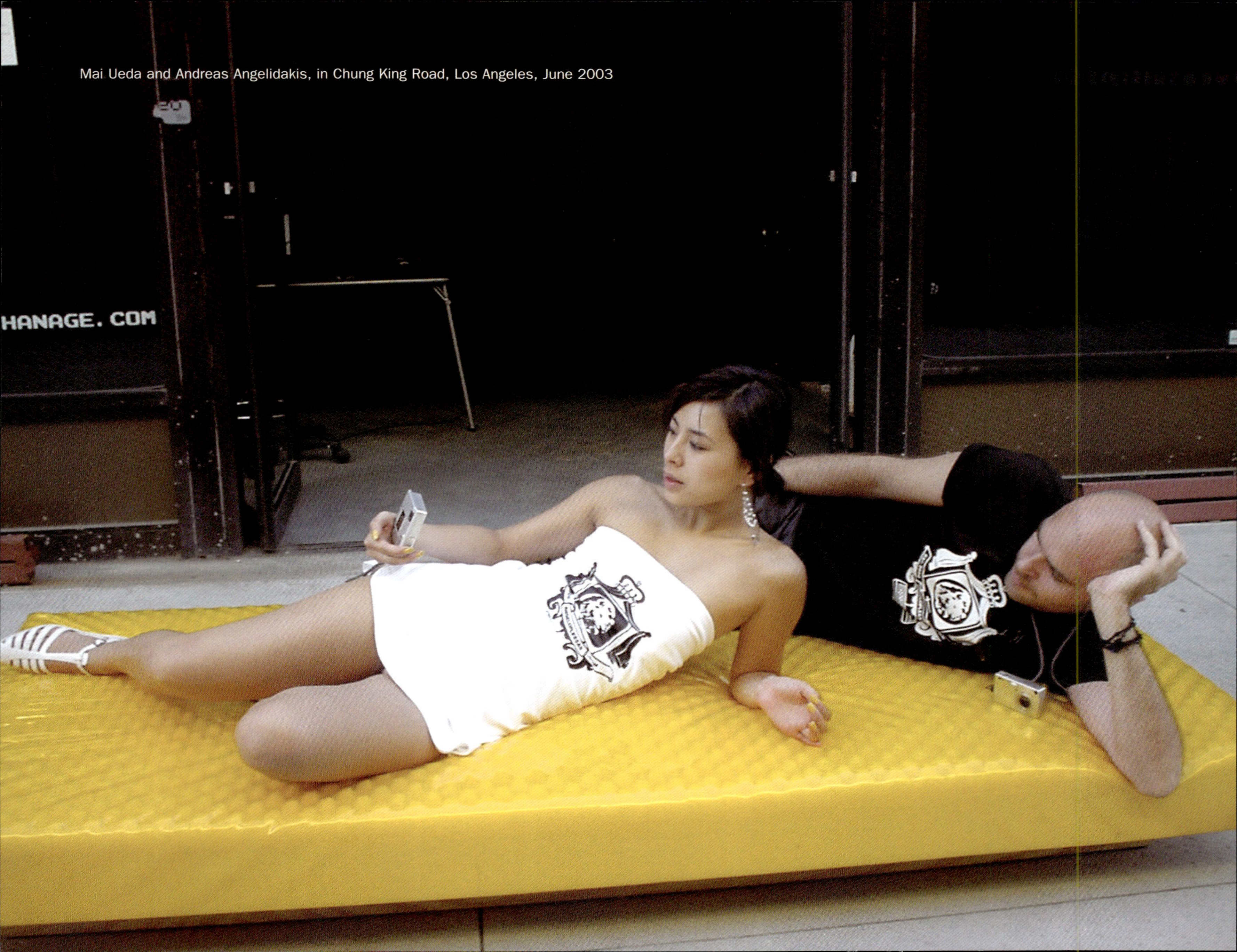

Mai Ueda and Andreas Angelidakis, in Chung King Road, Los Angeles, June 2003

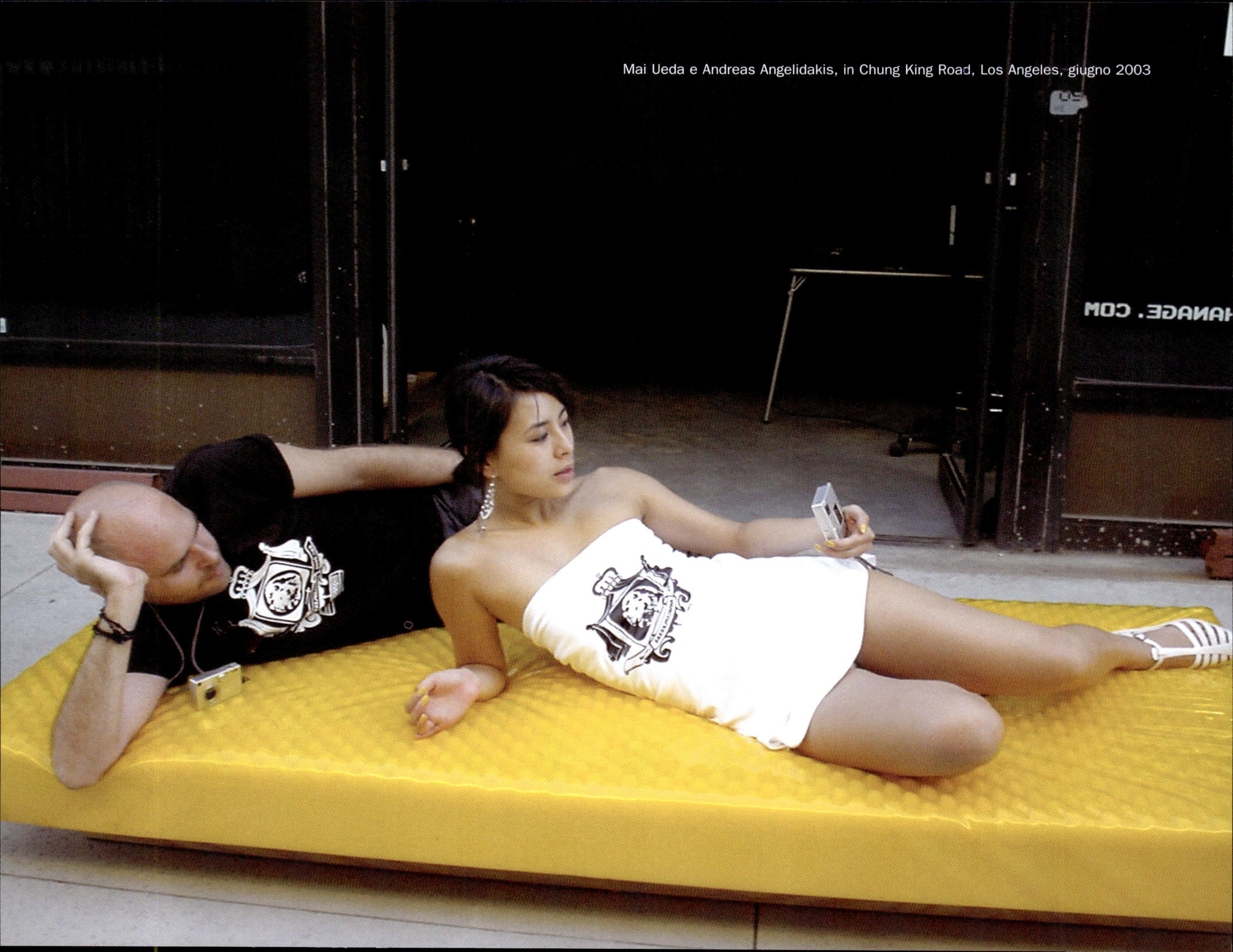

Mai Ueda e Andreas Angelidakis, in Chung King Road, Los Angeles, giugno 2003

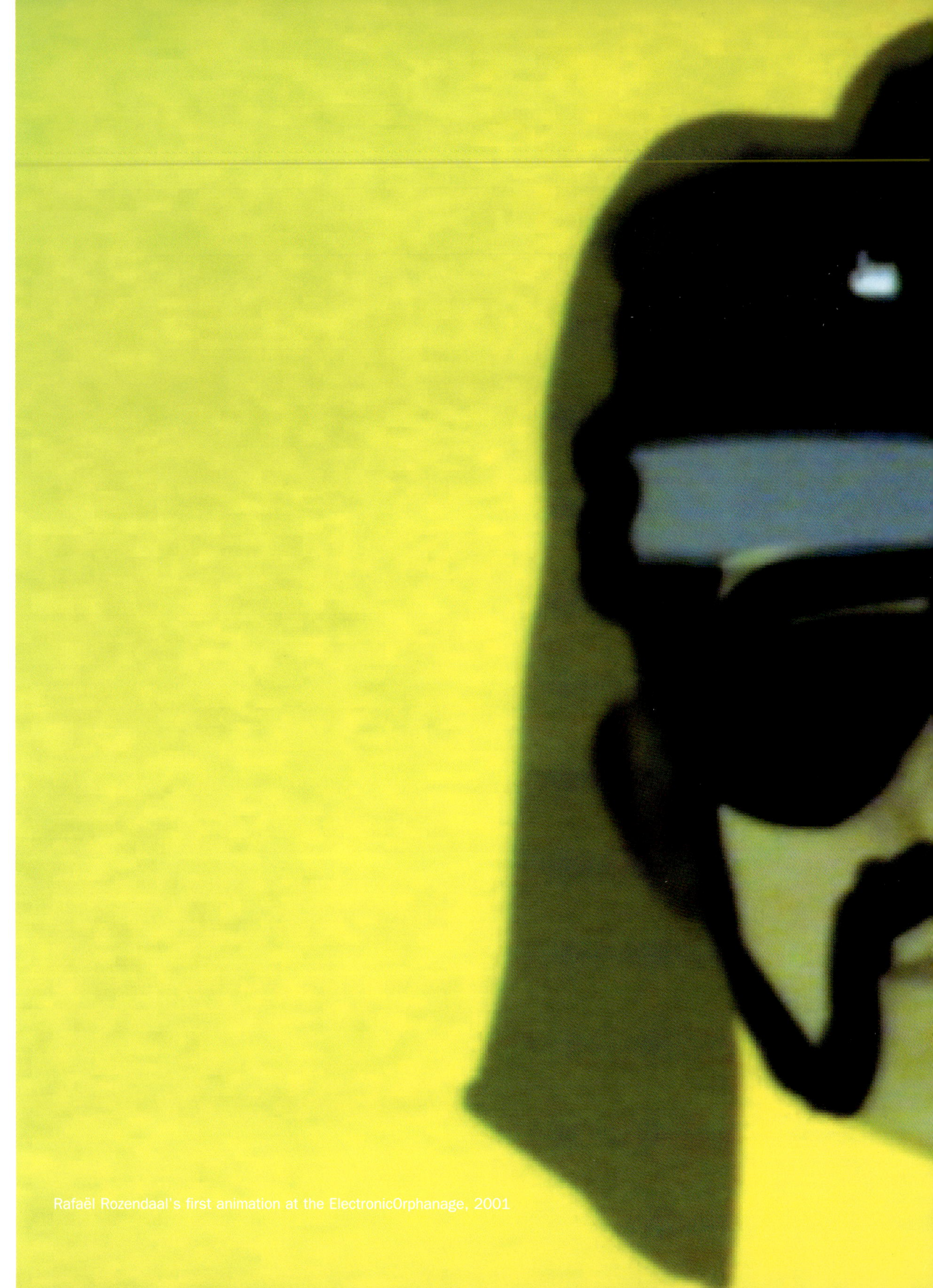

Rafaël Rozendaal's first animation at the ElectronicOrphanage, 2001

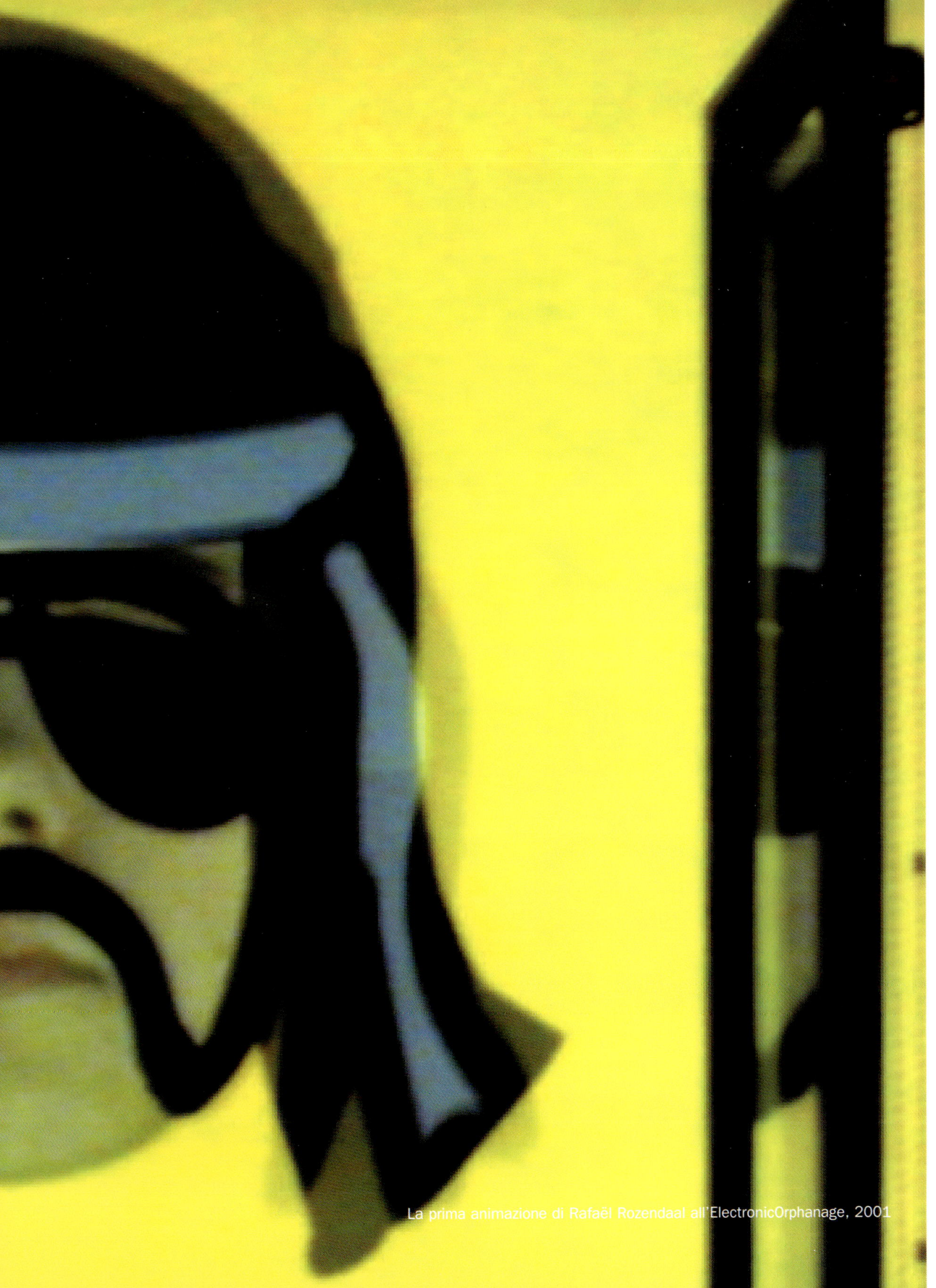

La prima animazione di Rafaël Rozendaal all'ElectronicOrphanage, 2001

The Neen Paradise

Interview with Miltos Manetas by Olivier Zahm, Drawings Mai Ueda

Greek artist Miltos Manetas has migrated from Athens to Millano to New York City, finally settling in Los Angeles, a city lying at the very limits of the West's Greek heritage. He has made videos and performance pieces, becoming a computer fanatic and eventually turning to making paintings of and for computer screens. He manipulates video games and now talks about the end of art and his newly created fantasy of an art of the future which he calls "neen"—a youthful-sounding word he bought from professional logo creators and applied to his end-all, begin-all art scheme. A corrosive humor lies at the core of the end-game strategy he has constructed out of commercial ideas, commercial products, and a publicist's view of art.

Olivier Zahm: You created a new art or esthetic movement and called it NEEN. How did it start?
Miltos Manetas: For a long time I asked friends, curators and writers to invent a new movement, or at least to find a name for one. I was tired of being seen and categorized as a contemporary artist—artists who do mostly photography, objects, and installations, and with whom I feel no affiliation. Someone like Damien Hirst, for example. I wanted something similar to movements like Dada or Cubism. The question was to find a name with glory which would also function as a barrier to keep away any art that doesn't really matter to or concern it. But no one came up with a usable name. There were some trials. Nicolas Bourriaud, introduced, in 1995, Relational Esthetics and, in 1996, the Purple group came with *Beige*. But I couldn't go to my father and say: "I do Relational Aesthetics," he would say something like, "Oh god, my son is a scientist, or social worker or something." *Beige* was very good for a moment and there are still things happening which are *Beige*. During 1995-1997 *Beige* was the spirit of the times more than anything that British artists were doing. Then, in 1998, everything changed and *Beige* could not cover my theories or those of my new friends. Even computers ceased to be *Beige* and all the suggestive romantic misery started to look fake and really cheap. Therefore, there was an urgency for a new name.

How did you come up with the name NEEN?
I happened to read a story in *Wired* magazine about Lexicon Branding, the company that created the names Pentium

and PowerBook. Suddenly I knew that these were the people who I should ask for a name. They were professionals. They find names for whatever. They charge an average of $100 to $150,000, and they offer different names from which to choose and to purchase.

So you paid for it.
Of course not. I contacted Yvonne Force and Art Production Fund and we realized the project together. She actually suggested that we offer the name to the public in a performative and glamorous way, with important personalities as guest stars. This is how we decided to do a big Demo at the Gagosian gallery in Chelsea, and write an elaborate press release. We did it on the last day of May 2000. We set up a panel with the president of Lexicon, David Placec; MIT neurolinguist Steven Pinker; games critic and the writer of *Videogames Nation*, J. C. Herz; art theorist Peter Lunenfeld; and a special appearance via video of Joseph Kosuth. We had a Sony Vaio laptop introduce it, using its robotic voice: "Ladies and Gentleman," it said to a shocked public, "the new name for contemporary art is NEEN. We hope that you like it! N-E-E-N. A computer program found the name. Have a nice evening." We had Warhol paintings of the diamond shadows all around, and we projected NEEN samples. And Gnac wrote the music : the NEEN scene.

How did you get Lexicon to go in such a semiotic direction ?
Yvonne and I went to their office in Sausalito, California,

and we showed them works by different artists, providing them with a frame of reference and the "landscape" of activities we were asking a name for. We explained to them that the name should represent mostly things not yet made, that it should recall technology, new media, computer screens, and computer culture, and that most of all, it should allude to works which are apparently unrelated, such as a sliced canvas by Lucio Fontana; the Capri Battery by Beuys, which is a yellow lemon next to a yellow light ball; the large paintings by Anselm Kiefer, which look so much like video games in reproduction and so obsolete in reality. I suppose that we confused them, but three months later they emailed us a list of about a hundred names, among them was NEEN.

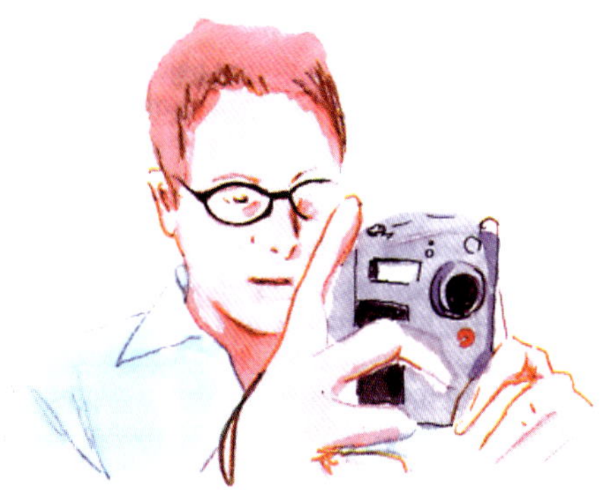

Is Lexicon *a computerized semiotic production company? How did they come up with the name?*
They use work groups composed of different types of people, who work together and separately to find names. They also have a proprietary software. A program was actually created for NEEN. I think they mixed the words "screen" and "seen" and were looking for a palindrome like Dada, because we told them that we wanted something as fresh and unpretentious as the word "dada".

What other names did they come up with?
I am not allowed to disclose them, but one was TELIC. Another was OLO which is a cubist word, others were ONQ and ESC.

Why did you choose NEEN?
Because Mai Ueda [Miltos's girlfriend] and other Japanese people really liked it. Mai immediately started to call herself a NEENster. She likes art, but she feels slightly embarrassed calling herself an artist. NEENster worked fine for her. Later, another friend from Tokyo explained to me that when Japanese do branding, they always try to include an 'n' and an 'e' because, for them, the sound of those letters are a successful combination. Think about Sony, Nintendo, Pokemon, etc. After we chose it, it also occurred to me that NEEN, in ancient Greek, means now.

Is NEEN *an art category or is it a nonartistic term?*
It functions like a third category: good, bad, and NEEN, or

art, nonart, and NEEN. It refers, in a way, to the Internet and to computer art, to software and hardware, and even to architecture and design. For example, the new Apple Cinema display is NEEN and the fat monitors we used to have on our desktops are not. The way Sony builds laptops is NEEN, and Apple's laptops were once NEEN, but now they're not—they look like covers for toilet seats. Emulation software and Macromedia's Flash is NEEN, while Microsoft's products are never NEEN. In terms of architecture, we want to separate conservative solutions, such as the architecture of Bernard Tsumi, from visionary works, such as 3-D world building, the book *S, M, L, XL* by Rem Koolhaas, the architectural work by Andreas Angelidakis (angelidakis.com), or the computer engineering, nonbuilding architecture of Takehiko Nagakura.

Is NEEN *a political word?*
We wanted a name that would defend the open source, freeware movement. Freeware is NEEN, while serial numbers and registrations aren't. We are currently doing a website against intellectual property and copyright (iamgonnacopy.com), where creators can vote if they agree that everything should be allowed to be copied or if they are for IPs and copyrights.

Why does NEEN *fight against copyright laws?*
The copyright is one of the most urgent social and political issues for NEENsters. Our world is largely composed of information, in the same way that yesterday's world was mostly about trees and land. We must keep information free and available to anyone. It's stupid to consider yourself the owner of an idea just because you think of something. It's also criminal: States use police to stop poor people from copying entertainment products (such as Harry Potter in China), and they try to stop the poor from using tools (such as Microsoft, in China again) without paying

for them, so that they stay poor forever. Piracy is good: let's copy as much as possible and encourage others to copy our products.

How do you decide what is NEEN and what is not NEEN?
The difference between a NEEN work and a non-NEEN work is like the difference between the sympathy we feel for a child as opposed to our irrational aversion to a midget.

Are you a NEENster yourself?
I hope, but maybe I'm just a boring painter. At least I try to live in a NEEN way, having divided my personality in different Websites. And my paintings are mostly sketches for JPEG computer images. That's the way I enjoy them.

What is important for a NEENster?
To become a public persona not only using the available media but transforming oneself into media, which is more than being a popstar or a flaming sun. A NEENster is a producer, not a product. NEENsters do things not as a job— and not even for creativity or self expression.

What's the difference between a NEEN artwork and contemporary art?
Installations, photographs, and art made with found objects are the stuff that today fills the empty spaces of museums and illustrates the pages of magazines and catalogues. They are conventional products for an old niche market. Any art student knows how to produce them nicely and professionally. The same happens to pop design and blobby architecture. While the SodaConstructor animal by Soda, the Objok by Golan Levin, the Vines by Deconcept, Experimental Jetset's designs, the Flash animations by Mike Calvert and Joel Fox, and the square watermelons produced in the Japanese town of Zentsuji are nothing like that. These works require the creation of a new market, and a new type of person who will collect and maybe consume them.

Is NEEN directly connected to the idea of a screen?
That's what we say to the public for promotional reasons, but even SCREEN is not NEEN. If it was NEEN, it should have no volume and no support, it should simply float around or be activated on a regular wall for a while and then dis-

appear. NEEN, for the moment, is more of a state of mind or an undefined psychology than a piece of art, design, or architecture. Building a movement around NEEN is like saving a bookmark for a dream we had the night before.

What were the first notable reactions to NEEN?
We didn't try to push NEEN in the magazines or in the media. It would have been too easy—immediately after we introduced it—to fill every glossy magazine, and dangerous too, because NEEN would have expired quickly. We preferred instead to present NEEN on the Net, and to see how corporations, young people, scientists, etc., would react.

What happened on the Net?
I receive emails every week from people who declare themselves to be NEEN. They send me samples of their work. Most of it is terrible, but a few works are very interesting. Some Japanese companies, such as Toshiba and Shiseido have asked for details about this new American trend. The most remarkable response was from a group of Greek philosophers, who created the site, greekworks.com. They asked us if September 11 was NEEN!

So, was 9-11 NEEN?
Unfortunately it was, at least in terms of spectacle and technology. The fact that they succeeded by only using cheap technology—some box cutters and a few pilot-training lessons—to wipe out two enormous towers, symbols of capitalism, of the capitalist empire. . . . It was like an artist who, for example, takes the ".fla" of a Flash animation and even though he doesn't know how to use Flash, he changes the objects in its library and produces a great artwork.

NEEN is necessarily low tech?
It's more like easy tech—using what's available and optimizing it with the least effort possible. Artists in the nineties were producers. Think of Matthew Barney, etc. NEEN people are editors and optimizers.

Who are NEENsters? Are they coming out of art schools?
Some come from art schools, but they are not the usual *Artforum* readers. They like Design's Republik, newstoday.com and shift.org more than Paul McCarthy. Some are working scientists, computer addicts, designers. Most don't have jobs, only computers and lot of free time.

In Los Angeles you opened a space called Electronic Orphanage. Why did you choose Chung King Road, in Chinatown?
Chinatown, which is in East LA, near downtown, is a very different place from the New York Chinatown. It was built in the 50s as a simulation of a Chinese neighborhood—a stage more than a real place, destined for tourists who never really came. Today, it's a cheap poetic area, completely alien to the Hollywood reality, but very suggestive for artists and musicians, who of course took the opportunity to transform Chung King Road into one of the hottest places in LA. Chung King Road is a pedestrian road which hosts young vanguard galleries, such as China Art Objects, Inmo gallery, and lately Aaron Rose's gallery, as well as fashion designers Loyd and Ford.

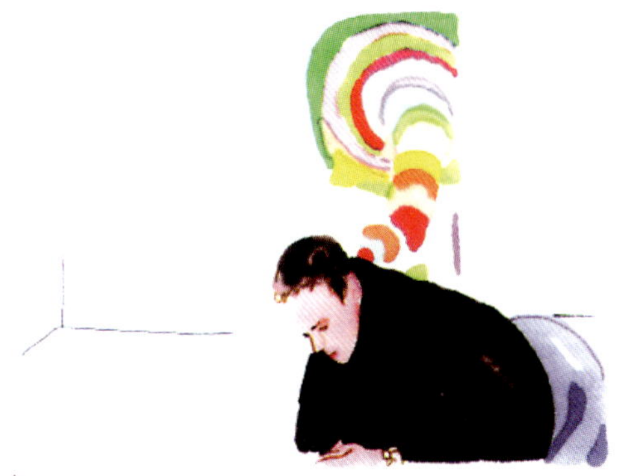

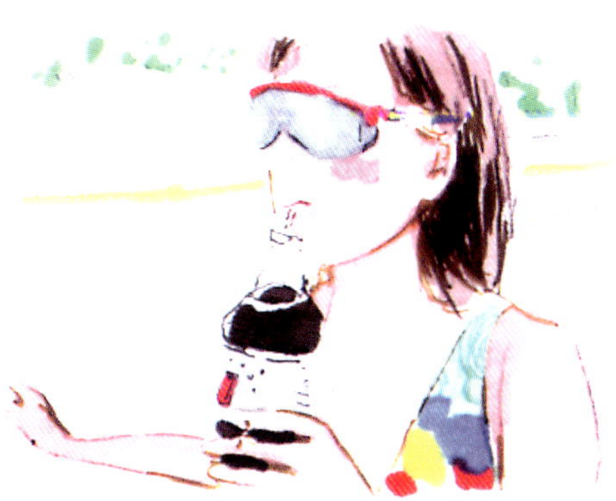

Does Electronic Orphanage function like a gallery?
It's more like a club for screen safaris and for theories. I didn't want to open a gallery myself, but the public was there anyway, and we could have visitors without sending invitations, because of other openings. We open it whenever there are gallery openings around and we project a NEEN piece which we either discover on the Internet or get from artists we run across. The space is an empty storefront, basically a black cube with a white wall that serves for the screenings. Visitors watch projections from the street. The doors are open, but for the most part, the public is not allowed inside. There is a sofa in the street where they can sit to watch the screening. Nobody explains anything to them. Visitors have to go on EO's Website to obtain further information. Those visitors who are invited in become "orphans" once they're inside. I arrange for some of them to go to other countries on the Internet, and to be orphans there for a while. Some return for other visits. Some send other visitors. All activities can been seen on-line at electronicorphanage.com. The rest of the time, the EO becomes a studio/office for different NEENsters. I provide the computers etc., and they take Internet safaris, play videogames, talk, build Websites, etc.

Who are some of the orphans?
They are a mix of different generations, from very young girls, who don't know about Karl Marx, to intellectuals like Norman Klein, who is one of the most astute California writers and the author of *The History of Forgetting,* Lev Manovich, a pioneer of new media theory, and Peter Lunenfeld, who wrote *Digital Dialectics.* They keep an eye on us and sometimes curate events. There's Mai Ueda and her robotic sister Juribot; Mike Calvert, Joel Fox, Tim Kho, and Steven Scholne, who are constantly producing pieces and finding other people on the Web and in real life. Collaborators include Rafaele Rozendall from white-trash.nl, Amy Franceschini from Future Farmers, who is one of the best animation designers on the Web in the US as well as a very charismatic artist; architects like Andreas Angelidakis and Francois Perrin, cofounders of World++, which is a virtual world in Active Worlds—a sequence from the art and architecture, chelsea.com. There are designers like Nicola Tosic (nekada.com), and Angelo

Plessas and Jonathan Maghen from textfield.org; and composers such as Mark Tranmer from Gnac and Ryan Francesconi, who wrote the software program, Spongefork, which is a great software to use as an instrument. Everyone's works and ideas are discussed and criticized and ultimately debugged and optimized. Everything is welcome as long as it doesn't look like the stuff in the galleries next door.

What are other EO activities, besides the public projections?
We work on Websites like iamgonnacopy.com and whomadewhat.com, which is a Web archive that documents inventions in the arts, such as Andy Warhol's Coca Cola paintings, circa 1967, and Jeff Koons' Michael Jackson sculpture from 1988, etc. It's a fast, self-generating art history, where the public is invited to contribute. Another EO project was biennale.net, a Website that shows the best art now made for screens. We did the first version of biennale.net as a commission for *Flash Art* magazine, which will be shown for the Tirana Biennale in Albania. We're working on an anti-show for the Whitney Biennial : whitneybiennial.com. And of course, we work on the World++ project, which is the ActiveWorlds' 3-D city.

Is the huge NEVER tattoo on your back the result of a love story. Is it too personal to speak about?
Mike Calvert, my collaborator in the EO, and Mai Udea, my girlfriend, traveled together to Europe for the biennale.net at Tirana, in Amsterdam, where Mai created a performance and Mike Calvert made a lecture. On September 11th, on a train to Italy, they fell in love and Mike was stupid enough to email me the news. He thought I would be cool enough to accept a three-way situation. I am not. I somehow wished that this had never happened and even that my love for Mai had never evolved. It was the days of the World Trade Center attack, and I felt that "never" had suddenly become actual and permanent. When Mai came back I asked her if I should write the word "never" on my back. She felt very positive about it. If she wouldn't have liked it, I wouldn't have done it, therefore the tattoo is her work because she "animated" it.

Is the tattoo a NEEN act?
It's definitely NEEN. This tattoo is a work by Mai Ueda, although she didn't thought of it. She asked Mike Calvert to design it. Some NEEN acts are very different from the usual contemporary art projects. In contemporary art, artists prepare situations—performances, videos, installations—in order to produce something, a product, that is more or less predictable. NEEN people, by contrast, create without a scenario or standard forms, such as my NEVER tattoo. The person whose style looks more closely like the final form becomes the creator of the piece even if he or she did not think of it. The different participants behave like interconnected peripherals, but at the end, all actions revert to one person. Think of the final artwork as a disease, where the one who looks the most sick from it is its creator. Unlike many collective works, this working method is multiprocessing but not collaborative. It's the work of a single person, even if that person didn't know that he or she wanted to create it.

Does NEEN affect your art and your vision of everyday life?
We are trying to define what could be a NEEN lifestyle. To do that we've borrowed the theory of multiple universes from quantum physics. For example, because of the 11 September incident in New York, I am simultaneously alive and dead. I'm alive because the airplanes hit the towers while I was observing them from a friend's flat in Harlem. I'm dead because in some other universe the planes missed the World Trade Center and fell in Harlem instead, where I was killed.

Does that mean that ever since 9-11 you are a vampire, half alive, half dead? This is the contemporary condition, according to the French philosopher, Mehdi Belhaj Kacem: a state in which we are not able to die, nor able to live.
Correct. We must now determine the vampire behavior, and how it applies to all the people who were in New York on the 11th of September. It would be an interesting exercise for Mehdi.

Do you mean that according to NEEN, our life is made up of multiple universes that we can activate? Are these multiple experiences equally real and virtual?
More or less. All this is under construction. But again I'm not a philosopher. Yet what we call virtual and real are no longer different—if they ever were different, which I doubt. According to the multiple universes theory, there is, for example, a Miltos Manetas who never undertook art as an occupation and is now teaching letters in Greece, as his mother suggested. There is also a successful but frustrated installation artist named Miltos, because I have had success in art since leaving art school in 1992, and had no reason to start painting but did. All these versions of myself exist in a parallel universe to this one, from which I am now writing this email to you. It would be NEEN to think that if not all universes are real then at least the one closest to what you consider your reality is real.

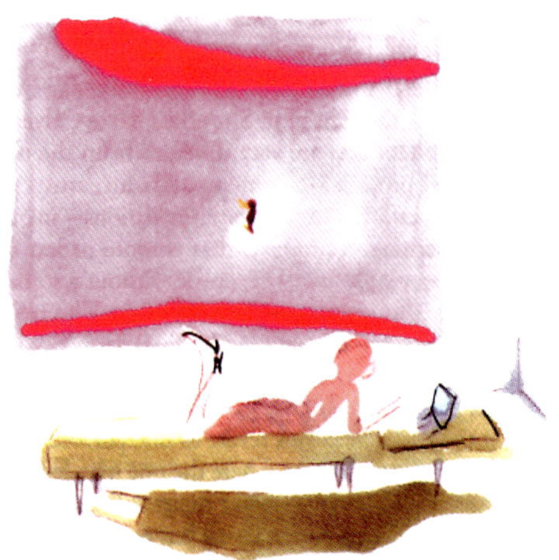

How do NEENsters see the present and future?
One NEEN idea is the hypothesis that the past is not fixed, that it's a combination of features from the pool of possibilities that your life has created. I am now a painter, even if I had absolutely no talent until six years ago, because I decided to become a painter. Therefore, I select from the past the version of myself where I had an interest in painting.

How do you see the art world today in which you are a successful non-NEEN artist?
I don't read any magazines and I don't know who the famous artists of the moment are. I sometimes try to read them, but I get bored so I give up. I also don't believe in exhibitions. I'm sorry for all the curators around, but today most of them are less important than cafeteria waiters. Eventually, as contemporary art becomes something of local pride, each curator will be a personal museum. What would be nice, would be if we allowed them to pass their museums to their sons and daughters.

Do you still consider the work of any artists from your generation?
I still think Vanessa Beecroft's work is surprising and beautiful. And I have fun with Maurizio Cattelan's pieces. The rest I find unremarkable.

Who are the worst artists today, from a NEEN perspective?
Most of the famous British artists.

Does NEEN have a political meaning which might be an extension of an empire?
I wish it did, because that would be fun. We're looking for philosophers who can put together ideas for something like that. I recently discovered Antonio Negri, but he's a bit too Marxist for my taste, although I like his idea of a "multitude" in contrast to people. He inspired me to install a cordon at EO, to separate VIPs from guests in our exhibitions. Democracy today involves ways to protect yourself and your friends from the public.

By categorizing visitors to your shows as VIP and visitors—by separating your public—are you calling the public the enemy? Are you questioning not what is the next revolution, but who has to be fought? If so, who is the enemy?
There's no enemy, there's only the annoying and the beloved. You want to keep the two apart, just like you would close the door of your room when you were fifteen when you and your friends were smoking dope and you didn't want your parents to bother you—even if it informed them that something sinister was going on.

Do you think that promoting piracy is a way to fight capitalism, because they will make fewer products and give away more information (as product)?
I think it's good when creative people lose money because then other people will be recycling their ideas. Most of the

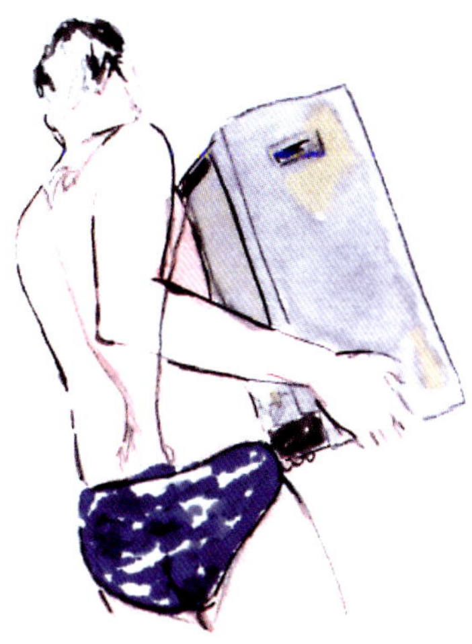

interesting people I know, immediately after they started to earn serious money, they became monkeys, ready for the zoo. I think if we get rid of IP and copyright, the large companies will pay even more for ideas, because the payment will be the only way for them to distinguish themselves from others who use the information or products for free. All jeans companies can put my picture in their campaign, but only Levis has the power to pay me enough to endorse their campaign. There are, of course, people, including Noam Chomsky, who disagree (writing to us at <u>iamgonna-copy.com</u>) with our anti-copyright agenda and who support the idea that creators who are *not* famous or connected will be left out and their works will be stolen. We believe that because of the Internet everybody is already famous and well-connected.

Does the NEEN project contradict your painting activity?
Not really, because I paint like a cleaning lady. I take the dust away from my images and prepare them to be used for the screen. An architect friend says my paintings fit well inside his constructions, while paintings by, say John Currin, look like shit. That's a reason to continue, I suppose.

You mean that your paintings look better as JPEG pictures on the Net than they do in a livingroom in Paris's 16th arrondissement?
In both places they look fine. I just consider their presence in the computer screen more important, because that will be the livingroom of the future.

What are the countries or places in the world that inspire you now?
Just Internet.

Do you think that, as Sloterdijk said, alternative people are the children of catastrophe, in a civilization of panic? Are you as cynical as some people think?
I'm not cynical at all. My role model is Socrates and not Diogenes. Anyway, it would be impossible to be cynical today because the establishment is so cynical already. I tend to see the capitalist machine as an operating system that is more digital than analog and therefore easy to hack. Hacking and piracy are our tools. It's more funny than dramatic, or at least it seems that way from this side of the ocean. This fact, or illusion, is the reason that I would never return to Europe. I was thinking today that I can't think of one reason that would bring me back to Europe, not for all the money, power, love, or success in the world. I'm better off as a little stone near the Pacific than an institution in the Euroworld.

Are NEEN artists conformist?
Yes, they are conformist. Being conformist means to fake your concession to a system. When a system becomes dangerous, to collaborate with it is the only way to continue to realize your dreams. That's what Negri did when he escaped to France and became an academic in the service of his enemies. Revolution is cooler, but artists are usually too lazy for revolution. Remember that the main occupation of an artist is to be close to the center of corruption so that it can be more easily observed and represented. We always want to be like Goya in the company of princes and kings.

Why do you often use the word 'fun' to describe art?
Not 'fun'— that's more for artists like Maurizio Cattelan— but 'cute'. I want to see really cute stuff —not like Mike Kelley's trash, but things that are cute like the clean-shaven face of Jesus in Caravaggio's *Supper at Emmaus*, or cute like the "Strawberries and Pizza" flash animation by Mike Calvert. Cute and NEEN.

IL PARADISO NEEN

Intervista a Miltos Manetas di Olivier Zahm. Disegni di Mai Ueda

L'artista greco Miltos Manetas è migrato da Atene a Milano e New York, per poi approdare a Los Angeles, una città ai limiti estremi della tradizione greca d'Occidente. Ha realizzato video e performance, è diventato un fanatico del computer e in seguito è passato a creare dipinti di e per schermi di computer. Manipola videogiochi e oggi parla della fine dell'arte e della sua neonata fantasia di un'arte del futuro che chiama "Neen", una parola dal suono giovanilistico che ha acquistato da una società di creatori di logo e ha applicato al suo progetto artistico onnicomprensivo. Un umorismo corrosivo caratterizza il nucleo di questa strategia da finale di partita che ha costruito partendo da idee commerciali, da prodotti commerciali e da una visione pubblicitaria dell'arte.

Olivier Zahm: Tu hai creato un nuovo movimento artistico o estetico e lo hai chiamato NEEN. Come è iniziato?
Miltos Manetas: Per molto tempo ho chiesto ad amici, curatori e scrittori di inventare un nuovo movimento, o almeno di trovargli un nome. Ero stanco di essere visto ed etichettato come un artista contemporaneo, dato che gli artisti contemporanei fanno perlopiù fotografia, oggetti e installazioni e io non mi sento in alcun modo vicino a loro. Gente come Damien Hirst, per esempio. Volevo qualcosa di simile a movimenti come il Dada o il cubismo. La questione era trovare un bel nome che facesse anche da barriera per tenere lontana tutta l'arte che non c'entra nulla. Ma nessuno se ne uscì con un nome utilizzabile. Vi fu qualche tentativo. Nicolas Bourriaud nel 1995 presentò il nome Estetica Relazionale e nel 1996 il gruppo di *Purple* propose *Beige*. Ma io non potevo andare da mio padre a dirgli: "Io faccio Estetica Relazionale". Avrebbe pensato qualcosa del tipo: "Oddio, mio figlio è uno scienziato o un assistente sociale o roba del genere". *Beige* fu un ottimo nome per un po' e ancora oggi succedono delle cose *Beige*. Nel 1995-1997 *Beige* era lo spirito del tempi più di qualsiasi cosa facessero gli artisti inglesi. Poi, nel 1998 cambiò tutto e *Beige* non bastava più a coprire le mie teorie o quelle dei miei amici. Anche i computer smisero di essere *Beige* e tutta quella suggestiva tristezza romantica iniziò a sembrare falsa ed estremamente *cheap*. E quindi serviva un nuovo nome.

Come hai trovato il nome NEEN?
Ho letto un articolo sulla rivista *Wired* in cui si parlava della Lexicon Branding, la società che aveva creato i nomi Pentium e PowerBook. Capii immediatamente che erano loro le persone a cui avrei dovuto chiedere quel nome. Erano professionisti. Trovano nomi per qualsiasi cosa. In media fanno pagare tra i 100 e i 150 000 dollari e offrono diversi nomi da scegliere e acquistare.

Così hai pagato per quel nome.
Certo che no. Ho contattato Yvonne Force e l'Art Production Fund e abbiamo realizzato il progetto insieme. È stata lei a proporre di presentare il nome al pubblico in un modo performativo e *glamour*, invitando come ospiti delle personalità importanti. È così che abbiamo deciso di fare una grande demo alla Gagosian Gallery di Chelsea e scrivere un elaborato comunicato stampa. L'abbiamo fatto l'ultimo giorno del maggio 2000. Abbiamo organizzato una conferenza con il presidente della Lexicon, David Placek, il neurolinguista del MIT Steven Pinker, la critica di videogiochi e autrice di *Il popolo del joystick* J.C. Herz, il teorico dell'arte Peter Lunenfeld e un'apparizione speciale in video di Joseph Kosuth. La presentazione l'abbiamo fatta fare a un portatile Sony Vaio, con la sua voce robotica: "Signore e signori", disse al pubblico scioccato, "il nuovo nome per l'arte contemporanea è NEEN. Speriamo che vi piaccia! N-E-E-N. Il nome è stato trovato da un programma informatico. Buona serata." Avevamo messo dappertutto dipinti di Warhol (le "diamond shadows") e abbiamo proiettato degli esempi di NEEN. E Gnac ha scritto la musica: la scena NEEN.

Come avete fatto entrare la Lexicon in una dimensione così semiotica?
Io e Yvonne siamo andati alla loro sede di Sausalito, in California, e abbiamo mostrato loro dei lavori di diversi artisti, fornendo anche un quadro di riferimento e il panorama di attività per il quale stavamo chiedendo un nome. Abbiamo spiegato loro che il nome avrebbe dovuto rappresentare soprattutto cose

non ancora fatte, che avrebbe dovuto richiamare la tecnologia, i nuovi media, gli schermi di computer e la cultura informatica e che, soprattutto, avrebbe dovuto alludere a lavori che apparentemente non avevano alcun rapporto tra loro, come le tele tagliate di Lucio Fontana, *Capri Battery* di Beuys (ovvero un limone giallo accanto a una lampadina gialla), i grandi dipinti di Anselm Kiefer, che riprodotti assomigliano molto a videogiochi mentre dal vivo appaiono così obsoleti. Immagino che li abbiamo confusi parecchio, ma tre mesi dopo ci hanno inviato via e-mail un elenco di un centinaio di nomi, e tra questi c'era NEEN.

La Lexicon è una società di produzione semiotica informatizzata? Come hanno trovato il nome?
Utilizzano gruppi di lavoro composti da diversi tipi di persone che lavorano sia insieme sia separatamente per trovare i nomi. E hanno anche un software di proprietà. Per NEEN è stato creato un programma apposito. Credo abbiamo mixato le parole "screen" e "seen" e cercato un palindromo come Dada, perché avevamo detto loro che volevamo qualcosa di fresco e poco pretenzioso come la parola "dada".

Quali altri nomi vi hanno proposto?
Non posso parlarne, ma uno era TELIC. Un altro era OLO, che è una parola cubista, e altri erano ONQ ed ESC.

Perché avete scelto NEEN?
Perché è piaciuto molto a Mai Ueda (la ragazza di Miltos) e ad altri giapponesi. Mai ha iniziato subito a definirsi una "NEENstar". A lei piace l'arte, ma prova un certo imbarazzo a definirsi un'artista. NEENstar le suonava bene. E poi un altro amico di Tokyo mi ha spiegato che quando i giapponesi si occupano di *branding* cercano sempre di includere nel nome una "n" e una "e" perché per loro il suono di queste lettere è una combinazione di successo. Pensa a Sony, Nintendo, Pokemon ecc. Dopo che lo avevamo scelto mi è anche venuto in mente che NEEN in greco antico significa "ora".

NEEN è una categoria artistica o un nome non-artistico?
Funziona come una terza categoria: buono, cattivo e NEEN, oppure arte, non-arte e NEEN. In un certo senso si riferisce all'arte di Internet e all'arte informatica, al software e all'hardware, e anche all'architettura e al design. Per esempio il nuovo Apple Cinema è NEEN e i grossi schermi che ingombravano le nostre scrivanie non lo sono. Il modo in cui la Sony costruisce i PC portatili è NEEN e i portatili Apple una volta erano NEEN ma adesso non lo sono più,

sembrano dei copritavola da toilette. Il software di emulazione e Flash di Macromedia sono NEEN, mentre i prodotti Microsoft non lo sono mai. In termini architettonici vogliamo separare le soluzioni conservatrici, come l'architettura di Bernard Tschumi, dai lavori visionari, come la costruzione di mondi 3D, il libro *S, M, L, XL* di Rem Koolhaas, il lavoro architettonico di Andreas Angelidakis (angelidakis.com) o l'architettura non-fisica di ingegneria informatica di Takehiko Nagakura.

NEEN è una parola politica?
Volevamo un nome che difendesse il movimento open source e freeware. Il freeware è NEEN, mentre i numeri seriali e i processi di registrazione non lo sono. Al momento stiamo realizzando un sito contro la proprietà intellettuale e il copyright (iamgonnacopy.com), dove dei creatori di contenuti possono votare per dire se ritengono che tutto possa essere copiabile o se sono a favore della proprietà intellettuale e del copyright.

Perché NEEN lotta contro le leggi sul copyright?
Il copyright è uno dei temi sociali e politici più pressanti per i NEENster. Il nostro mondo è composto in larga parte da informazione, proprio come il mondo di ieri era perlopiù fatto di alberi e terra. Dobbiamo mantenere l'informazione libera e disponibile a tutti.
È stupido considerarsi proprietari di un'idea solo perché si è pensato a qualcosa. Ed è anche criminale: gli stati usano la polizia per impedire ai poveri di copiare i prodotti di intrattenimento (come Harry Potter in Cina) e cercano di impedire loro di utilizzare degli strumenti (come quelli Microsoft, ancora in Cina) senza pagare, in modo che restino poveri per sempre. La pirateria è un bene: copiamo tutto il possibile e incoraggiamo gli altri a copiare i nostri prodotti.

Come decidi cosa è NEEN e cosa non lo è?
La differenza tra un lavoro NEEN e un lavoro non-NEEN è come quella tra la simpatia che proviamo per un bambino e la repulsione irrazionale nei confronti di un nano.

Tu sei un NEENster?
Lo spero, ma forse sono solo un noioso pittore. Quantomeno provo a vivere in modo NEEN, avendo diviso la mia personalità in diversi siti Web. E i miei dipinti sono perlopiù bozzetti per immagini digitali JPEG. È così che mi piace pensarli.

Cosa è importante per un NEENster?
Diventare una persona pubblica, non solo usando i
media disponibili ma trasformandosi in un medium,
il che è più che essere una popstar o un sole splendente.
Un NEENster è un produttore, non un prodotto.
I NEENster fanno delle cose non come un lavoro…
e nemmeno per la creatività o per l'espressione di sé.

*Qual è la differenza tra un'opera d'arte NEEN e l'arte
contemporanea?*
Installazioni, fotografie e arte fatta con oggetti trovati
sono la materia che oggi riempie gli spazi vuoti dei
musei e illustra le pagine di riviste e cataloghi. Sono
prodotti convenzionali per un vecchio mercato di
nicchia. Qualsiasi studente d'arte sa come produrli in
modo carino e professionale. Lo stesso accade per il
design pop e il blob architettonico. Invece, l'animale
Soda Constructor di Soda, l'Objok di Golan Levin,
i Vines di Deconcept, il design di Experimental Jetset,
le animazioni Flash di Mike Calvert e Joel Fox e le
angurie quadrate prodotte nella cittadina giapponese
di Zentsuji, sono tutt'altra cosa. Questi lavori
richiedono la creazione di un nuovo mercato e di un
nuovo tipo di persona che li collezioni e forse li consumi.

NEEN è collegato direttamente all'idea di schermo?
È quello che diciamo al pubblico per ragioni
promozionali, ma anche SCREEN non è NEEN.
Se fosse NEEN non dovrebbe avere né volume né
supporto, dovrebbe semplicemente fluttuare in aria
o essere attivato per un po' su un muro qualsiasi
e poi sparire. NEEN, per il momento, è più uno stato
mentale o una psicologia indefinita che un'opera
d'arte, di design o di architettura. Costruire un
movimento attorno a NEEN è come salvare un
Preferito per un sogno che abbiamo avuto la notte
precedente.

Quali sono state le reazioni più notevoli a NEEN?
Non abbiamo cercato di spingere NEEN sulle riviste
o sui media. Sarebbe stato troppo facile – subito
dopo averlo introdotto – riempire le pagine di tutte le
riviste patinate, e sarebbe stato anche pericoloso,
perché NEEN sarebbe morto in fretta. Abbiamo preferito presentare NEEN in rete e vedere come avrebbero
reagito le imprese, i giovani, gli scienziati ecc.

Cosa è successo in Rete?
Ogni settimana ricevo e-mail da gente che dichiara di
essere NEEN. Mi mandano degli esempi del loro
lavoro. La maggior parte è terribile, ma qualcuno è
molto interessante. Alcune imprese giapponesi, come

la Toshiba e la Shiseido, hanno chiesto di avere più
informazioni su questa nuova tendenza americana.
La reazione più notevole è stata quella di un gruppo di
filosofi greci che hanno creato il sito greekworks.com.
Ci hanno chiesto se l'11 settembre è stato NEEN!

E lo è stato?
Purtroppo sì, almeno in termini di spettacolo
e tecnologia. Il fatto che usando solo tecnologia poco
costosa – qualche taglierino e un po' di lezioni di volo
– siano riusciti a spazzare via due enormi grattacieli,
simboli del capitalismo, dell'impero capitalista…
È stato come un artista che per esempio prende il
".fla" di un'animazione Flash e, anche se non sa
usare Flash, cambia gli oggetti della *library* e produce
una grande opera d'arte.

NEEN è necessariamente low-tech?
È più *easy-tech*: usare quello che è disponibile e
ottimizzarlo con il minor sforzo possibile. Gli artisti
negli anni Novanta erano produttori. Pensa a Matthew
Barney ecc. I NEEN sono montatori e ottimizzatori.

Chi sono i NEENster? Escono dalle scuole d'arte?
Qualcuno sì, ma non sono i soliti lettori di *Artforum*.
Apprezzano più Design's Republik, newstoday.com
e shift.org che Paul McCarthy. Alcuni sono scienziati,
computerdipendenti, designer. La maggior parte non ha
un lavoro, solo dei computer e un sacco di tempo libero.

*A Los Angeles hai aperto uno spazio che si chiama
ElectronicOrphanage. Perché hai scelto Chung King
Road, a Chinatown?*
Chinatown si trova nell'East L.A., vicino a *downtown*,
ed è un posto molto diverso dalla Chinatown di New
York. È stata costruita negli anni Cinquanta per
simulare un quartiere cinese: è più un palco che un
posto reale, destinato a turisti che in realtà non sono
mai arrivati. Oggi è un'area poetica e poco costosa,
completamente aliena dalla realtà di Hollywood, ma molto
suggestiva per artisti e musicisti, che naturalmente
hanno colto l'opportunità di trasformare Chung King
Road in uno dei posti più fighi di Los Angeles. Chung
King Road è una zona pedonale dove si trovano
gallerie d'avanguardia come la China Art Objects, la
Inmo Gallery e ultimamente anche la galleria di Aaron
Rose, oltre agli stilisti Loyd e Ford.

L'ElectronicOrphanage funziona come una galleria?
È più un club per safari informatici e teorie. Non
volevo aprire un'altra galleria, ma il pubblico c'era
in ogni caso e potevamo avere dei visitatori senza

spedire alcun invito, grazie ad altre inaugurazioni.
Noi apriamo ogni volta che ci sono delle inaugurazioni
nelle gallerie della zona e proiettiamo un lavoro NEEN
che scopriamo su Internet o che ci viene dato da un
artista in cui ci siamo imbattuti. Lo spazio è una
vetrina vuota, fondamentalmente un cubo nero con
una parete bianca che serve per le proiezioni.
I visitatori guardano le proiezioni dalla strada.
Le porte sono aperte, ma il pubblico non è ammesso
all'interno. C'è un divano in strada dove la gente si
può sedere a guardare la proiezione. Nessuno spiega
nulla. I visitatori devono andare sul sito dell'E.O. per
ottenere altre informazioni. I visitatori che vengono
invitati a entrare, una volta dentro
diventano "orfani". Io organizzo le cose perché
possano andare in altri paesi con Internet ed essere
orfani lì per un po'. Qualcuno torna per altre visite.
Qualcuno manda altri visitatori. Tutte le attività
possono essere viste on line all'indirizzo
electronicorphanage.com. Per il resto del tempo l'E.O.
diventa lo studio/ufficio di diversi NEENster.
Io fornisco i computer ecc. e loro fanno safari in Internet,
giocano a videogiochi, parlano, creano siti ecc.

Chi sono gli orfani?
C'è un mix di generazioni diverse, da ragazze
giovanissime che non sanno chi sia Karl Marx a
intellettuali come Norman Klein, uno dei più sagaci
scrittori californiani e autore di *The History of
Forgetting*, Lev Manovich, un pioniere della teoria dei
nuovi media, e Peter Lunenfeld, che ha scritto *The
Digital Dialectic*. Loro ci tengono d'occhio e a volte
curano degli eventi. Ci sono Mai Ueda e la sua sorella
robotica Juribot, Mike Calvert, Joel Fox, Tim Kho e
Steven Schkolne, che producono costantemente lavori
e trovano altre persone sul Web e nella vita reale.
Tra i collaboratori ci sono Rafaël Rozendaal di
whitetrash.nl, Amy Franceschini di Future Farmers,
una delle migliori *animation designer* americane per il
Web nonché artista molto carismatica; architetti come
Andreas Angelidakis e Francois Perrin, cofondatori di
World++, un mondo virtuale di Active World – una
sequenza dall'arte e dall'architettura, chelsea.com.
Ci sono designer come Nikola Tosic (nekada.com)
e Angelo Plessas e Jonathan Maghen di textfield.org
e compositori come Mark Tranmer di Gnac e Ryan
Francescani, che ha scritto il software Spongefork, un
programma fantastico da usare come uno strumento.
I lavori e le idee di tutti vengono discussi e criticati,
in sostanza, ripuliti e ottimizzati. È tutto benaccetto,
purché non assomigli alla roba che si trova nelle
gallerie della porta accanto.

*Quali sono le altre attività dell'E.O., a parte le
proiezioni pubbliche?*
Lavoriamo su siti come iamgonnacopy.com e
whomadewhat.com, un archivio su Internet che
documenta le invenzioni nelle arti, come i dipinti della
Coca-Cola di Warhol del 1967 circa e la scultura di
Michael Jackson di Jeff Koons del 1988 ecc. È una
storia dell'arte veloce e autogenerante alla quale il
pubblico è invitato a contribuire. Un altro progetto
dell'E.O. è stato biennale.net, un sito che mostra la
migliore arte prodotta al momento per lo schermo.
Abbiamo realizzato la prima versione di biennale.net
su commissione della rivista *Flash Art* e verrà esposta
per la Biennale di Tirana, in Albania. Ora stiamo
lavorando a una anti-mostra per la Whitney Biennial:
whitneybiennial.com. E naturalmente lavoriamo al
progetto World++, la città 3D di Active World.

*Il grande tatuaggio NEVER che hai sulla schiena è
l'eredità di una storia d'amore. È troppo personale
per parlarne?*
Mike Calvert, il mio collaboratore all'E.O., e Mai Ueda,
la mia ragazza, sono andati insieme in Europa per la
biennale.net a Tirana. Sono andati ad Amsterdam,
dove Mai ha fatto una performance e Mike Calvert ha
tenuto una conferenza. L'11 settembre, su un treno
per l'Italia, si sono innamorati e Mike è stato tanto
stupido da mandarmi la notizia via e-mail.
Ha pensato che io fossi tanto *cool* da accettare una
storia a tre. Non lo sono. Desiderai che non fosse mai
successo e anche che il mio amore per Mai non si
fosse mai evoluto. Erano i giorni dell'attentato al
World Trade Center e sentii che "never" all'improvviso
era una parola reale e permanente. Quando Mai tornò
le chiesi se avrei dovuto scrivermi la parola "never"
sulla schiena. Lei fu d'accordo. Se la cosa non le
fosse piaciuta non l'avrei fatto, per cui il tatuaggio
è un suo lavoro, perché è lei che lo ha "animato".

Il tatuaggio è un atto NEEN?
Decisamente sì. Questo tatuaggio è un lavoro di Mai
Ueda, anche se non è stata lei a pensarlo. Ha chiesto
a Mike Calvert di disegnarlo. Alcuni atti NEEN sono
molto diversi dai soliti progetti di arte contemporanea.
Nell'arte contemporanea gli artisti preparano delle
situazioni – performance, video, installazioni – allo
scopo di produrre qualcosa, un prodotto, che sia più
o meno prevedibile. La gente NEEN invece crea senza
una sceneggiatura e senza forme standard, come nel
caso del mio tatuaggio NEVER. La persona, il cui stile
si avvicina di più alla forma finale, diventa il creatore
dell'opera, anche se non è stata lei a pensarci.

I diversi partecipanti si comportano come periferiche interconnesse, ma alla fine tutte le azioni riconducono a un'unica persona. Pensa all'opera finale come a una malattia: quello che ne sembra più malato è considerato il creatore. A differenza di molti lavori collettivi, questo metodo funziona in *multiprocessing* ma non è collaborativo. È il lavoro di un'unica persona, anche se quella persona non sapeva di volerlo creare.

NEEN influenza la tua arte e la tua visione della vita quotidiana?
Noi stiamo cercando di definire quello che potrebbe essere uno stile di vita NEEN. Per farlo abbiamo preso a prestito la teoria degli universi multipli dalla fisica quantistica. Per esempio, a causa dell'attentato dell'11 settembre a New York io sono, al tempo stesso, vivo e morto. Sono vivo perché gli aerei hanno colpito le torri mentre io li guardavo dalla casa di un amico ad Harlem. Sono morto perché in un qualche altro universo gli aerei hanno mancato il World Trade Center e sono caduti su Harlem, dove io sono stato ucciso.

Questo significa che dall'11 settembre tu sei un vampiro, mezzo vivo e mezzo morto? Questa è la condizione contemporanea, secondo il filosofo francese Mehdi Belhaj Kacem: uno stato in cui non siamo in grado né di morire né di vivere.
Giusto. Ora dobbiamo determinare il comportamento vampiresco e come si applica a tutte le persone che si trovavano a New York l'11 settembre. Sarebbe un esercizio interessante per Mehdi.

Vuoi dire che secondo NEEN la nostra vita è composta di universi multipli che possiamo attivare? Queste esperienze multiple sono ugualmente reali e virtuali?
Più o meno. È tutto in fase di costruzione. E comunque io non sono un filosofo. Ma ciò che chiamiamo virtuale e reale, ormai non è più diverso, se mai lo sia stato, cosa di cui dubito. Secondo la teoria degli universi multipli c'è per esempio un Miltos Manetas che non si è mai occupato di arte e oggi insegna letteratura in Grecia, come avrebbe voluto sua madre. C'è anche un artista di nome Miltos che si occupa di installazioni, ha avuto successo ma è frustrato, perché ha avuto successo nell'arte da quando è uscito dalla scuola d'arte nel 1992 e non aveva alcun motivo di iniziare a dipingere, ma l'ha fatto. Tutte queste versioni di me stesso esistono in un universo parallelo a questo, dal quale in questo momento ti sto scrivendo questa e-mail. Sarebbe NEEN pensare che se non tutti gli universi sono reali lo è almeno quello più vicino a quello che consideri la tua realtà.

Come vedono il presente e il futuro i NEENster?
Un'idea NEEN è l'ipotesi che il passato non sia fissato, che sia una combinazione di caratteristiche del *pool* di possibilità che la tua vita ha creato. Io oggi sono un pittore, anche se fino a sei anni fa non avevo assolutamente alcun talento, perché ho deciso di diventare un pittore. E quindi, seleziono dal passato la versione di me stesso in cui ero interessato alla pittura.

Come vedi il mondo dell'arte attuale in cui tu sei un artista non-NEEN di successo?
Non leggo le riviste e non so chi siano gli artisti famosi del momento. A volte ci provo, ma mi annoio e lascio perdere. E poi non credo nelle mostre. Mi dispiace per i curatori, ma oggi la maggior parte di loro è meno importante del cameriere di una caffetteria. Alla fine, mano a mano che l'arte contemporanea diventerà una questione di orgoglio locale, ogni curatore sarà un museo personale. La cosa carina sarebbe se consentissimo loro di lasciare in eredità i loro musei ai loro figli.

Prendi ancora in considerazione il lavoro di qualche artista della tua generazione?
Ritengo ancora che il lavoro di Vanessa Beecroft sia sorprendente e bello. E mi diverto con le opere di Maurizio Cattelan. Il resto lo trovo insignificante.

Chi sono i peggiori artisti di oggi, da un punto di vista NEEN?
La maggior parte degli artisti inglesi famosi.

NEEN ha un significato politico che potrebbe essere un'estensione di un impero?
Mi piacerebbe, perché sarebbe divertente. Stiamo cercando dei filosofi che riescano a mettere insieme le idee per qualcosa del genere. Ho scoperto di recente Toni Negri, ma è un po' troppo marxista per i miei gusti, anche se mi piace la sua idea di "moltitudine" in opposizione a quella di "gente". Mi ha ispirato a installare un cordone all'E.O., per separare i V.I.P. dagli ospiti nelle nostre mostre. Oggi la democrazia implica dei modi per proteggere te e i tuoi amici dal pubblico.

Suddividendo i visitatori delle tue mostre in V.I.P. e visitatori comuni – separando il tuo pubblico – definisci il pubblico come il nemico? Ti chiedi non

*quale sarà la prossima rivoluzione ma chi si deve
combattere? E in questo caso, chi è il nemico?*
Non c'è nessun nemico, ci sono solo i fastidiosi
e gli adorati. E il desiderio di tenerli separati, come
quando chiudevi la porta della tua stanza quando avevi
quindici anni e tu e i tuoi amici vi facevate le canne
e non volevi che i tuoi genitori vi rompessero
le scatole… anche se quella chiusura li informava del
fatto che stava succedendo qualcosa di sinistro.

*Pensi che promuovere la pirateria sia un modo per
combattere il capitalismo, perché così creeranno
meno prodotti e diffonderanno più informazione (come
prodotto)?*
Credo sia positivo se i creativi perdono soldi, perché
allora altre persone ricicleranno le loro idee.
La maggior parte delle persone interessanti che
conosco, subito dopo avere iniziato a fare soldi sul
serio, sono diventate delle scimmie, pronte per lo zoo.
Penso che se ci sbarazziamo della proprietà
intellettuale e del copyright, le grandi aziende
pagheranno ancora di più per le idee, perché per loro
il pagamento sarà l'unico modo per distinguersi da
chi usa le informazioni o i prodotti gratuitamente.
Tutte le aziende che producono jeans possono usare
le mie immagini nelle loro campagne, ma solo la Levis
ha il potere di pagarmi abbastanza per appoggiare la
sua campagna. Naturalmente, ci sono persone, tra cui
Noam Chomsky, che non sono d'accordo (e ci scrivono
a iamgonnacopy.com) con il nostro programma
anti-copyright e sostengono l'idea che i creatori che
non sono famosi o che non hanno agganci, resteranno
esclusi e i loro lavori verranno rubati. Noi crediamo
che, grazie a Internet, tutti sono già famosi e con
buoni contatti.

Il progetto NEEN contraddice la tua attività di pittore?
No, perché io dipingo come una donna delle pulizie.
Tolgo la polvere dalle mie immagini e le preparo a
essere usate per lo schermo. Un mio amico architetto
dice che i miei dipinti si adattano bene all'interno
delle sue costruzioni, mentre quelli, per esempio
di John Currin, fanno cagare. È una ragione per
continuare, direi.

*Vuoi dire che i tuoi dipinti hanno un aspetto
migliore come JPEG in Rete che in un salotto
del XIV arrondissement di Parigi?*
Hanno un bell'aspetto in entrambi i casi. È solo che
considero più importante la loro presenza sullo
schermo di un computer, perché sarà quello
il salotto del futuro.

*Quali sono i paesi o i posti del mondo che ti
ispirano ora?*
Solo Internet.

*Pensi che, come ha detto Sloterdijk, le persone
alternative siano i figli della catastrofe, in una civiltà
di panico? Sei cinico come pensano alcuni?*
Non sono affatto cinico. Il mio modello è Socrate, non
Diogene. In ogni caso, sarebbe impossibile essere
cinici oggi perché l'establishment è già così cinico. Io
tendo a vedere la macchina capitalista come un sistema
operativo più digitale che analogico, e quindi facile da
piratare. I nostri strumenti sono *l'hacking* e la pirateria.
È più divertente che drammatico, o quantomeno così
sembra da questa parte dell'oceano. Questo fatto –
o questa illusione – è il motivo per cui non tornerei
mai in Europa. Oggi pensavo che non mi viene in
mente nemmeno un motivo che mi potrebbe riportare
in Europa, nemmeno per tutto il denaro, il potere,
l'amore o il successo del mondo. Preferisco essere
un sassolino vicino al Pacifico che un'istituzione a
Euroworld.

Gli artisti NEEN sono conformisti?
Sì, sono conformisti. Essere conformisti significa
falsificare la propria concessione al sistema. Quando
un sistema diventa pericoloso, collaborare con esso è
l'unico modo per continuare a realizzare i propri sogni.
È quello che ha fatto Negri quando è fuggito in Francia
ed è diventato un accademico al servizio del nemico.
La rivoluzione è più *cool*, ma gli artisti di solito sono
troppo pigri per la rivoluzione. Non dimenticare che
l'occupazione principale di un artista è stare vicino
al centro della corruzione per poterlo osservare
e rappresentare più facilmente. Vogliamo sempre
essere come Goya, in compagnia di principi e re.

*Perché usi spesso la parola "divertente" per
descrivere l'arte?*
Non "divertente" – è un aggettivo che funziona più per
artisti come Maurizio Cattelan – ma "carina". Io voglio
davvero vedere cose carine, non come l'immondizia di
Mike Kelley, ma cose carine come la faccia perfettamente
sbarbata di Cristo nella *Cena in Emmaus* di
Caravaggio o carine come l'animazione Flash
Strawberries and Pizza di Mike Calvert.
Carine e NEEN.

da Purple, n. 11, primavera 2002

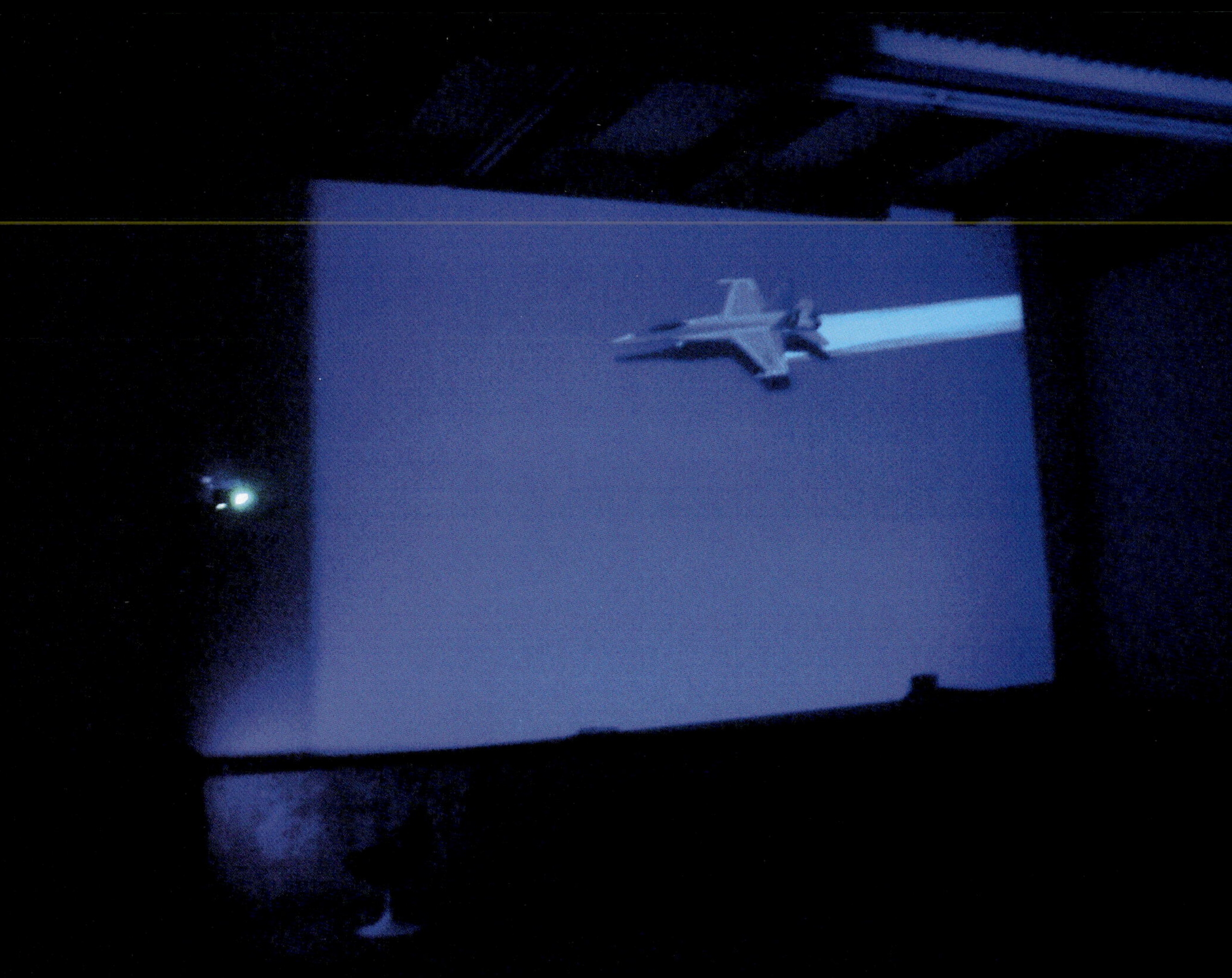

Miltos Manetas, *Miracle*, 1996, video after video game
right, Miltos Manetas, *SuperMario Sleeping*, 1998, video after video game

Q: Could you describe the orphans?
A: They are orphans in terms of an ideology. In the past, people would believe in a system of ideas
such as Marxism or anarchism or whatever: they would belong to an intellectual family.
Today, instead, we don't have any of those, even if most of us came from similar schools of thought
or from common life experiences. We are very different from each other, we are orphans
and we want to stay such.
But the ElectronicOrphans are also people who understand the power of computing: they are mastering
this power and build samples for the unconventional use of computing. In between the EOrphans,
there are two visible categories: people who are Telic and Neenstars. The Telic people are doing a lot
of research, theory, and planning. They have a sense of duty. The Neen people, instead, are careless
and they are doing only Neen. Telic is encouraged and respected in the ElectronicOrphanage,
but the real target of the club is Neen.

from an interview by Isabelle Arvers with Miltos Manetas, fluctuat.net, Paris, August 2002
http://www.fluctuat.net/1253-Miltos-Manetas-Andreas-Angelidakis

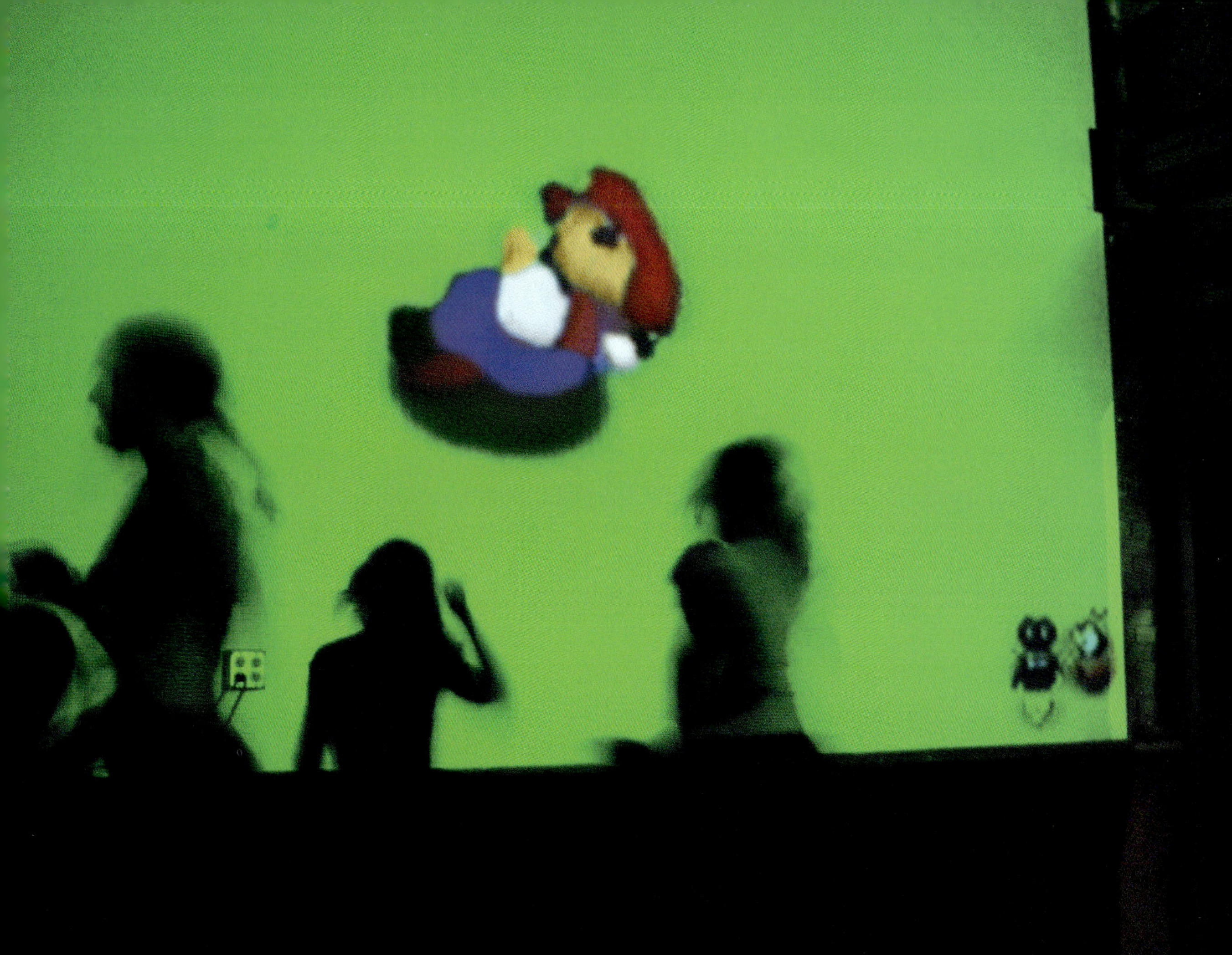

Miltos Manetas, *SuperMario Sleeping*, 1998, video da videogioco
a sinistra, Miltos Manetas, *Miracle*, 1996, video da videogioco

D: Puoi descrivere gli orfani?
R: Sono orfani in senso ideologico. Nel passato la gente credeva in un sistema di idee come il Marxismo
o l'anarchia o qualsiasi altra cosa: si sentivano parte di una famiglia intellettuale.
Oggi invece non abbiamo niente di tutto ciò, anche se la maggior parte di noi viene da scuole di
pensiero simili o da esperienze di vita comuni. Siamo molto differenti l'uno dall'altro, siamo orfani
e vogliamo esserlo.
Ma gli ElectronicOrphans sono anche persone che capiscono il potere della programmazione
al computer: padroneggiano questa potenza e costruiscono campioni per un uso non convenzionale
dei computer. Peraltro, tra gli orfani ci sono due categorie visibili: persone che sono Telic e le Neenstar.
Le persone Telic fanno un sacco di ricerca, teoria e progetti. Hanno il senso del dovere.
Le persone Neen invece sono senza preoccupazioni e fanno solo il Neen.
Telic è incoraggiato e rispettato all'ElectronicOrphanage, ma il vero obiettivo del club è il Neen.

da un'intervista di Isabelle Arvers a Miltos Manetas, fluctuat.net, Parigi, agosto 2002
http://www.fluctuat.net/1253-Miltos-Manetas-Andreas-Angelidakis

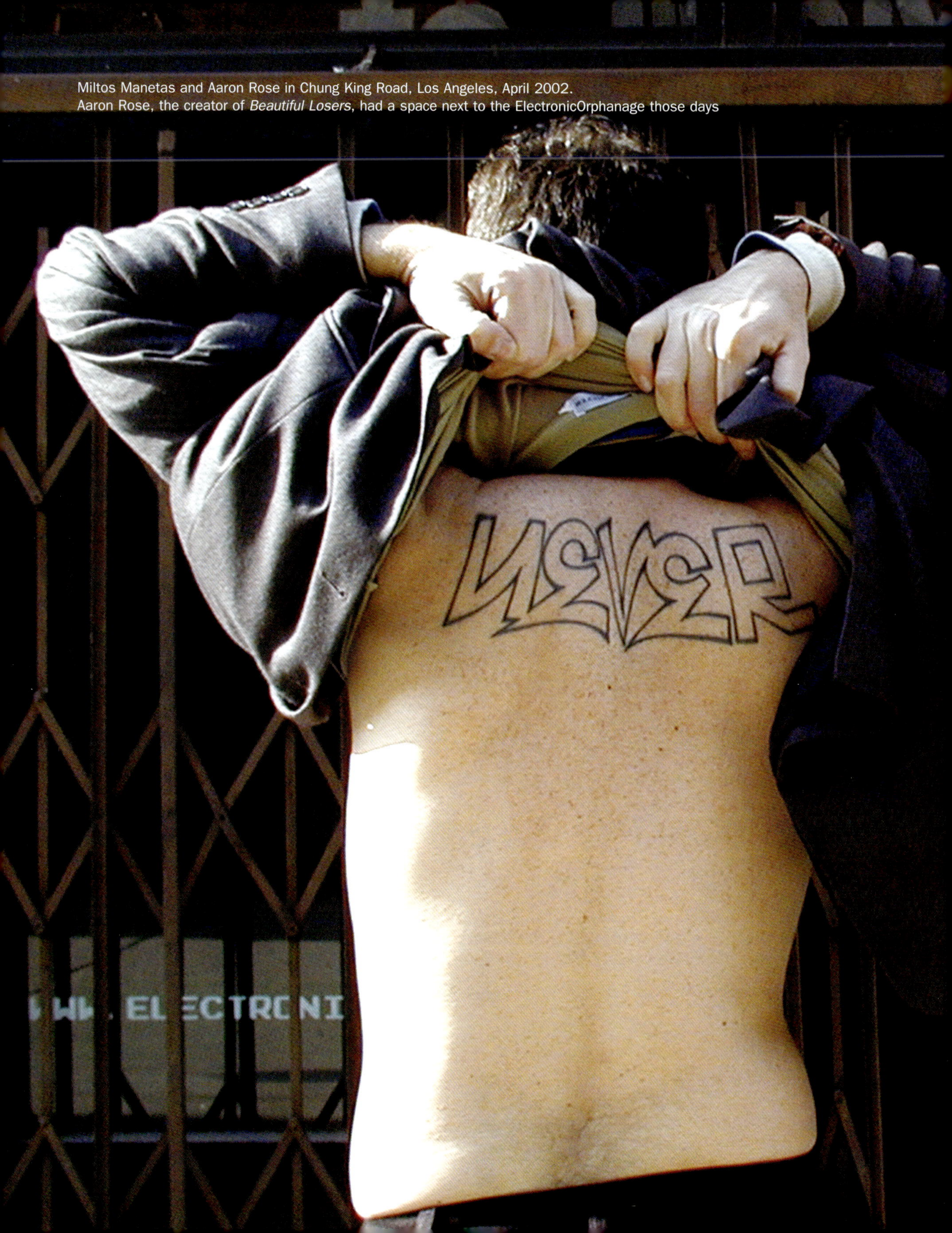

Miltos Manetas and Aaron Rose in Chung King Road, Los Angeles, April 2002.
Aaron Rose, the creator of *Beautiful Losers*, had a space next to the ElectronicOrphanage those days

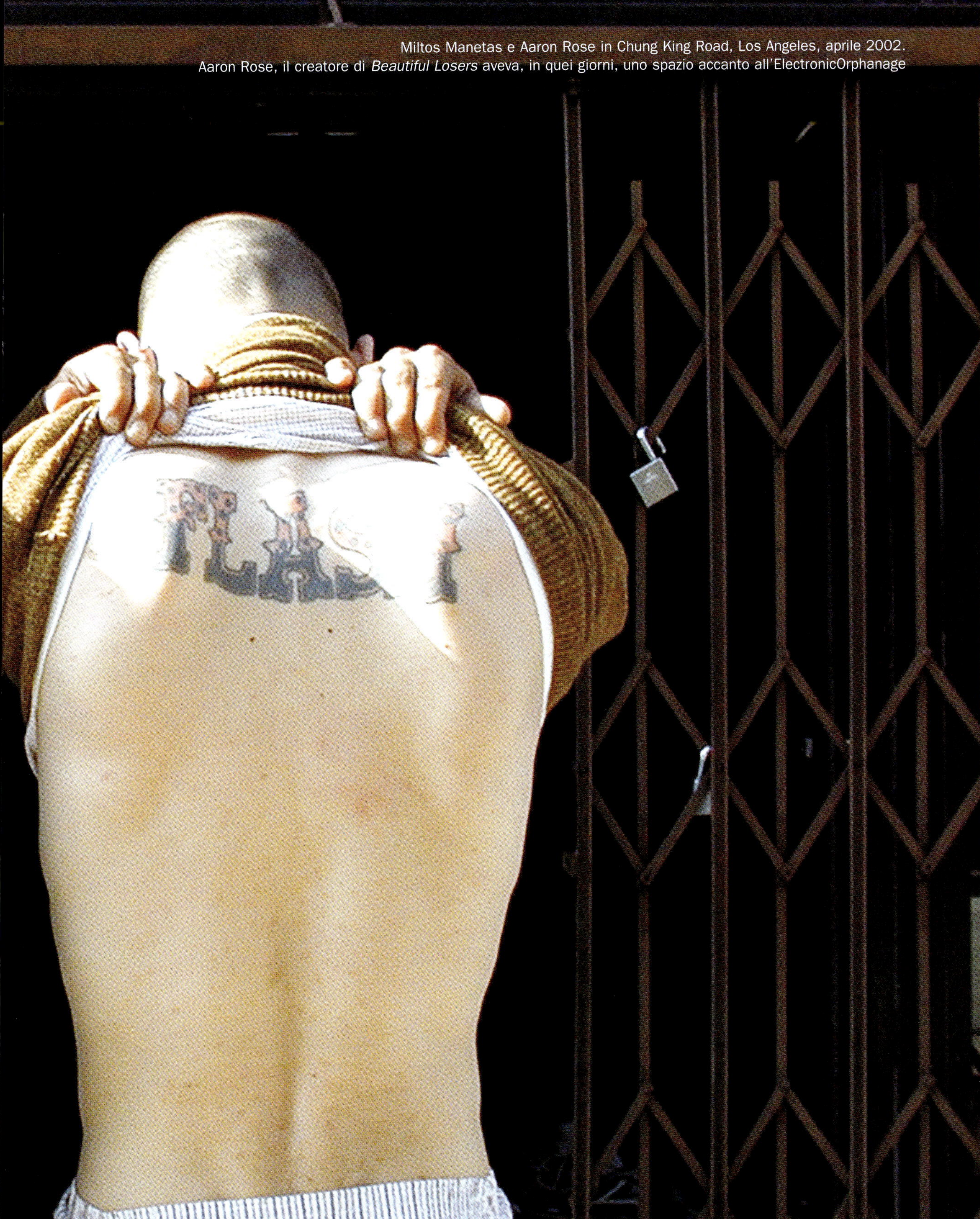

Miltos Manetas e Aaron Rose in Chung King Road, Los Angeles, aprile 2002.
Aaron Rose, il creatore di *Beautiful Losers* aveva, in quei giorni, uno spazio accanto all'ElectronicOrphanage

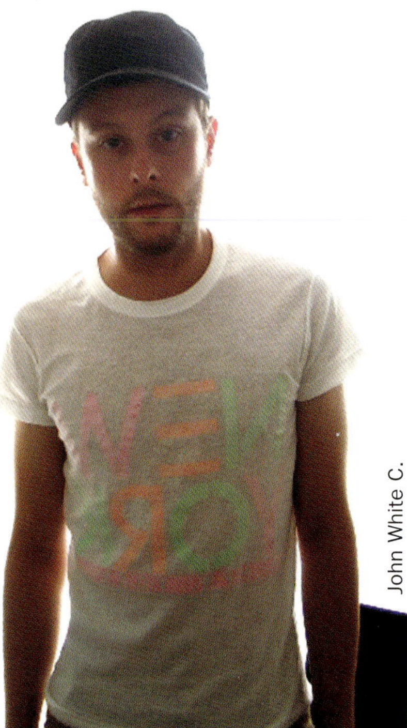

John White C.

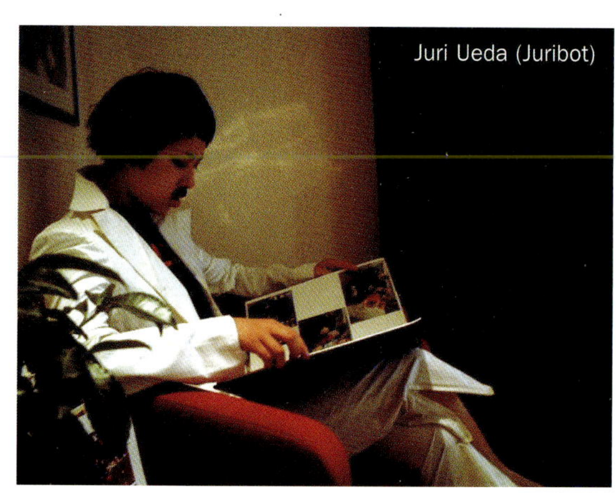

Juri Ueda (Juribot)

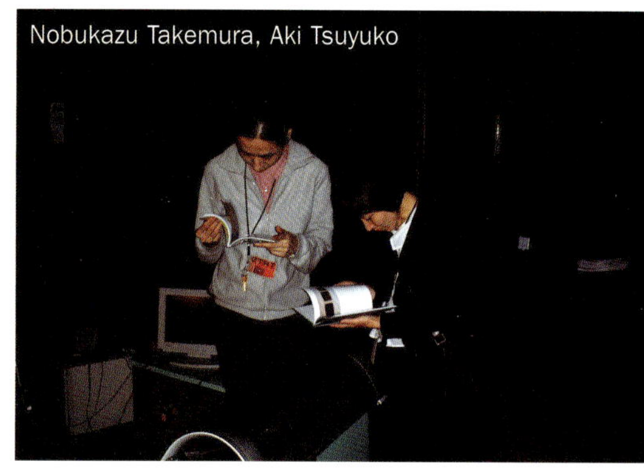

Nobukazu Takemura, Aki Tsuyuko

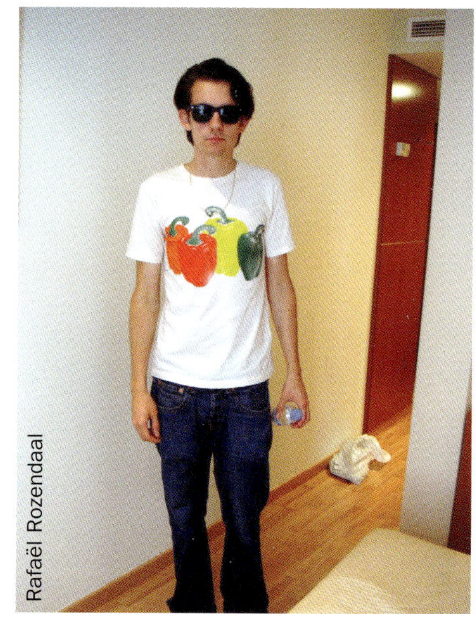

Rafaël Rozendaal

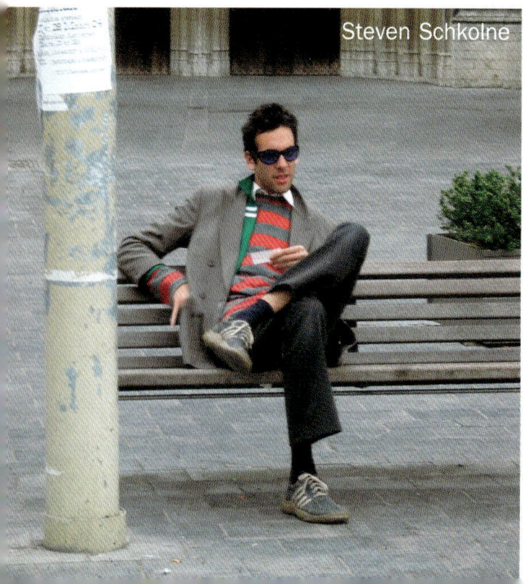

Steven Schkolne

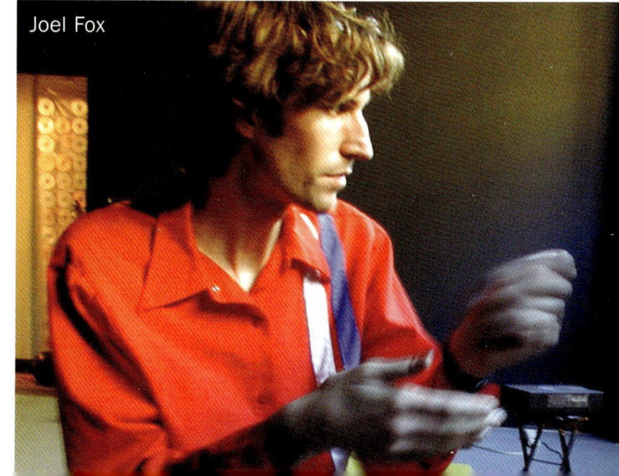

Joel Fox

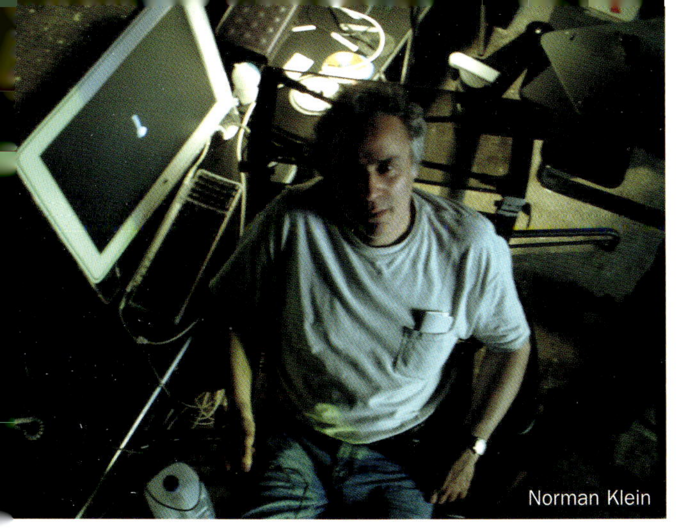

Norman Klein

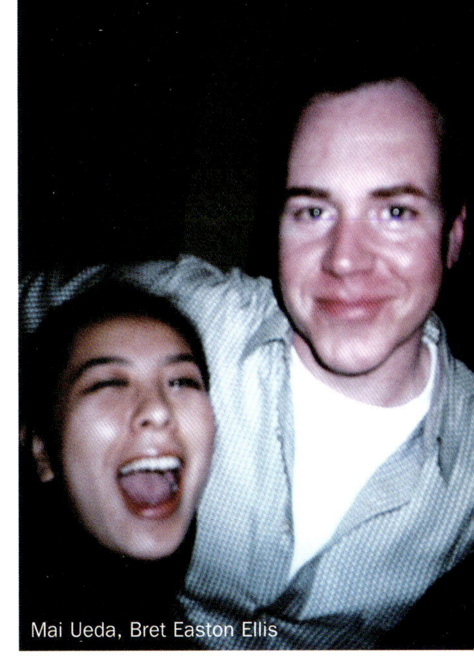

Mai Ueda, Bret Easton Ellis

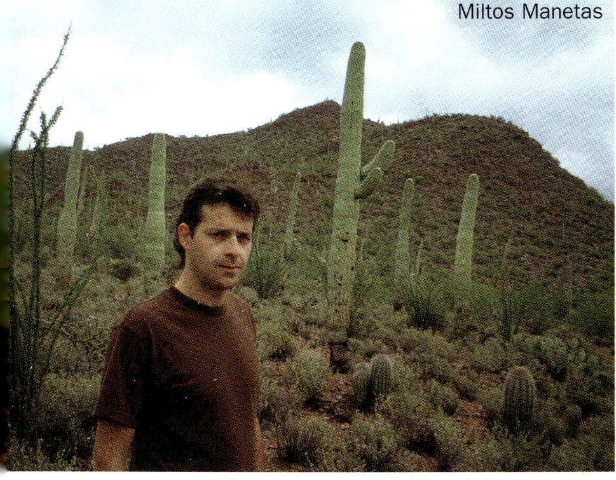

Miltos Manetas

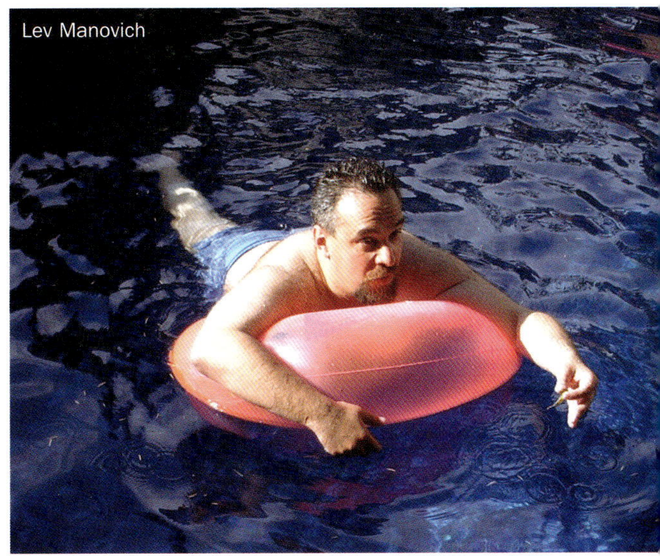

Lev Manovich

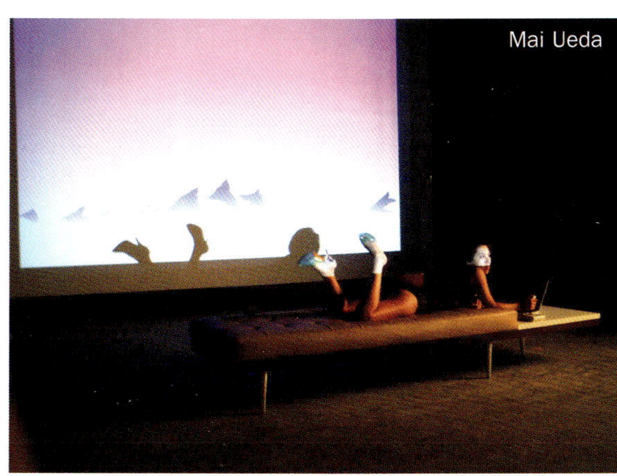

Mai Ueda

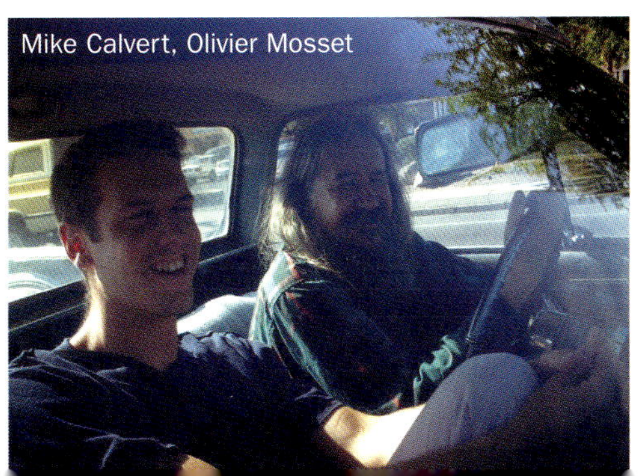

Mike Calvert, Olivier Mosset

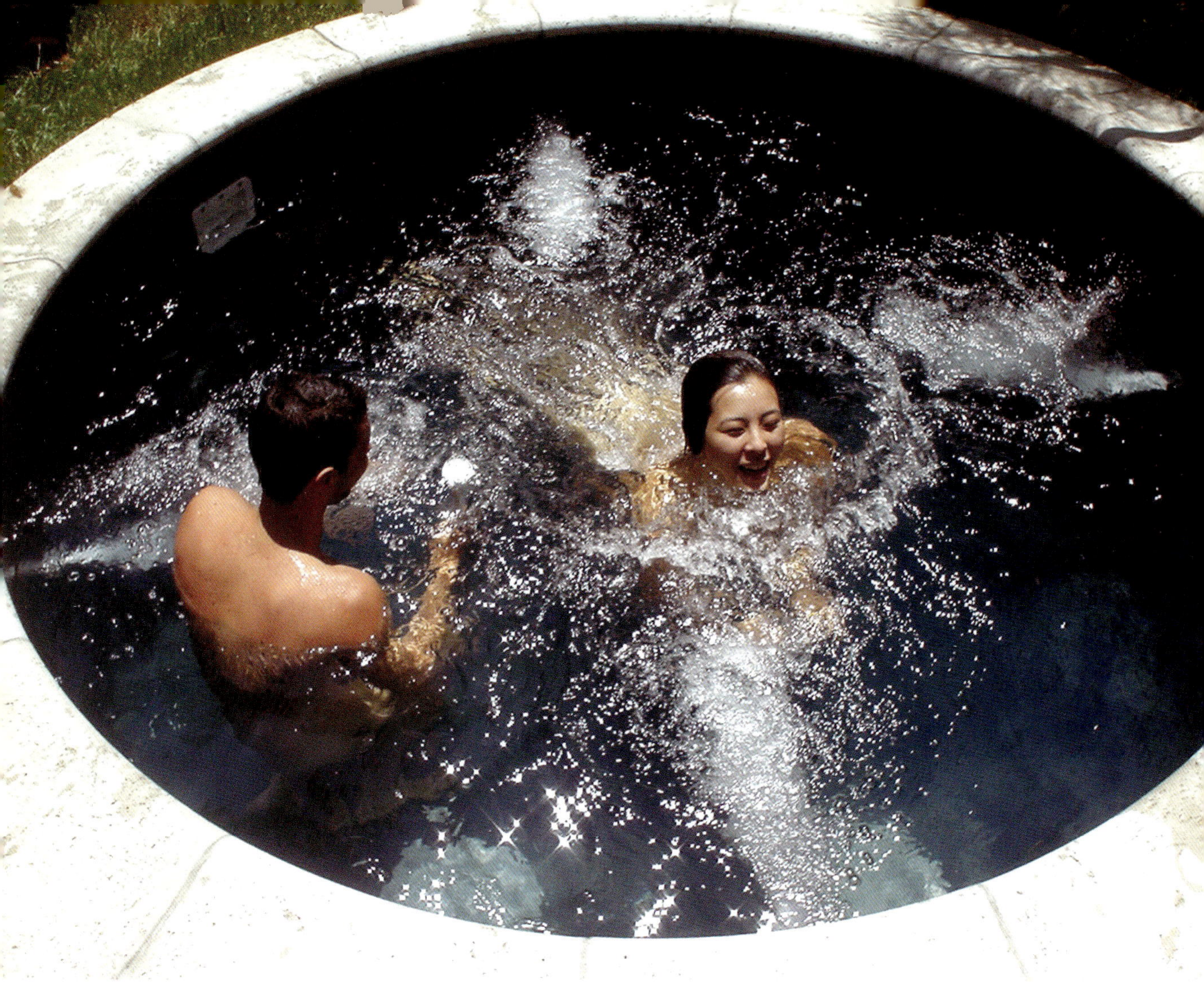

I use Web sites as my main form of expression. These Web sites are animations
or semi-animations of strangeness, wit, and abstract feelings.
They are not talking about social or moral issues. We had enough of them.

Angelo Plessas, 2005

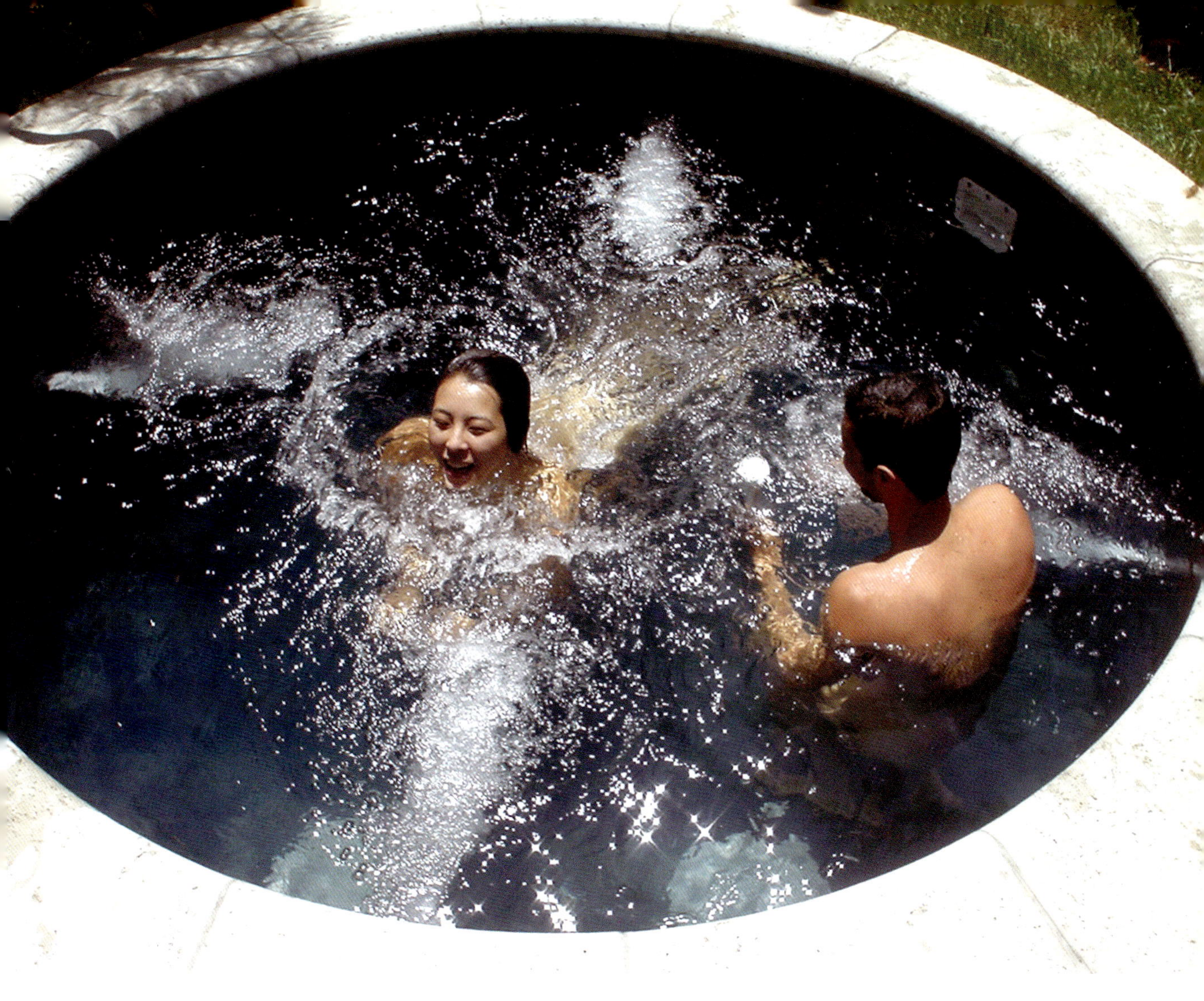

Uso i siti Web come la mia principale forma di espressione. Questi siti sono animazioni
o semianimazioni di cose strane, con un sentimento astratto e arguto.
Non parlano di questioni morali o sociali, di tali argomenti ne abbiamo già abbastanza.

Angelo Plessas, 2005

After two years of E.O. activities in Los Angeles, I missed New York and went back there.
New York was not Neen at all. Things have to have business outlets or academic explanations
to survive. Neen does have those, but it is so avant-garde you have to be
even more advanced to make immediate connections to it.
After two years of fighting, suffering, and going to therapists, all the Neen went to Europe.

Mai Ueda, *Mai Ueda Times*, 2006

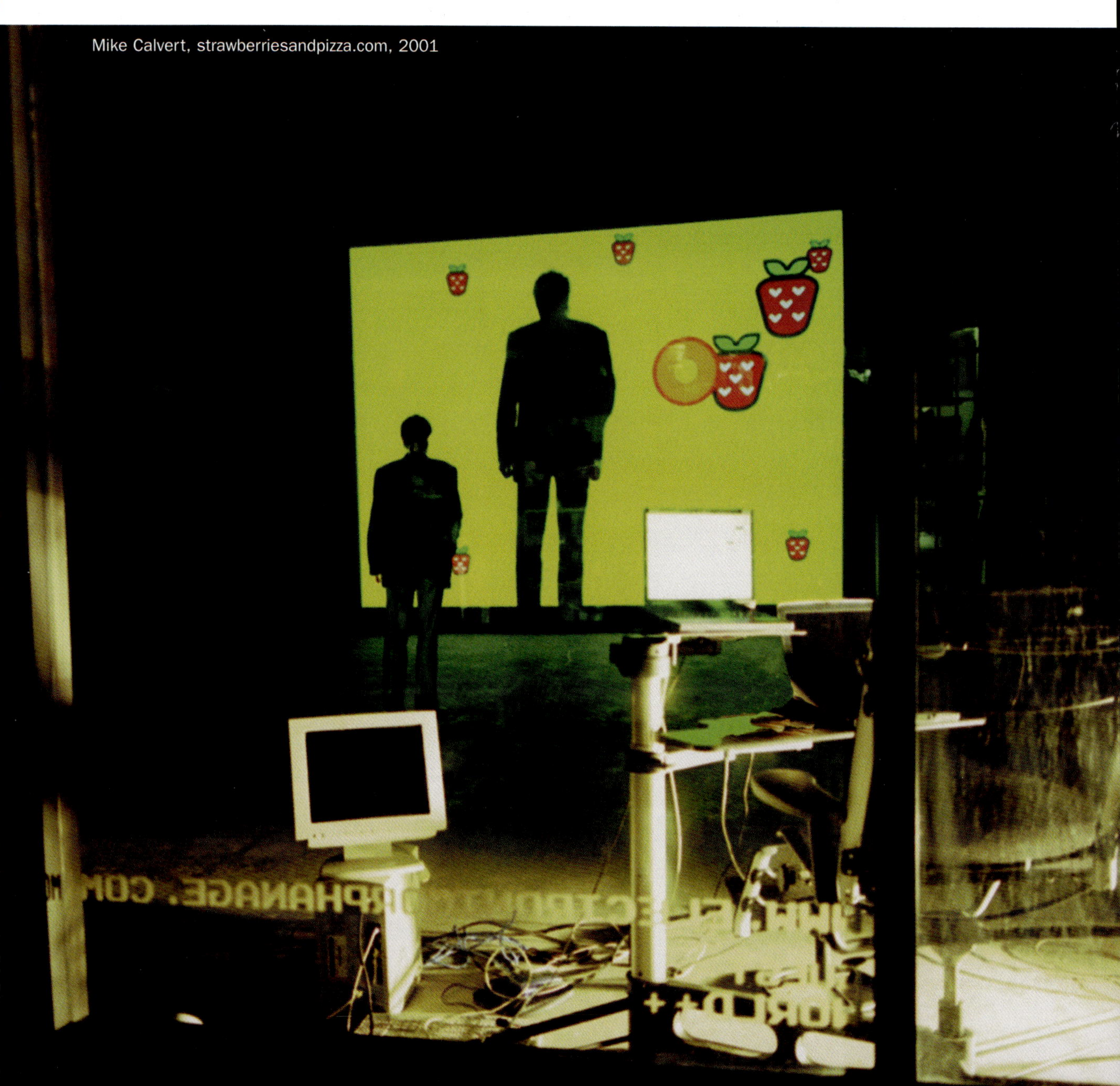

Mike Calvert, strawberriesandpizza.com, 2001

Dopo due anni di attività all'E.O. di Los Angeles, ho sentito la mancanza di New York e sono tornata lì.
New York non era assolutamente Neen. Le cose, per sopravvivere, dovevano essere commerciali
o sostenute accademicamente. Neen deve essere tutto ciò, ma è così all'avanguardia che tu devi sempre
essere più avanti per realizzare delle connessioni immediate con esso.
Dopo due anni di lotta, di sofferenza e di visite dall'analista, tutto il Neen si è mosso verso l'Europa.

Mai Ueda, *Mai Ueda Times*, 2006

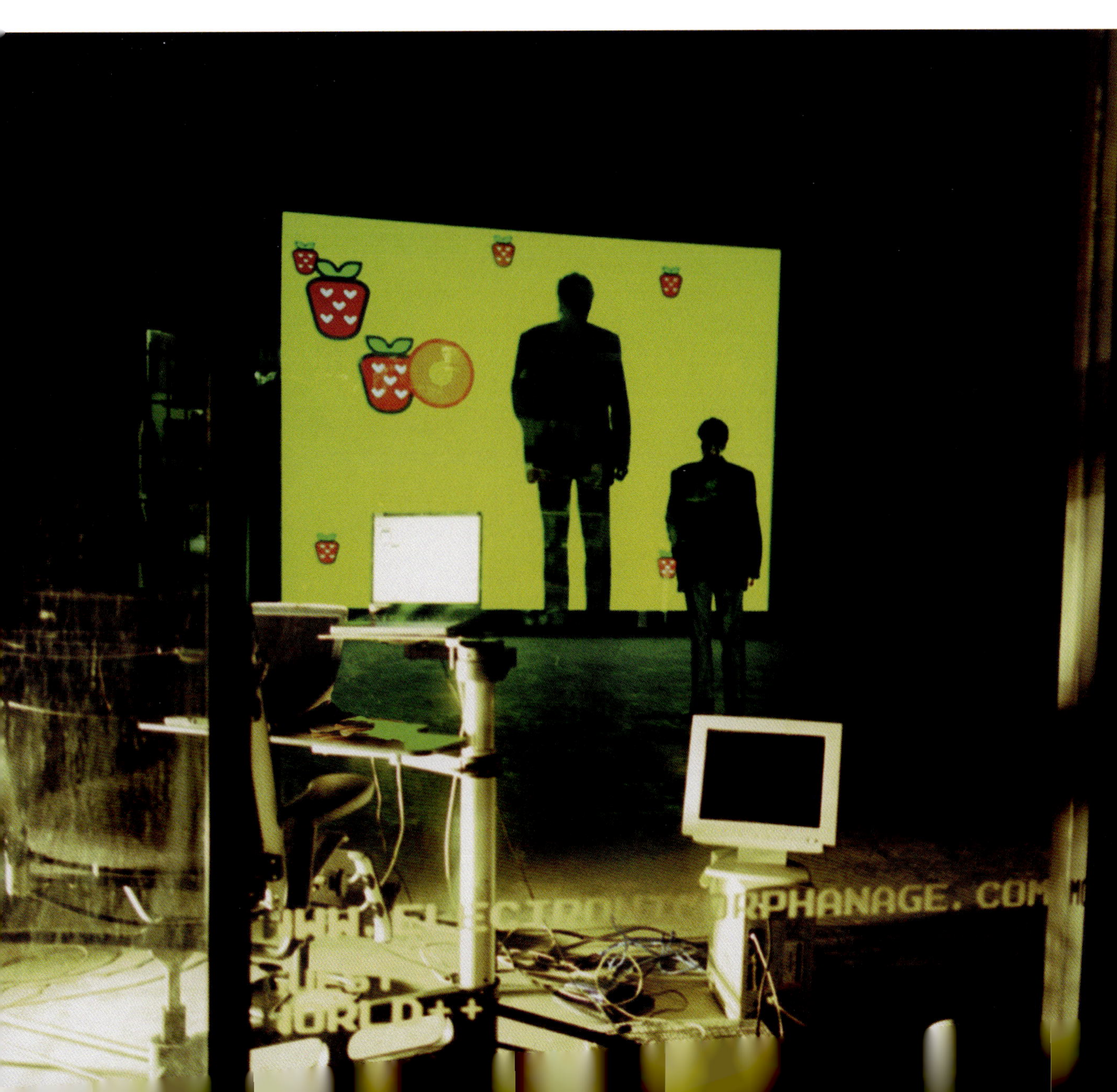

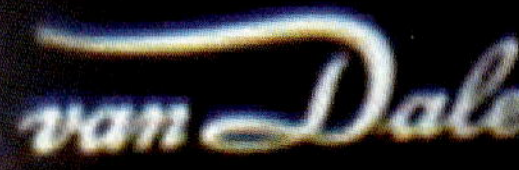

Dictionaries found at the library of MU, Eindhoven

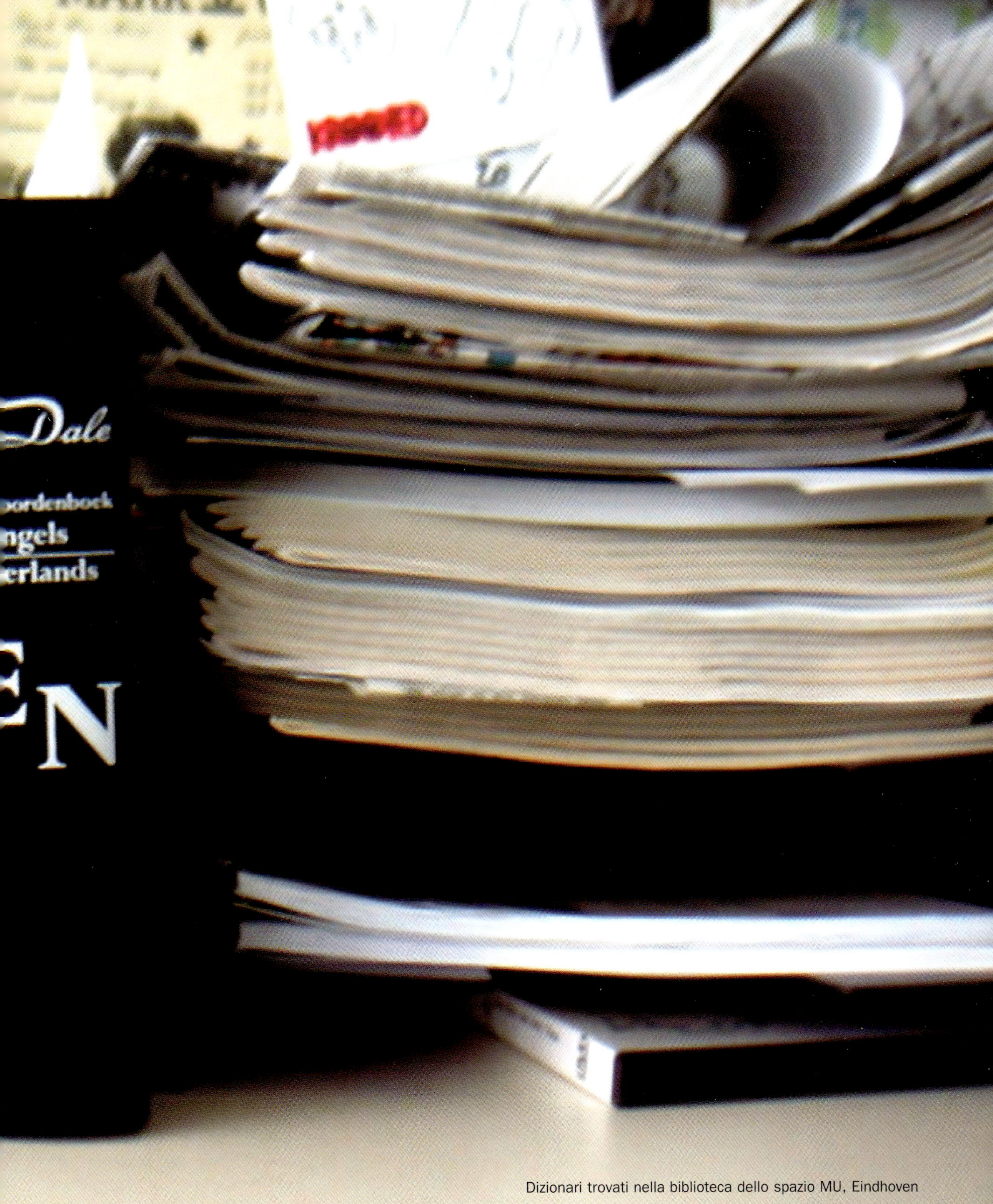

Dizionari trovati nella biblioteca dello spazio MU, Eindhoven

another Neenstar if he needs to do so. But this works also on reverse: a Neenstar can create artwork for another Neenstar and that is the major difference between Neen and contemporary art. While in contemporary art you need to be yourself all the time, a certain type of "hero" who is polishing always his image until he becomes a mirror of his lifetime, in Neen, you are a kind of "screen". A Neenstar projects a temporary self that stays always under construction and moves from the present to past and future without limitations. And because a Neenstar will publish everything on the web, his state of mind reflects the public taste. Neenstars are public personas.

If fantasy brought surrealists to the ridiculous and revolution drove communists to failure, it will be curious to observe where computing will bring Neen.

Miltos Manetas, 2000 – 2006

Neenstar crei l'opera di un altra Neenstar e questa è la maggiore differenza tra Neen e l'arte contemporanea.

Mentre nell'arte contemporanea devi essere te stesso tutto il tempo, una specie di "eroe" intento sempre a distinguere la propria immagine finché non diventerà uno specchio della propria vita, nel Neen sei una specie di "schermo". Un progetto neenstar è un lo temporaneo sempre in costruzione, che si muove dal presente al passato al futuro, senza limiti. Poiché una Neenstar pubblicherà tutto sul web, il proprio stato mentale si rifletterà nel pubblico. Le Neenstar sono persone pubbliche.

Se la fantasia ha portato i surrealisti al ridicolo e la rivoluzione ha condotto il comunismo al fallimento, sarà interessante osservare dove la rivoluzione informatica porterà Neen.

Miltos Manetas, 2000 – 2006

From / Da: Marx & Marinetti & Miltos & Manetas

Manifesto
Manifesto

A Few Things I Know About Neen

Neen stands for Neenstars: a still-undefined generation of visual artists. Some of them belong to the contemporary art world; others are software creators, web designers, and video game directors or animators.

Our official theories about reality – quantum physics, etc. – proved that the taste of our life is the taste of a simulation. Machines help us feel comfortable with this condition: they simulate the simulation we call Nature. Opening the door of your room or clicking on a folder on your computer's desktop will send you to similar destinations – two versions of reality that are seemingly perfect and dense, but they will start dissolving after you analyze them.

Computing is to Neen as what fantasy was to surrealism and freedom to communism. It creates its context, but it can also be postponed. Neenstars buy the newest products and they study how to create momentum.
They glorify machines, but they get easily bored with them. Sometimes they prefer just watching others operating them. Neenstars find their pleasure in the in-between actions. Neen is about losing time on different operating systems.

Neenstars love copying in the same way that the city of Hong Kong multiplies its most successful buildings. The same, but a little different: Names, Clothes, Style, Art and Architecture are important for Neenstars. So they create all that from scratch, as if what has been done before them

Alcune Cose Che Conosco Circa il Neen

Neen sta per Neenstar: una generazione ancora indefinita di artisti visivi. Alcuni di essi appartengono al mondo dell'arte contemporanea, altri sono creatori di software, web designer e registi o animatori di videogiochi.

Le nostre teorie ufficiali circa la realtà – la fisica dei quanti ecc. – provano che il sapore delle nostre vite è il sapore di una simulazione. Le macchine ci aiutano a sentirci a nostro agio in questa situazione: esse simulano la simulazione che chiamiamo Natura.
Aprire un documento di un computer è come aprire la porta di una stanza: due versioni della realtà apparentemente perfette e dense che cominceranno a dissolversi quando inizierai ad analizzarle.

La rivoluzione informatica sta al Neen come la fantasia stava al surrealismo e la libertà al comunismo. Crea il contesto ma può essere anche posposta. Le Neenstar vogliono sempre avere i prodotti più nuovi per creare il momentum. Glorificano le macchine ma si annoiano anche di esse, qualche volta preferiscono osservare, altre volte utilizzarle. Le Neenstars provano piacere nelle azioni intermedie. Neen è perdere tempo tra differenti sistemi operativi.

Le Neenstar amano copiare alla stessa maniera della città di Hong Kong che moltiplica i propri edifici di maggior successo: nomi, abiti, stili, arte e architettura sono importanti per le Neenstar che però fanno tutto da zero come se quello

all that from scratch, as if what has been done before them
is not so important.

Neen is very sentimental, but it is not about identity, although
Neenstars occasionally use their identities as passwords in
order to obtain certain privileges. Because the identity of a
Neenstar is his state of mind, he is free to use the identity of
another Neenstar if he needs to do so. But this works also on
reverse: a Neenstar can create artwork for another Neenstar
and that is the major difference between Neen and
contemporary art. While in contemporary art you need to be
yourself all the time, a certain type of "hero" who is polishing
always his image until he becomes a mirror of his lifetime,
in Neen, you are a kind of "screen". A Neenstar projects a
temporary self that stays always under construction and
moves from the present to past and future without
limitations. And because a Neenstar will publish everything
on the web, his state of mind reflects the public taste.
Neenstars are public personas.

If fantasy brought surrealists to the ridiculous and revolution
drove communists to failure, it will be curious to observe
where computing will bring Neen.

Miltos Manetas, 2000 – 2006

per le Neenstar che però fanno tutto da zero come se quello
che è stato fatto prima di loro non fosse poi così importante.
Neen è molto sentimentale ma non è qualcosa che ha a che
fare con l'identità, sebbene le Neenstar utilizzino
occasionalmente le proprie identità come una password per
vivere situazioni privilegiate. Per una Neenstar l'identità
è uno stato mentale intercambiabile, può succedere che una
Neenstar crei l'opera di un altra Neenstar e questa è la
maggiore differenza tra Neen e l'arte contemporanea.

Mentre nell'arte contemporanea devi essere te stesso tutto il
tempo, una specie di "eroe" intento sempre a distinguere la
propria immagine finché non diventerà uno specchio della
propria vita, nel Neen sei una specie di "schermo". Un
progetto neenstar è un lo temporaneo sempre in costruzione,
che si muove dal presente al passato al futuro, senza limiti.
Poiché una Neenstar pubblicherà tutto sul web, il proprio
stato mentale si rifletterà nel pubblico. Le Neenstar sono
persone pubbliche.

Se la fantasia ha portato i surrealisti al ridicolo e la rivoluzione
ha condotto il comunismo al fallimento, sarà interessante
osservare dove la rivoluzione informatica porterà Neen.

Miltos Manetas, 2000 – 2006

From / Da: Marx&Marinetti&Miltos&Manetas

Manifesto
Manifesto

A Few Things I Know About Neen

Neen stands for Neenstars: a still-undefined generation
of visual artists. Some of them belong to the contemporary
art world; others are software creators, web designers, and
video game directors or animators.

Our official theories about reality – quantum physics, etc. –
proved that the taste of our life is the taste of a simulation.
Machines help us feel comfortable with this condition: they
simulate the simulation we call Nature. Opening the door of
your room or clicking on a folder on your computer's desktop
will send you to similar destinations – two versions of reality
that are seemingly perfect and dense, but they will start
dissolving after you analyze them.

Computing is to Neen as what fantasy was to surrealism and
freedom to communism. It creates its context, but it can also
be postponed. Neenstars buy the newest products and they
study how to create momentum.
They glorify machines, but they get easily bored with them.
Sometimes they prefer just watching others operating them.
Neenstars find their pleasure in the in-between actions.

Alcune Cose Che Conosco Circa il Neen

Neen sta per Neenstar: una generazione ancora indefinita
di artisti visivi. Alcuni di essi appartengono al mondo
dell'arte contemporanea, altri sono creatori di software, web
designer e registi o animatori di videogiochi.

Le nostre teorie ufficiali circa la realtà – la fisica dei quanti ecc.
– provano che il sapore delle nostre vite è il sapore di una
simulazione. Le macchine ci aiutano a sentirci a nostro agio
in questa situazione: esse simulano la simulazione che
chiamiamo Natura.
Aprire un documento di un computer è come aprire la porta
di una stanza: due versioni della realtà apparentemente
perfette e dense che cominceranno a dissolversi quando
inizierai ad analizzarle.

La rivoluzione informatica sta al Neen come la fantasia stava
al surrealismo e la libertà al comunismo. Crea il contesto ma
può essere anche posposta. Le Neenstar vogliono sempre
avere i prodotti più nuovi per creare il momentum.
Glorificano le macchine ma si annoiano anche di esse,
qualche volta preferiscono osservare, altre volte utilizzarle.

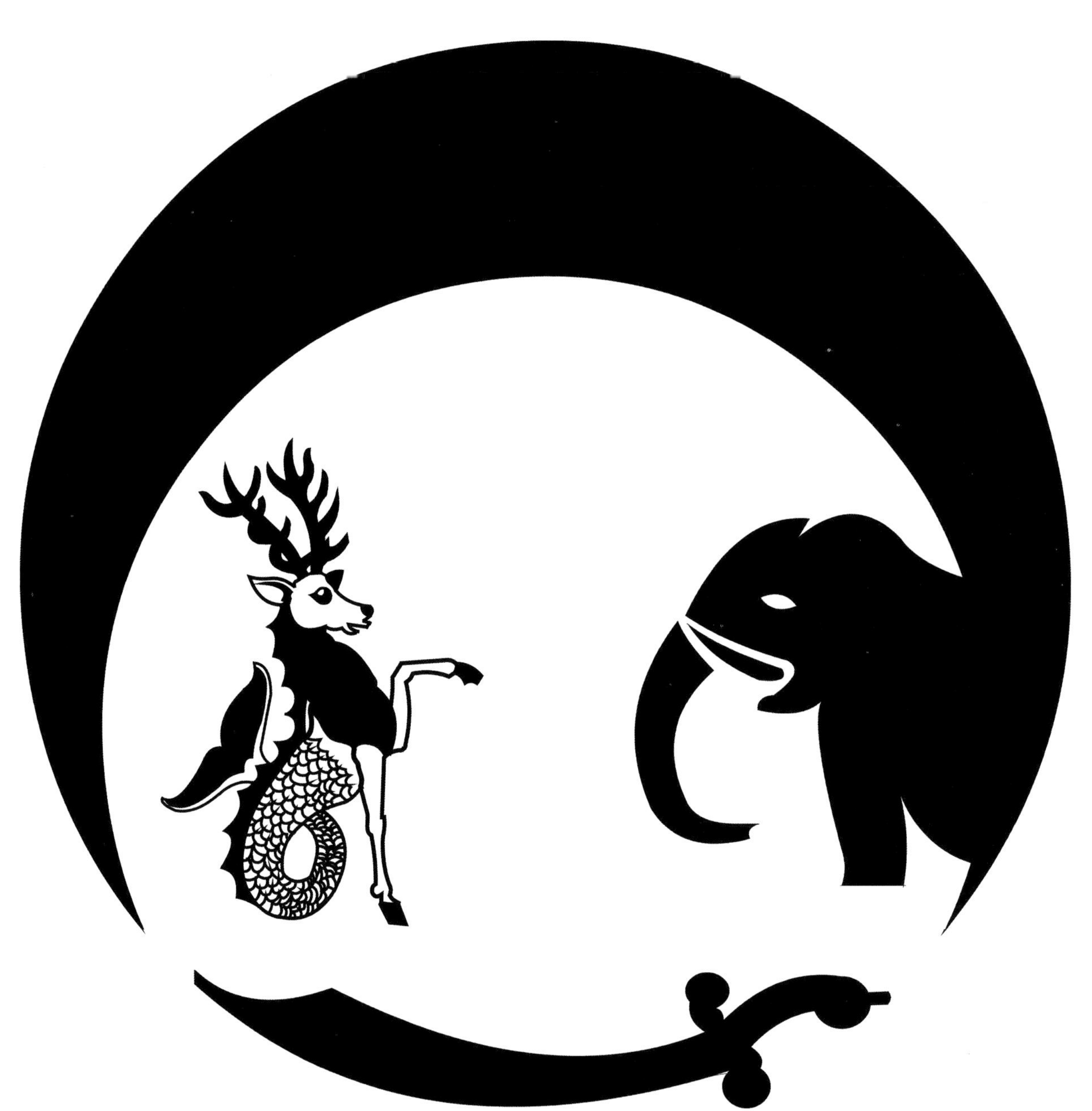

2002: ElectronicOrphanage
presents whitneybiennial.com

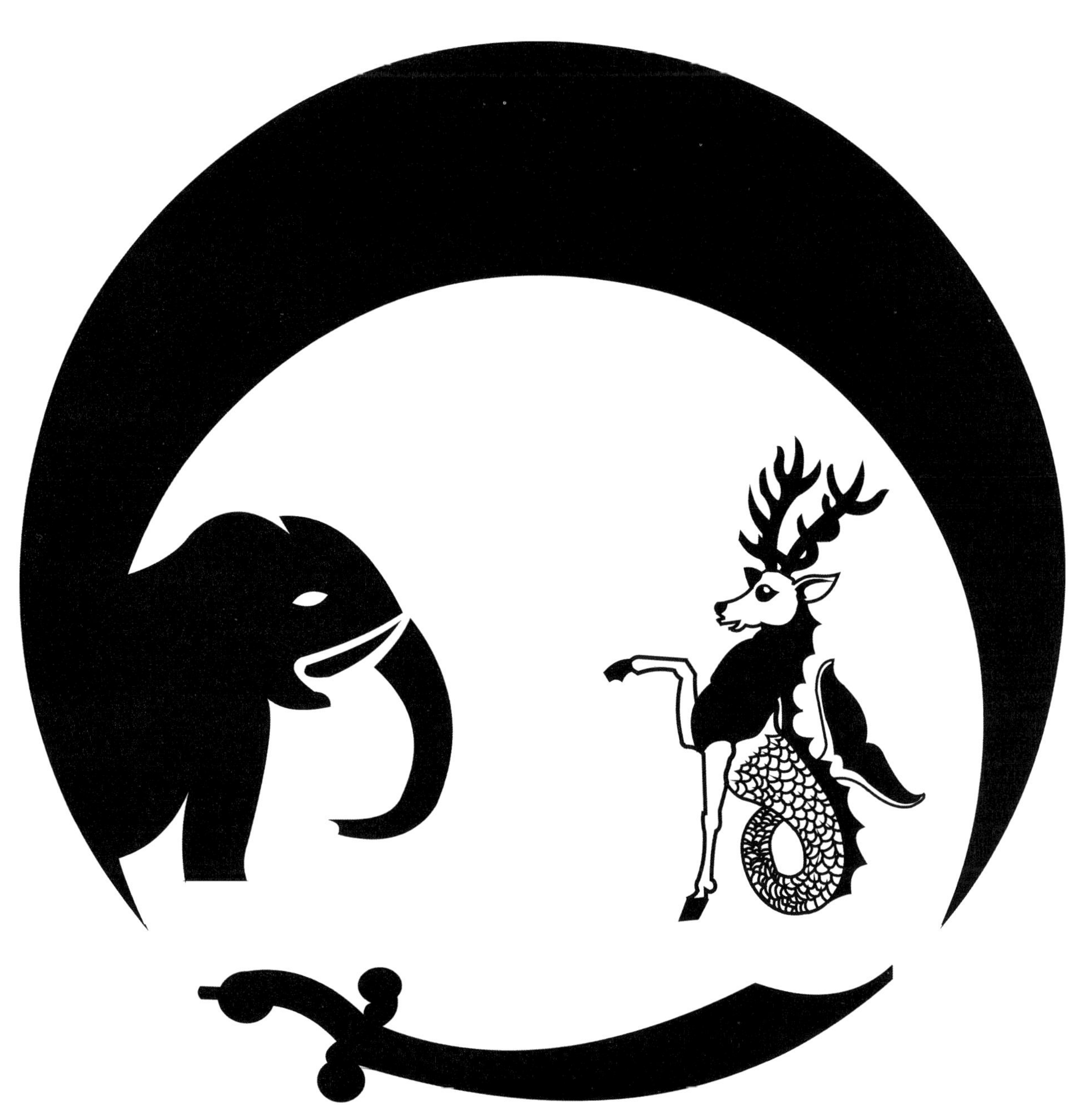

2002: ElectronicOrphanage
presents whitneybiennial.com

One night last December, after conducting his own review of the 113 artists selected for the biennial,
Miltos Manetas decided to set up a Web site on which he could publish his own thoughts
on the perpetually controversial exhibition.
. . .
(Manetas) checked an online database of Web addresses. He was surprised to learn that no one,
including the Museum, had staked a claim on an obvious address: whitneybiennial.com.
He registered it immediately. (The Museum's Web site is at whitney.org.)

Matthew Mirapaul, "If You Can't Join 'Em, You Can Always Tweak 'Em,"
The New York Times, March 4, 2002

Mr. Manetas has rented twenty-three U-Haul trucks that will circle
the Whitney during a V.I.P. biennial reception tomorrow evening.
Each truck will be turned into a mobile easel, with a computer inside projecting
the site's works onto a curtain of fabric stretched across the vehicle's back opening.
. . .
Mr. Manetas said he envisioned the procession as a live version of *Broadway Boogie-Woogie*, Mondrian's
Manhattan landscape. Told that his convoy might be mistaken for a legitimate entry in the biennial,
he said: "I want that."

Matthew Mirapaul, "If You Can't Join 'Em, You Can Always Tweak 'Em,"
The New York Times, March 4, 2002

Angelo Plessas, drawing for whitneybiennial.com

Una notte, lo scorso dicembre, dopo aver redatto la propria personale recensione dei 113 artisti selezionati per la
Biennale, Miltos Manetas decise di mettere su un sito Web, sul quale avrebbe potuto pubblicare i propri pensieri
sulla, perpetuamente controversa, esposizione.
…
(Manetas) consultò un archivio on line di indirizzi Web e fu sorpreso nello scoprire che nessuno,
nemmeno il museo, avesse richiesto un ovvio indirizzo come: whitneybiennial.com.
Lo registrò immediatamente. (Il sito Web del museo è all'indirizzo: www.whitney.org).

Matthew Mirapaul, "If You Can't Join 'Em, You Can Always Tweak 'Em'",
The New York Times, 4 marzo 2002

Manetas ha noleggiato ventitré camion U-Haul che domani
pomeriggio circonderanno il Whitney durante il ricevimento riservato ai V.I.P.
Ogni camion sarà trasformato in un cavalletto mobile, con un computer al suo interno
che proietterà i lavori su una tenda di tessuto stesa intorno al portellone posteriore del veicolo.
…
Manetas ha detto di aver immaginato la processione come una versione live di
Broadway Boogie-Woogie, il paesaggio di Manhattan realizzato da Mondrian. Riferitogli che il suo convoglio
poteva essere confuso per un'entrata regolare alla Biennale, ha detto: "È proprio quello che voglio".

Matthew Mirapaul, "If You Can't Join 'Em, You Can Always Tweak 'Em'",
The New York Times, 4 marzo 2002

Angelo Plessas, disegno per whitneybiennial.com

WHITNEYBIENNIAL.COM, 2002

a concept by Miltos Manetas

organized by the ElectronicOrphanage
and assisted by Michele Thursz

Web site design: carbonatedjazz, music: Gnac

Curators/writers and organizations: Jan Aman, Andreas Angelidakis, archinect.com, Stefano Chiodi, Joshua Decter, Laurence Dreyfus, Alex Galloway, Paul Groot, Patrick Lichty, Peter Lunenfeld, Lev Manovich, Magda Sawon, newstoday.com, Hans Ulrich Obrist, Marisa Olson, Michele Thursz, Roosavelt Savage, Philippe Vergne, Olivier Zahm, *Purple Magazine*

Artists: Andreas Angelidakis, Fia Backstorm, Tobias Bernstrup, Andrew Bucksbarg, Christophe Bruno, Mike Calvert, Carbonated Jazz, Larry Carlson, Mauro Ceolin, Sarah Ciracì, Kevin Chan, Sadie Chandler, Chiaki, Taro Chiezo, Aaron Clinger, John White C., Nic Clockworker, Claude Closky, Jennifer and Kevin McCoy, Joyce Charis, Andrew Childs, Jordan Crane, donleo.org, Dj Spooky, Gisela Domscheke, Decosterd & Rahm, Fat Architecture, Reinier Feijen/Marjan Lemmens, Adam Somlai-Fischer, Joseph Franklyn & Donna McElroy, Amy Franceschini, Ryan Francesconi, Foreign Office Architects, Joel Fox, Rainer Ganahl, Joaquin Ganez, Gnac, Valery Grancher, Stefan Gruber, Debra Hampton, Elsa Harkins, Heidrun Holzfeind, Han Hoogerbrugge, Alejandra Jarabo, Experimental Jetset, Roya Jakoby, Thorsten Iberl, Young Hae Chang Heavy Industries, Digital Sisters Indeed, Mitchell Kane, Yael Kanarek, Kol Mac Studio, Eleni Kostika, Ioanna Kostika, Jon Krusell, Katarina Iofstrom, Lot-ek Architecture, Marcos Lutyens, limiteazero.com, lostpixel.com, mashica.com, Miltos Manetas, Jonathan Maghen, Pablo Margaria, Ilias Marmaras, Aitor Mendez, Yucef Merhi, Marcello Mercado, Sascha Merg, Hidekazu Minami, Christian Moeller, Nanogod, Daisuke Nishimura, Josh On, Maria Papadimitriou, Paper Architecture, Scott Paterson, Francois Perrin, Angelo Plessas, Alexandros Psychoulis, Michael Rees, Autumn Rooney, Rafaël Rozendaal, Gerwald Rockenschaub, Rick Silva, Steven Schkolne, Scott Sona Snibbe, Leah Singer, Julia Scher, Nico Stumpo, Allan Tarantino, teleferique.org, Petra Trefzger, John Tremblay, Nikola Tosic, Mai Ueda, unclickable.com, uncontrol.com, Ritsko Utchida, Jordi Valls, Siebren Versteeg, Leo Villareal, Autumn Whitehurst, Jody Zellen, David Zerah, Yi Zhou.

Selected Press for the whitneybiennial.com:
The New York Times, March 8, 2002
The New York Times, March 4, 2002
Newsweek, March 19, 2002
Le Monde, March 26, 2002
El Pais, March 29, 2002
The Guardian, March 21, 2002
Artforum International, May 2002
salon.com
artnet.com
neural.it
artandjobmagazine.com
rhizome.org

whitneybiennial.com is dedicated to the Italian artist Gino De Dominicis (1947–1998)

other inspirations:

Forgotten Silver, New Zealand, 1995
a documentary by Peter Jackson and Costa Botes

and

When We Were Kings, USA, 1996
a documentary on Muhammad Ali, directed
by Leon Gast and Taylor Hackford

whitneybiennial.com è dedicata a Gino De Dominicis (1947-1998)

altre ispirazioni:

Forgotten Silver, Nuova Zelanda, 1995
un documentario di Peter Jackson e Costa Botes

e

When We Were Kings, USA, 1996
un documentario su Muhammad Ali, diretto
da Leon Gast e Taylor Hackford

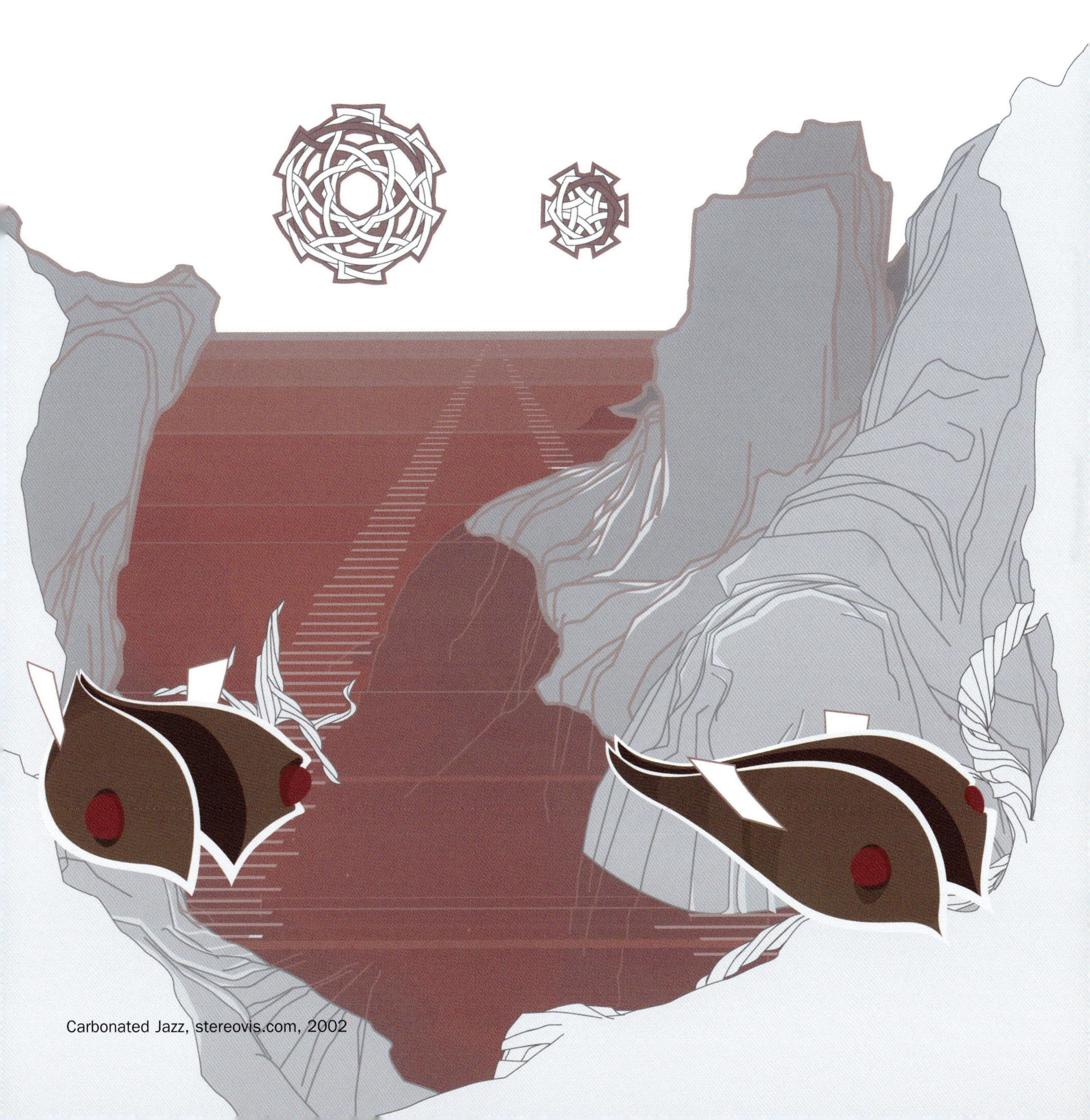

Carbonated Jazz, stereovis.com, 2002

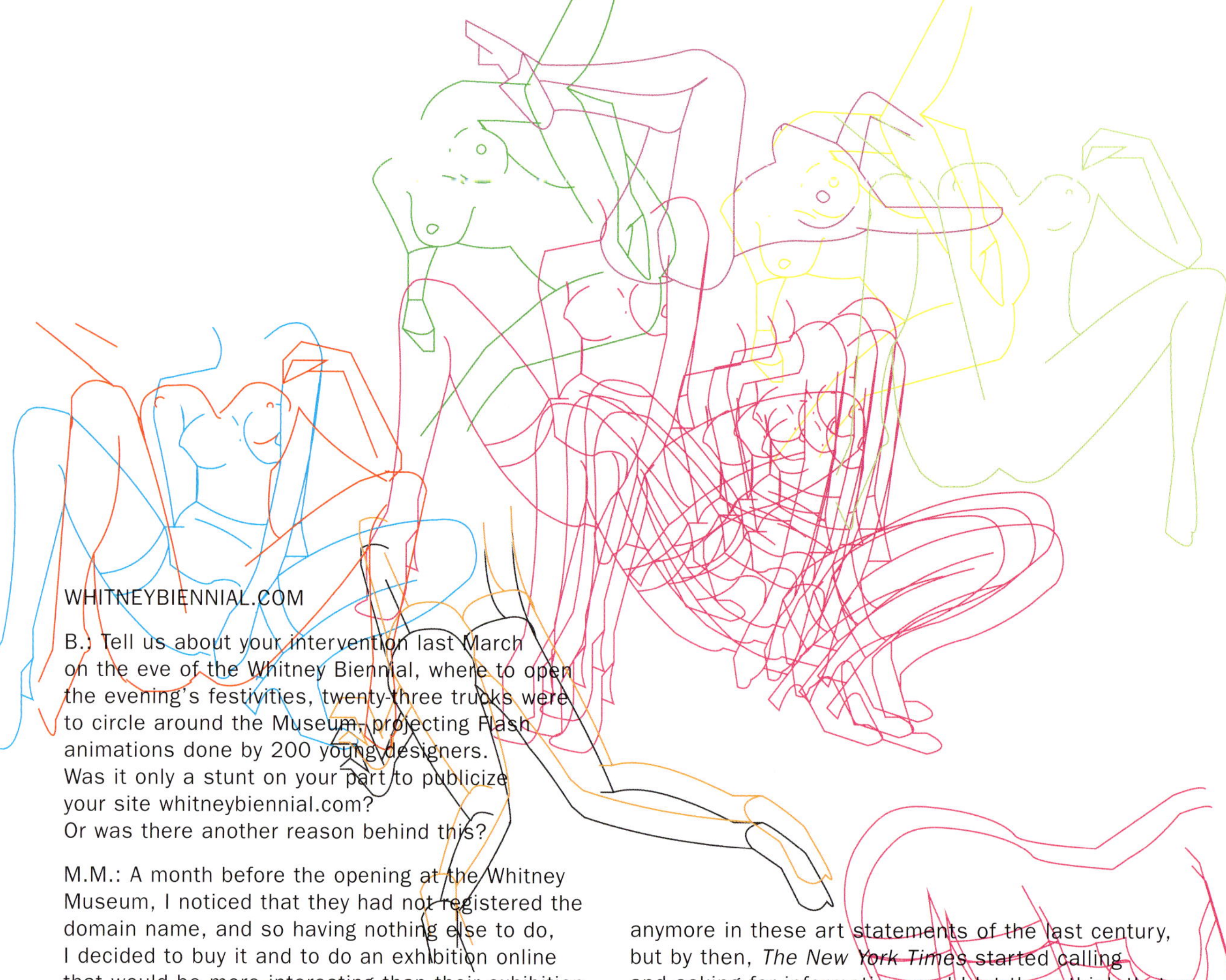

WHITNEYBIENNIAL.COM

B.) Tell us about your intervention last March
on the eve of the Whitney Biennial, where to open
the evening's festivities, twenty-three trucks were
to circle around the Museum, projecting Flash
animations done by 200 young designers.
Was it only a stunt on your part to publicize
your site whitneybiennial.com?
Or was there another reason behind this?

M.M.: A month before the opening at the Whitney
Museum, I noticed that they had not registered the
domain name, and so having nothing else to do,
I decided to buy it and to do an exhibition online
that would be more interesting than their exhibition.
I immediately called different curators, asking them
to suggest artists (and not only artists, but also
architects, designers, etc.) for the whitneybiennial.com.
I also contacted the organizers of the (official)
Whitney Biennial.
They invited me to discuss the idea, and they
proposed to do my exhibition at an empty bank
in front of the Museum.

I understood that it was their intention to offer me
a sort of Salon des Refuses. You can imagine it:
my friends and I with about a dozen computers
in an immense, miserable, empty bank in front
of the Museum where everyone is enjoying
themselves. In that moment, a terrorist idea
occurred to me, and I told them that instead
I would organize an army transformed into monitors
that would surround the Museum the day of the
opening. Naturally, I had no intention of really
doing it; I get bored even at the idea. I don't believe

anymore in these art statements of the last century,
but by then, *The New York Times* started calling
and asking for information, and I let them think that
I would actually do it. In the end, a lot of people
came the day of the opening to see the U-Haul
trucks of the whitneybiennial.com and many people
that were in the Museum came out to see them.
Many returned inside saying that they had seen
the U-Haul trucks, but that they were not anything
interesting after all. There was a lot of confusion
and everyone was talking about
the whitneybiennial.com instead of the official
exhibition, and today the story has become some
kind of urban legend. In other countries, the press
referred to how the U-Haul trucks had circled the
Museum, which is true in a certain sense because
the U-Haul trucks of the whitneybiennial.com are
invisible and omnipresent vehicles:
you can see their Web sites everywhere.

from an interview by Vito Campanelli with
Miltos Manetas, boilermag.it, 2003
http://www.boilermag.it/article.php?sid=173

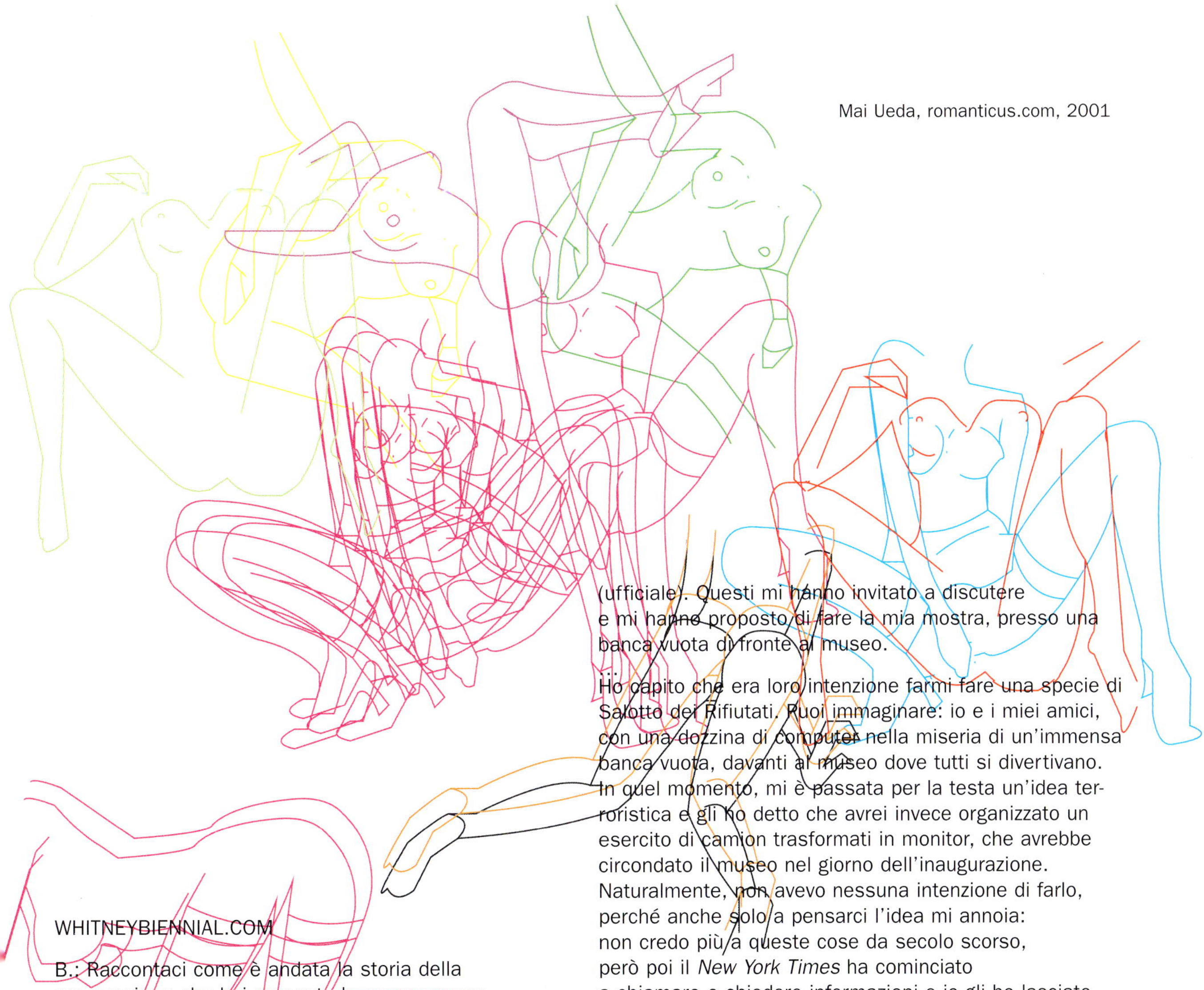

(ufficiale). Questi mi hanno invitato a discutere
e mi hanno proposto di fare la mia mostra, presso una
banca vuota di fronte al museo.

Ho capito che era loro intenzione farmi fare una specie di
Salotto dei Rifiutati. Puoi immaginare: io e i miei amici,
con una dozzina di computer nella miseria di un'immensa
banca vuota, davanti al museo dove tutti si divertivano.
In quel momento, mi è passata per la testa un'idea ter-
roristica e gli ho detto che avrei invece organizzato un
esercito di camion trasformati in monitor, che avrebbe
circondato il museo nel giorno dell'inaugurazione.
Naturalmente, non avevo nessuna intenzione di farlo,
perché anche solo a pensarci l'idea mi annoia:
non credo più a queste cose da secolo scorso,
però poi il *New York Times* ha cominciato
a chiamare e chiedere informazioni e io gli ho lasciato
credere che lo avrei fatto veramente. Alla fine, tantissime
persone sono venute il giorno dell'inaugurazione per
vedere i camion della whitneybiennial.com e molta della
gente che era nel museo, usciva fuori per cercarli.
Molti tornavano dentro e dicevano che avevano visto
i camion ma che, dopotutto, non erano granché!
Si è creata una tale confusione che alla fine tutti
parlavano della whitneybiennial.com invece
che della mostra ufficiale,e la storia è diventata
una leggenda metropolitana. In diversi paesi, la stampa
ha riferito che i camion avevano veramente circondato il
museo, il che è vero in un certo senso,
perché i camion della whitneybiennial.com
sono veicoli invisibili e onnipresenti: sono i suoi siti Web
che puoi vedere ovunque.

da un'intervista di Vito Campanelli a Miltos Manetas,
boilermag.it, 2003
http://www.boilermag.it/article.php?sid=173

WHITNEYBIENNIAL.COM

B.: Raccontaci come è andata la storia della
provocazione che hai proposto lo scorso marzo,
alla vigilia dell'inaugurazione della Whitney Biennial
Exhibition, di portare la sera del gala di apertura,
ventitré camion che avrebbero dovuto girare intorno
al museo e proiettare delle animazioni in Flash
realizzate da 200 giovani designer.
Si è trattato soltanto di un espediente per pubblicizzare
il sito whitneybiennial.com da te ideato?
Oppure esistevano altre motivazioni per pensare
a una simile azione dimostrativa?

M.M.: Un mese prima dell'apertura del Whitney
Museum, ho notato che non avevano registrato
il relativo dominio e poiché non avevo niente altro da
fare, ho deciso di comprarmelo e di fare una mostra
on line che sarebbe stata più interessante della loro.
Ho chiamato immediatamente diversi curatori chiedendo
loro di proporre artisti (e non solo, ma anche architetti,
designer ecc.) per la whitneybiennial.com
e ho contattato gli organizzatori della Whitney Biennial

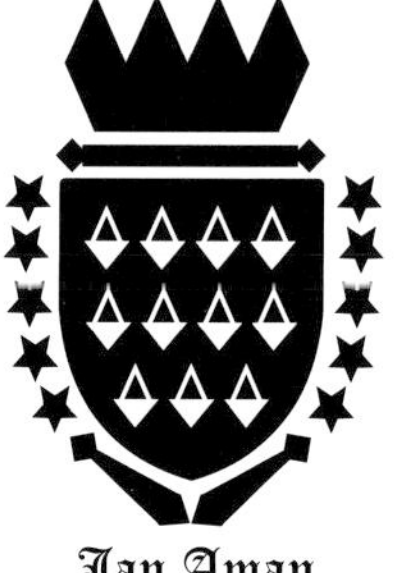

Jan Aman

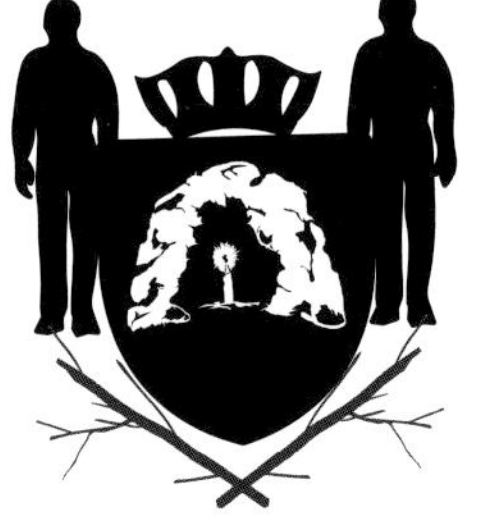

Andreas Angelidakis

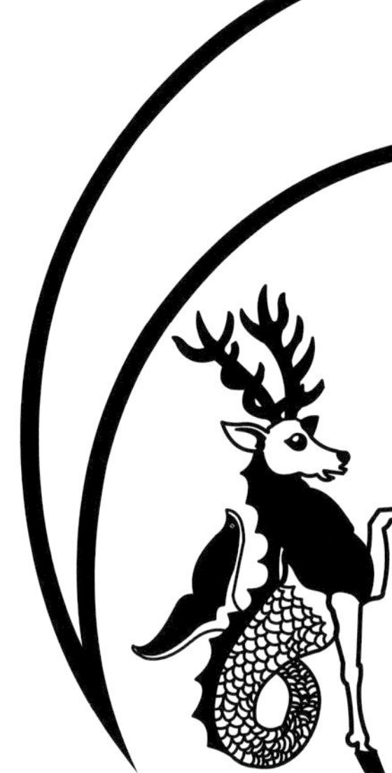

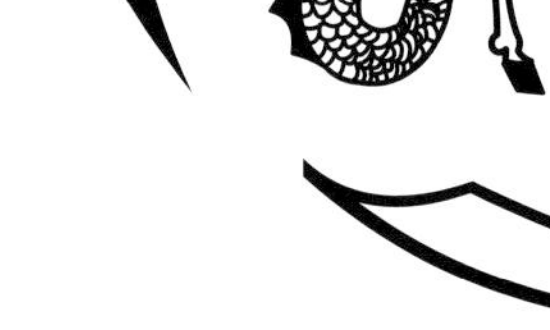

Celebra
Whitneybien

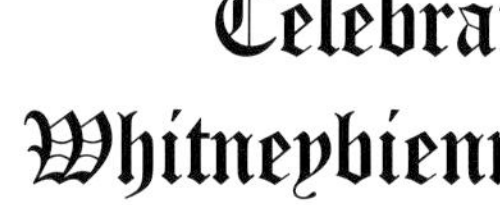

Mai Ueda

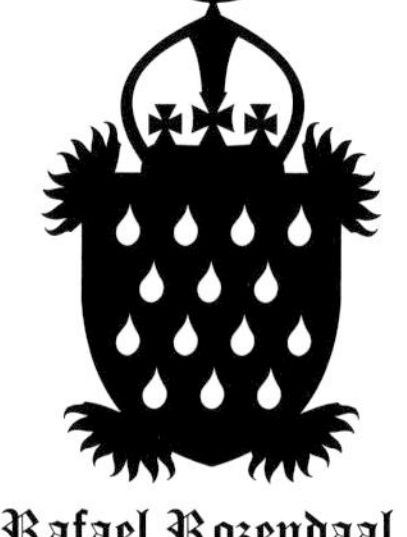

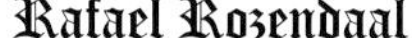

Joel Fox

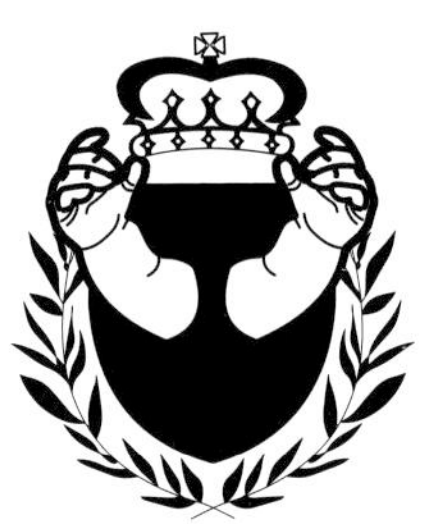

Rafael Rozendaal

Carbonated Jazz

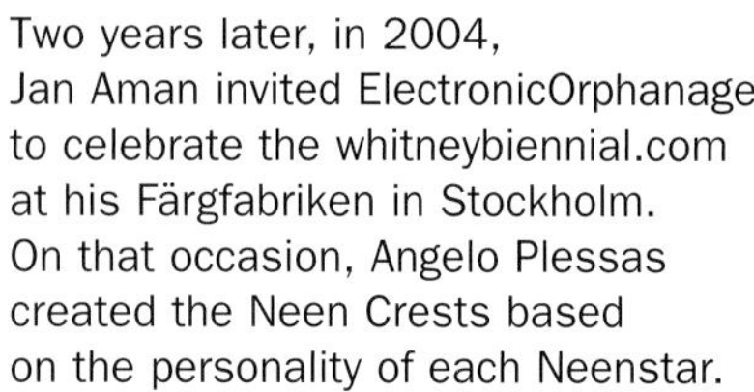

Two years later, in 2004,
Jan Aman invited ElectronicOrphanage
to celebrate the whitneybiennial.com
at his Färgfabriken in Stockholm.
On that occasion, Angelo Plessas
created the Neen Crests based
on the personality of each Neenstar.

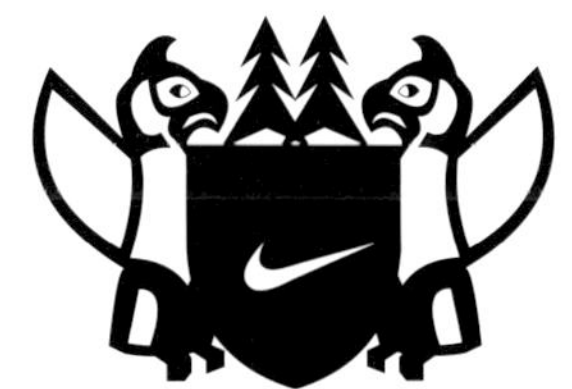

John White C.

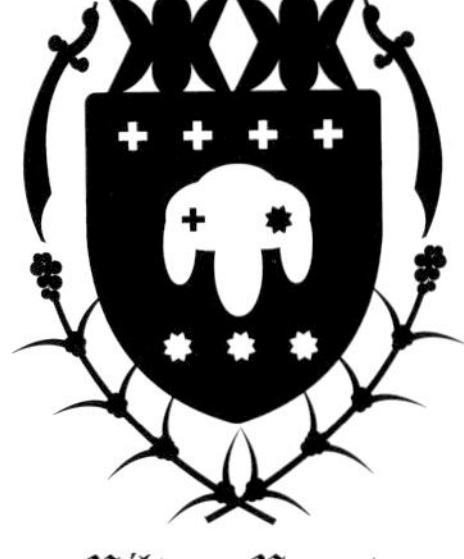

Miltos Manetas

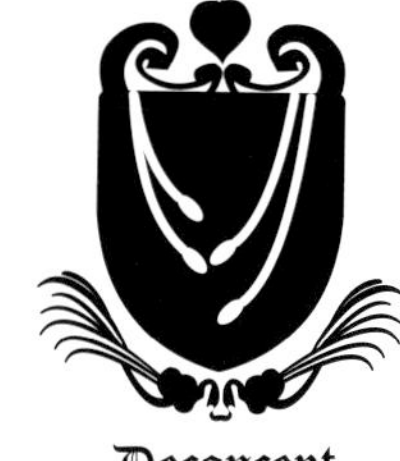

Deconcept

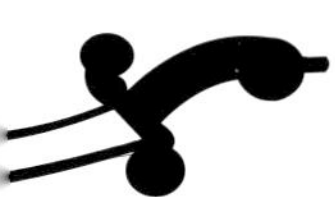

Demon:
2 years later

Nikola Tosic

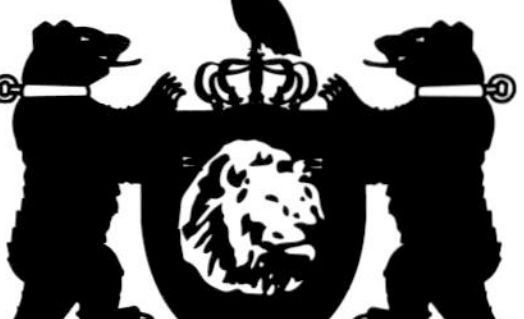

Angelo Plessas

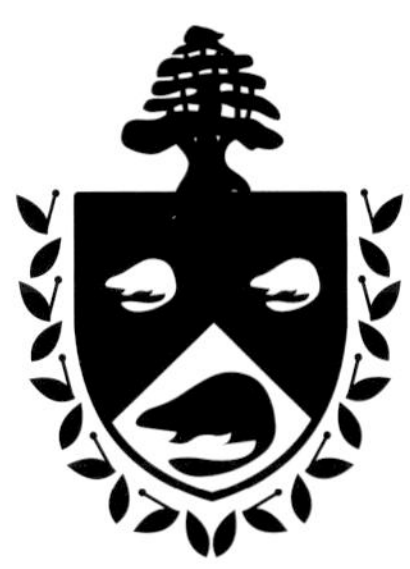

Aaron Clinger

Due anni dopo, nel 2004,
Jan Aman invitò l'ElectronicOrphanage
a celebrare la whitneybiennial.com
presso la Färgfabriken, a Stoccolma.
In quell'occasione, Angelo Plessas creò gli
Stemmi Neen, basati sulla personalità
di ciascuna Neenstar.

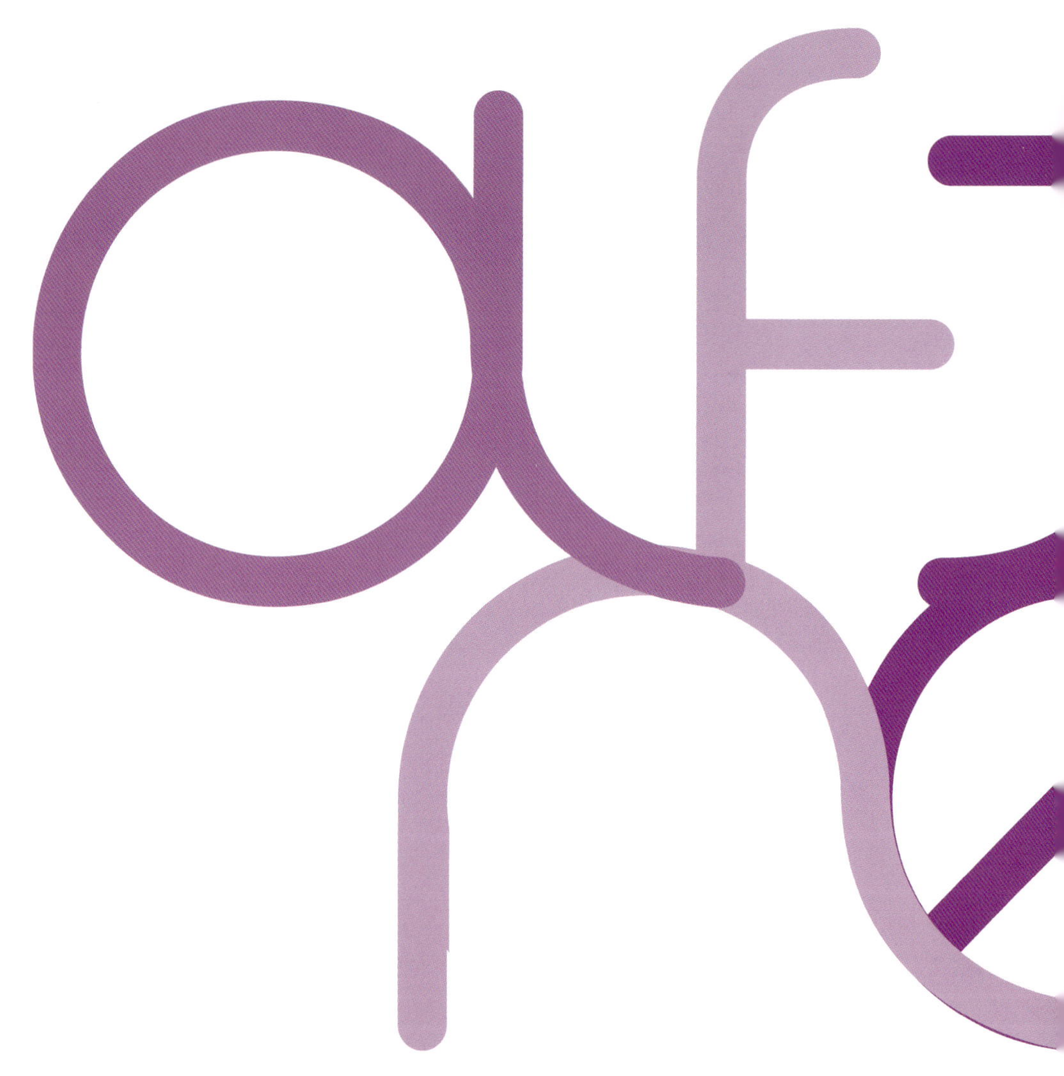

design Mike Calvert

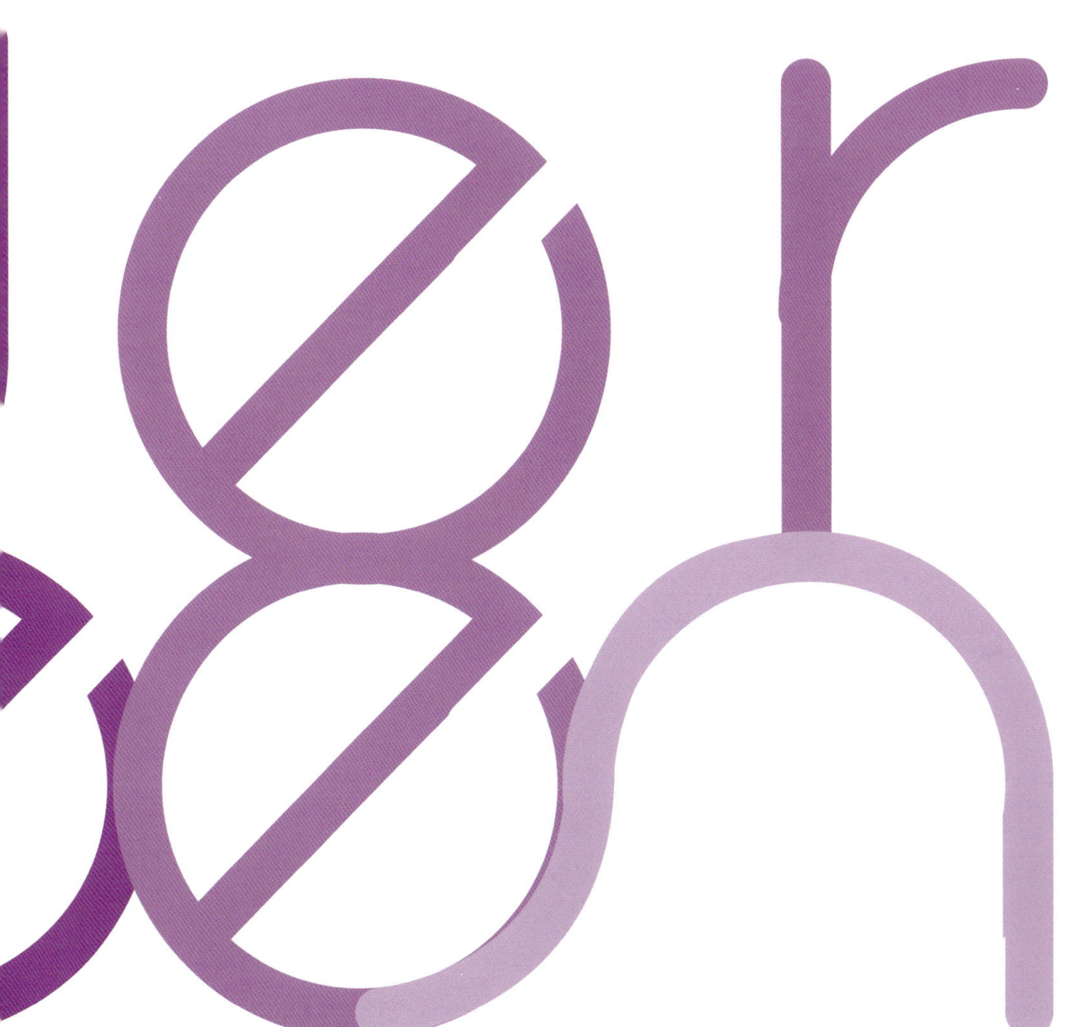

AFTERNEEN
NOVEMBER 16 – DECEMBER 15, 2002

AfterNeen was the first Neen exhibition.
Created for Casco, an alternative art space in Utrecht,
the Netherlands, it was conceived as a show
that challenges the real space where it is hosted.
At Casco, two computer projections were installed,
both connected to the Internet. In one of them the Neen
World of Andreas Angelidakis was displayed, while in
the second projection a Web browser was left empty.
A visitor in Casco could connect to the Neen World,
he would get assigned an avatar body, and he would
go around and eventually meet other people who
happen to be there.
If he met a Neenstar (the Neen World is a village made
by the studios of the different Neenstars) and if the
Neenstar were willing, he would be invited to see
some artworks that were hidden in domain names
over the Internet.
In that case, the Neenstar would activate—via
Internet—the second projection in the gallery
and show to the Casco visitor the hidden domain.
The idea was interesting, but after two days, no
Neenstar could be found anymore in the Neen World
and the *AfterNeen* show was kind of boring. And then,
a miracle happened. A computerized Mercedes, driven
by a drunken kid, collapsed at the space of Casco and
destroyed everything. It was a cruel accident because
one of the people who was working there was seriously
injured, but it was also significant: a real crash between
our World and the World of the computer screen.

These were the domains that were included at the
AfterNeen show:

abiraunken.com, Mai Ueda
abstractme.com, Roya Jakoby
angleviner.com, Joel Fox
brotherofvelvet.com, John White C.
oneaftertheother.com, Angelo Plessas
personality-stereotypes.com, Nikola Tosic
vines, Deconcept
stereovis.com, Carbonated Jazz
manproject.com, Aaron Clinger
wewillattack.com, Rafaël Rozendaal

In Casco, music written by Gnac (Mark Tranmer),
Essetesse, Sawako, and Aki Tsuyuko was playing
during the show.

Nikola Tosic, *AfterNeen* sticker

Questi sono i domini inclusi nella mostra *AfterNeen*:

abiraunken.com, Mai Ueda
abstractme.com, Roya Jakoby
angleviner.com, Joel Fox
brotherofvelvet.com, John White C.
oneaftertheother.com, Angelo Plessas
personality-stereotypes.com, Nikola Tosic
vines, Deconcept
stereovis.com, Carbonated Jazz
manproject.com, Aaron Clinger
wewillattack.com, Rafaël Rozendaal

Durante la mostra allo spazio Casco è stata diffusa musica composta da Gnac (Mark Tranmer), Essetesse, Sawako e Aki Tsuyuko.

after neen
is a show taking place at casco
which is a gallery in utrecht holland
i do not know what neen really is
i know that a greek artist manetas raised
$100 000
and paid someone to come up with
this word to represent a new art movement
it is a big tax deduction for someone
so come and see the show at casco
my name is nikola

Nikola Tosic, adesivo *AfterNeen*

AfterNeen è stata la prima mostra Neen. Creata per Casco, uno spazio d'arte alternativo a Utrecht (Paesi Bassi), è stata concepita come una mostra che mette alla prova lo spazio reale dove è ospitato.
A Casco sono stati istallati due computer per proiezioni, entrambi connessi a Internet. Uno mostrava il Neen World di Andreas Angelidakis, mentre l'altro fu lasciato su un browser vuoto. Il visitatore di Casco poteva connettersi al Neen World, gli veniva assegnato un avatar con il quale avrebbe potuto andare in giro ed eventualmente incontrare altre persone che passavano di lì. Se avesse incontrato una Neenstar (il Neen World è un villaggio creato dagli studi di differenti Neenstar), e se la Neenstar l'avesse desiderato, sarebbe stato invitato a vedere alcune opere, nascoste all'interno di domini Internet. In quel caso la Neenstar avrebbe attivato – attraverso Internet – il secondo proiettore della galleria e mostrato al visitatore il dominio nascosto. L'idea era interessante, ma dopo due giorni, non fu più possibile trovare alcuna Neenstar nel Neen World e *AfterNeen* divenne una cosa noiosa. A questo punto accadde un miracolo. Una Mercedes automatizzata, guidata da un ragazzo ubriaco, si schiantò nello spazio Casco e distrusse ogni cosa. Fu un incidente crudele, perché una delle persone che lavoravano lì si infortunò seriamente, ma fu anche significativo: un vero scontro tra il nostro mondo e il mondo rappresentato dallo schermo di un computer.

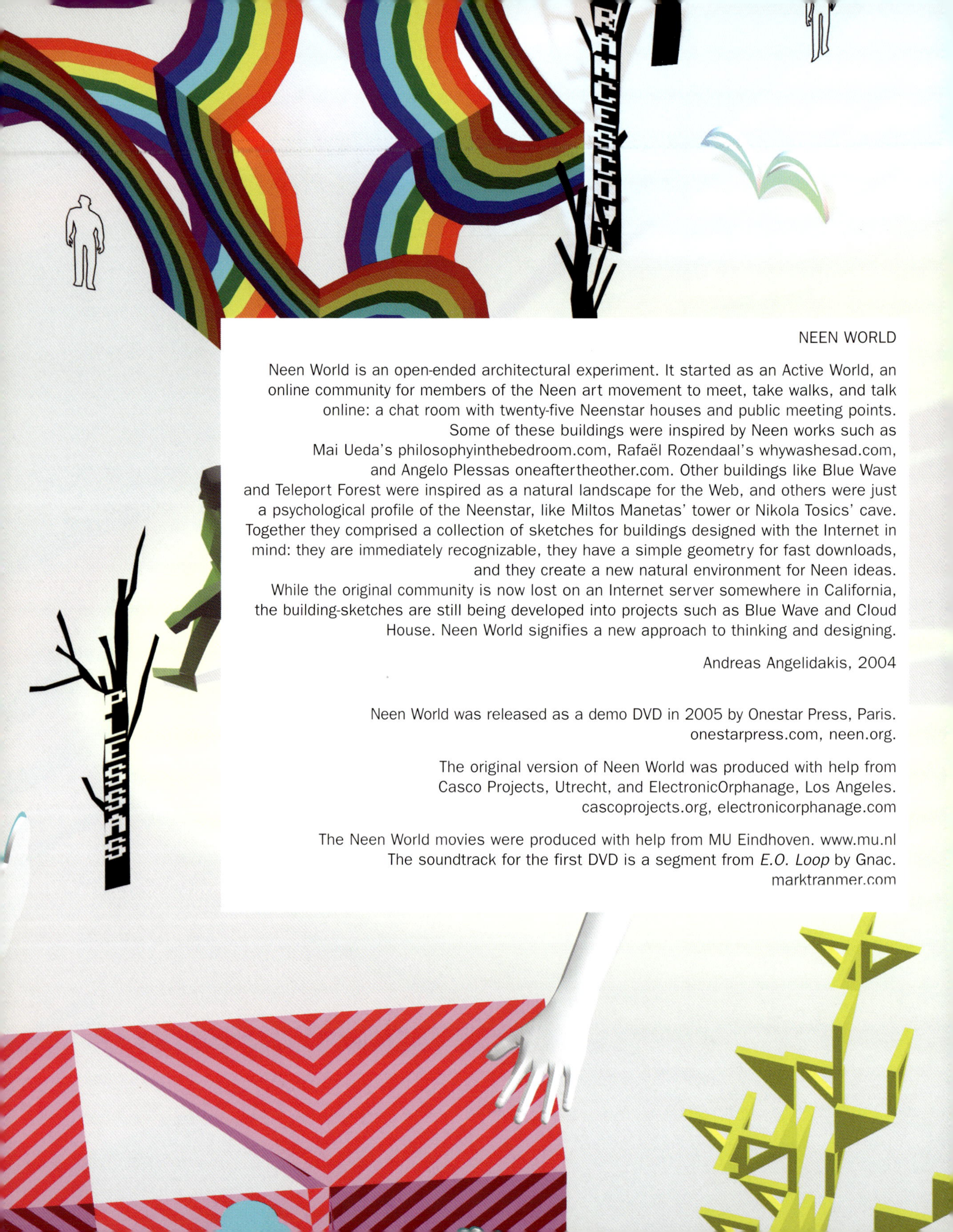

NEEN WORLD

Neen World is an open-ended architectural experiment. It started as an Active World, an online community for members of the Neen art movement to meet, take walks, and talk online: a chat room with twenty-five Neenstar houses and public meeting points. Some of these buildings were inspired by Neen works such as Mai Ueda's philosophyinthebedroom.com, Rafaël Rozendaal's whywashesad.com, and Angelo Plessas oneaftertheother.com. Other buildings like Blue Wave and Teleport Forest were inspired as a natural landscape for the Web, and others were just a psychological profile of the Neenstar, like Miltos Manetas' tower or Nikola Tosics' cave. Together they comprised a collection of sketches for buildings designed with the Internet in mind: they are immediately recognizable, they have a simple geometry for fast downloads, and they create a new natural environment for Neen ideas. While the original community is now lost on an Internet server somewhere in California, the building-sketches are still being developed into projects such as Blue Wave and Cloud House. Neen World signifies a new approach to thinking and designing.

Andreas Angelidakis, 2004

Neen World was released as a demo DVD in 2005 by Onestar Press, Paris. onestarpress.com, neen.org.

The original version of Neen World was produced with help from Casco Projects, Utrecht, and ElectronicOrphanage, Los Angeles. cascoprojects.org, electronicorphanage.com

The Neen World movies were produced with help from MU Eindhoven. www.mu.nl
The soundtrack for the first DVD is a segment from *E.O. Loop* by Gnac. marktranmer.com

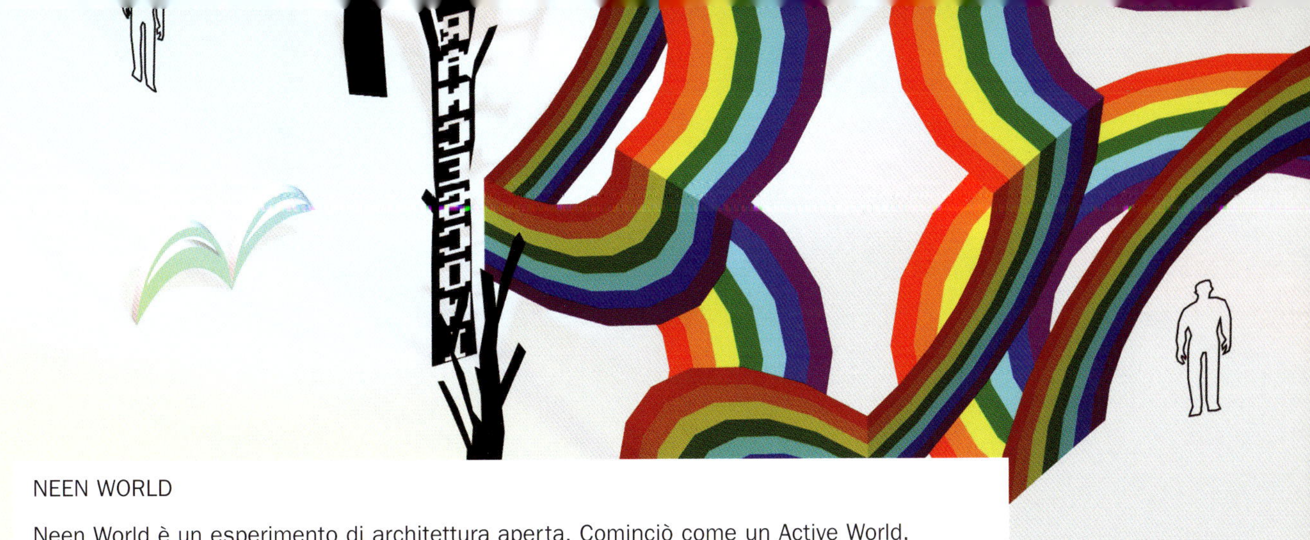

NEEN WORLD

Neen World è un esperimento di architettura aperta. Cominciò come un Active World,
una comunità on line per i membri del movimento Neen, per incontrarsi, passeggiare
e parlarsi on line: una chat room con venticinque case di Neenstar e luoghi di ritrovo pubblici.
Alcuni di questi edifici furono ispirati da opere Neen come philosophyinthebedroom.com
di Mai Ueda, whywashesad.com di Rafaël Rozendaal e oneaftertheother.com
di Angelo Plessas. Altri edifici, come Blue Wave e Teleport Forest, furono pensati come
paesaggi naturali per il Web, e altri ancora erano profili psicologici di Neenstar,
come la torre di Miltos Manetas o la grotta di Nikola Tosic. Insieme, comprendevano una
collezione di abbozzi di edifici progettati avendo Internet in mente: immediatamente
riconoscibili, hanno una geometria semplice per assicurare un download veloce, e creano un
nuovo ambiente naturale per le idee Neen. Mentre la comunità originale è al momento persa
su un server Web in qualche posto della California, gli abbozzi di edifici si stanno ancora
trasformando in progetti, come accade per Blue Wave e Cloud House. Il Neen World ha
significato un nuovo approccio teorico e progettuale.

Andreas Angelidakis, 2004

Il Neen World è stato pubblicato in un DVD demo nel 2005 dall'editore Onestar Press, Parigi.
onestarpress.com, neen.org

La versione originale del Neen World fu prodotta con l'aiuto
di Casco Projects, Utrecht e ElectronicOrphanage, Los Angeles.
cascoprojects.org, electronicorphanage.com

I film Neen World sono stati prodotti con l'aiuto di MU, Eindhoven. mu.nl
La cononna sonora per il primo DVD è tratta da *E.O. Loop* di Gnac.
marktranmer.com

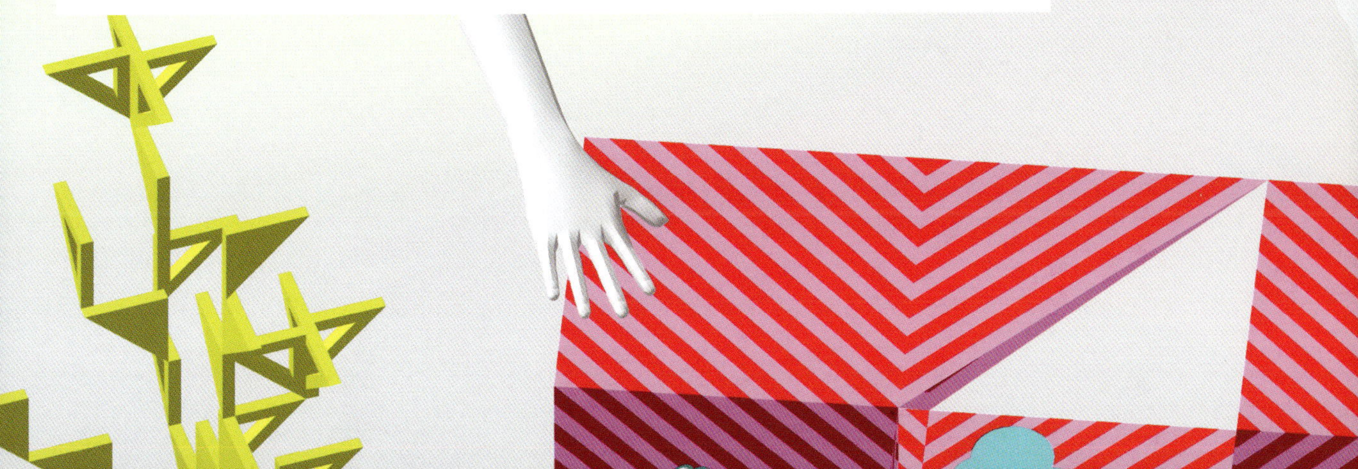

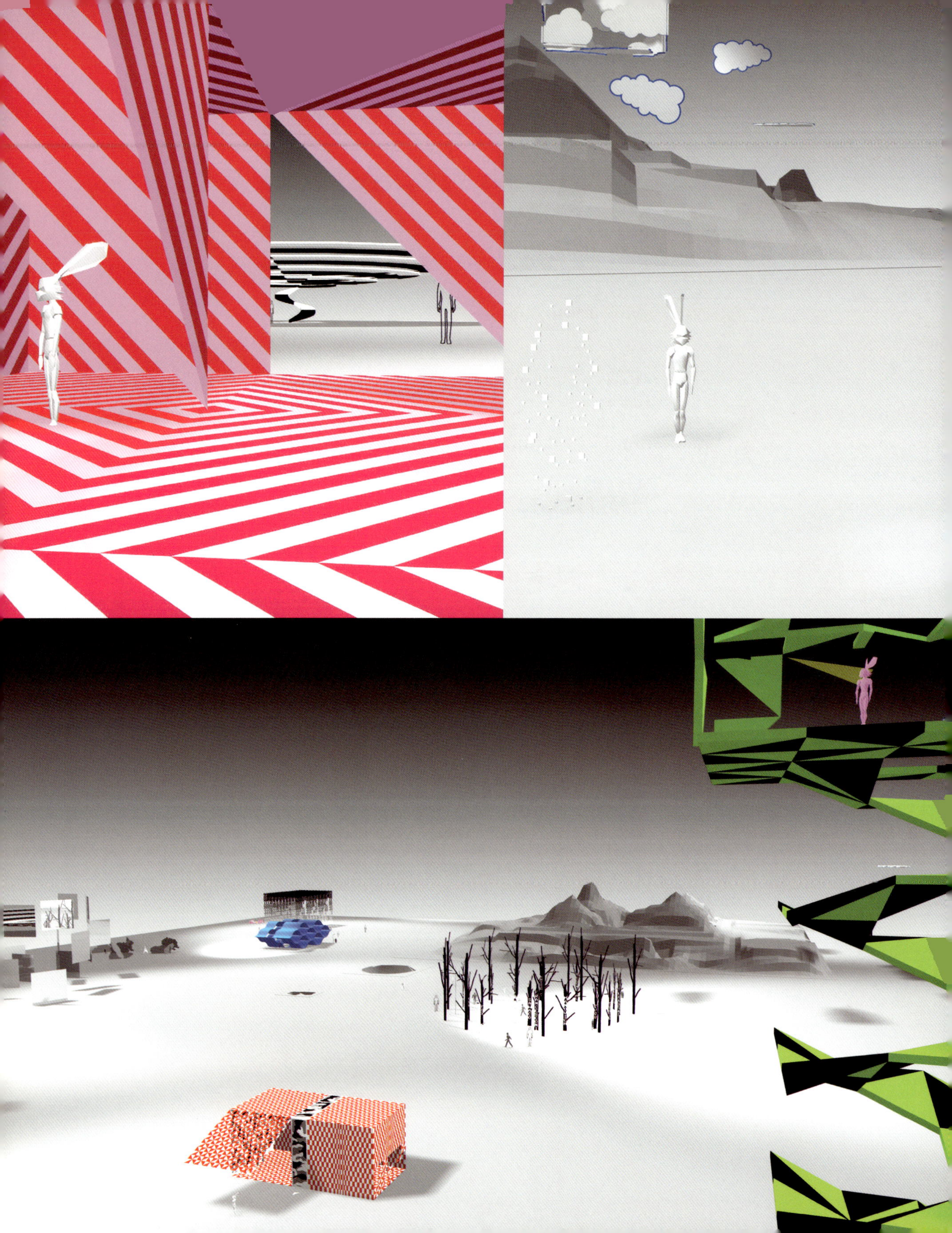

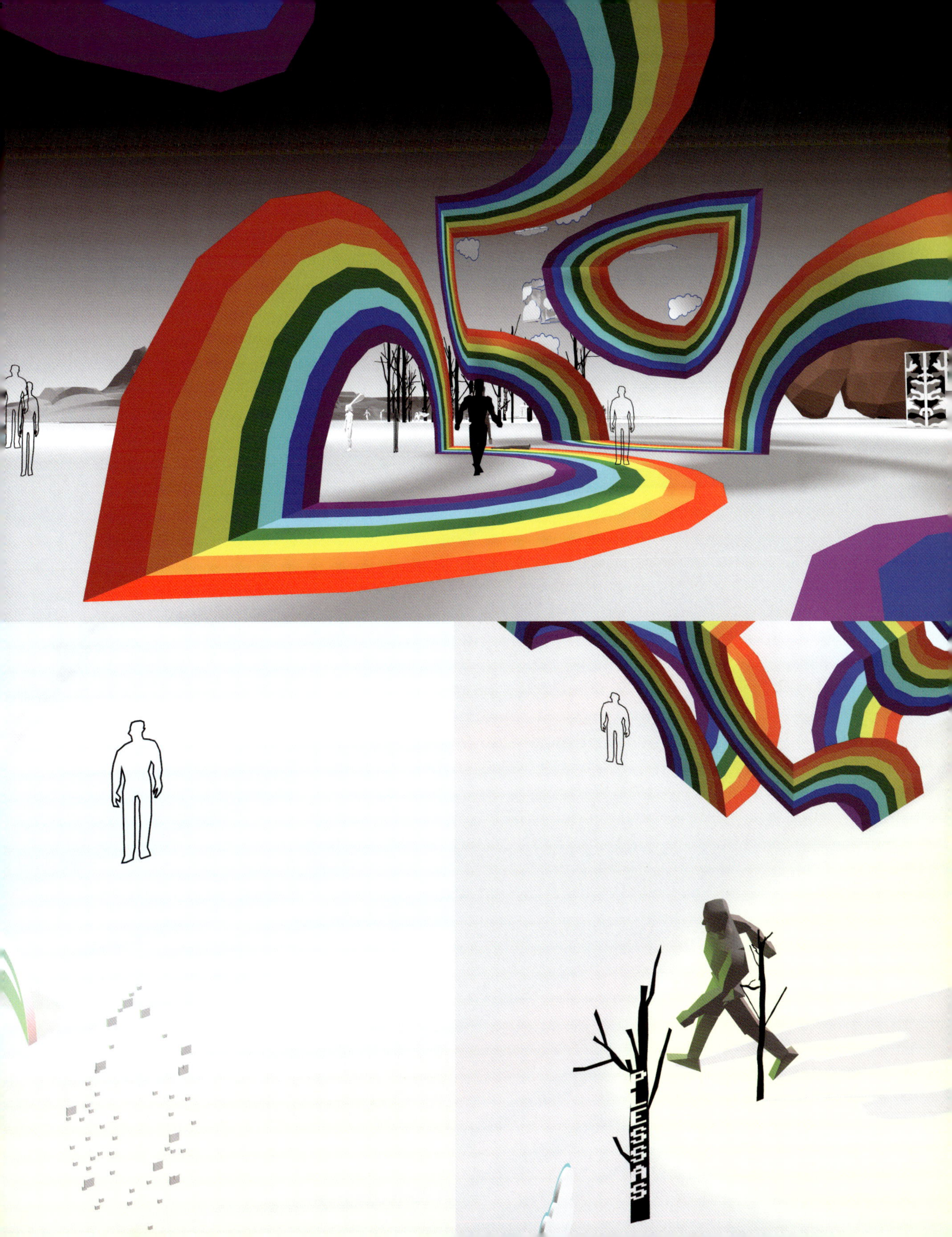
PIESSAS

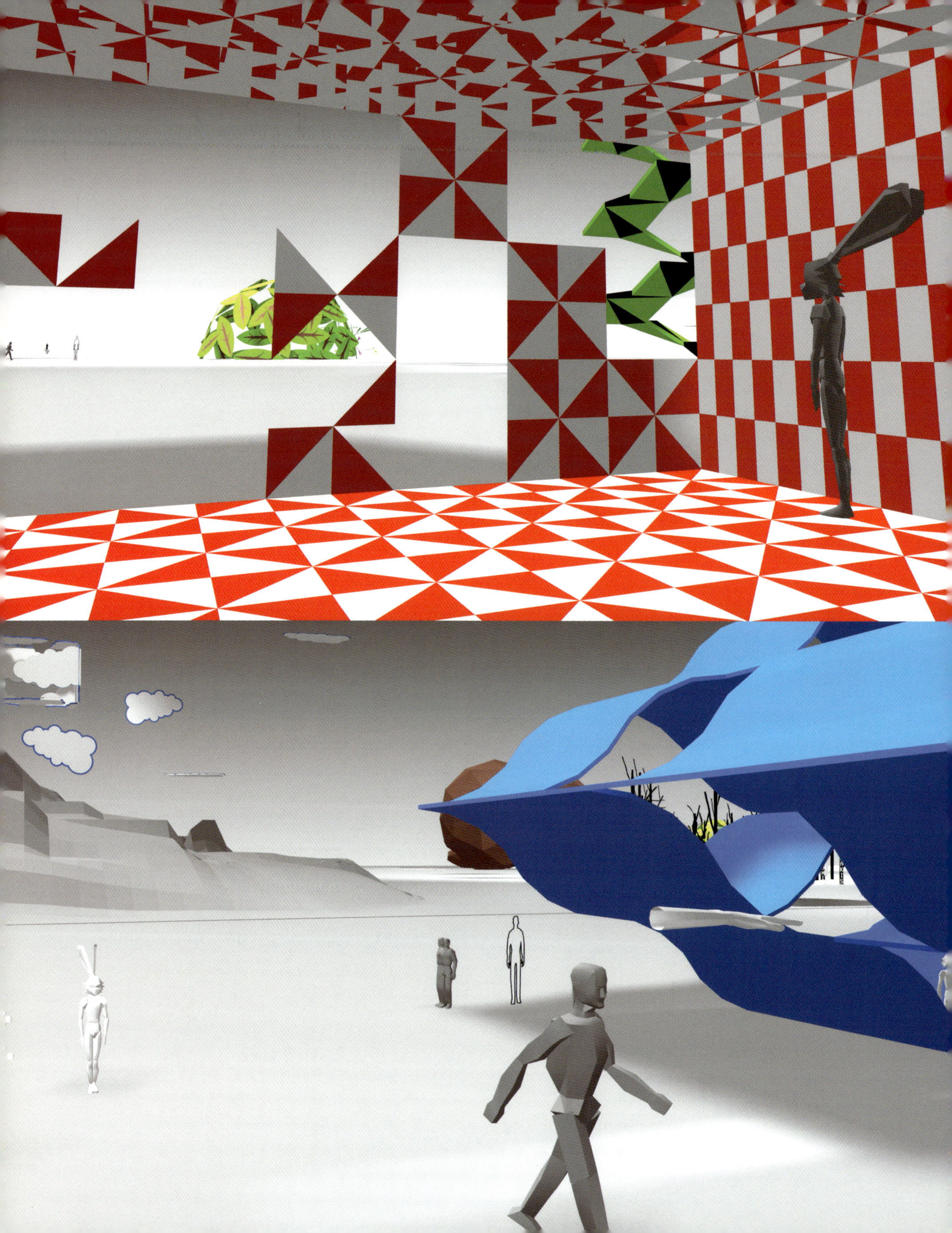

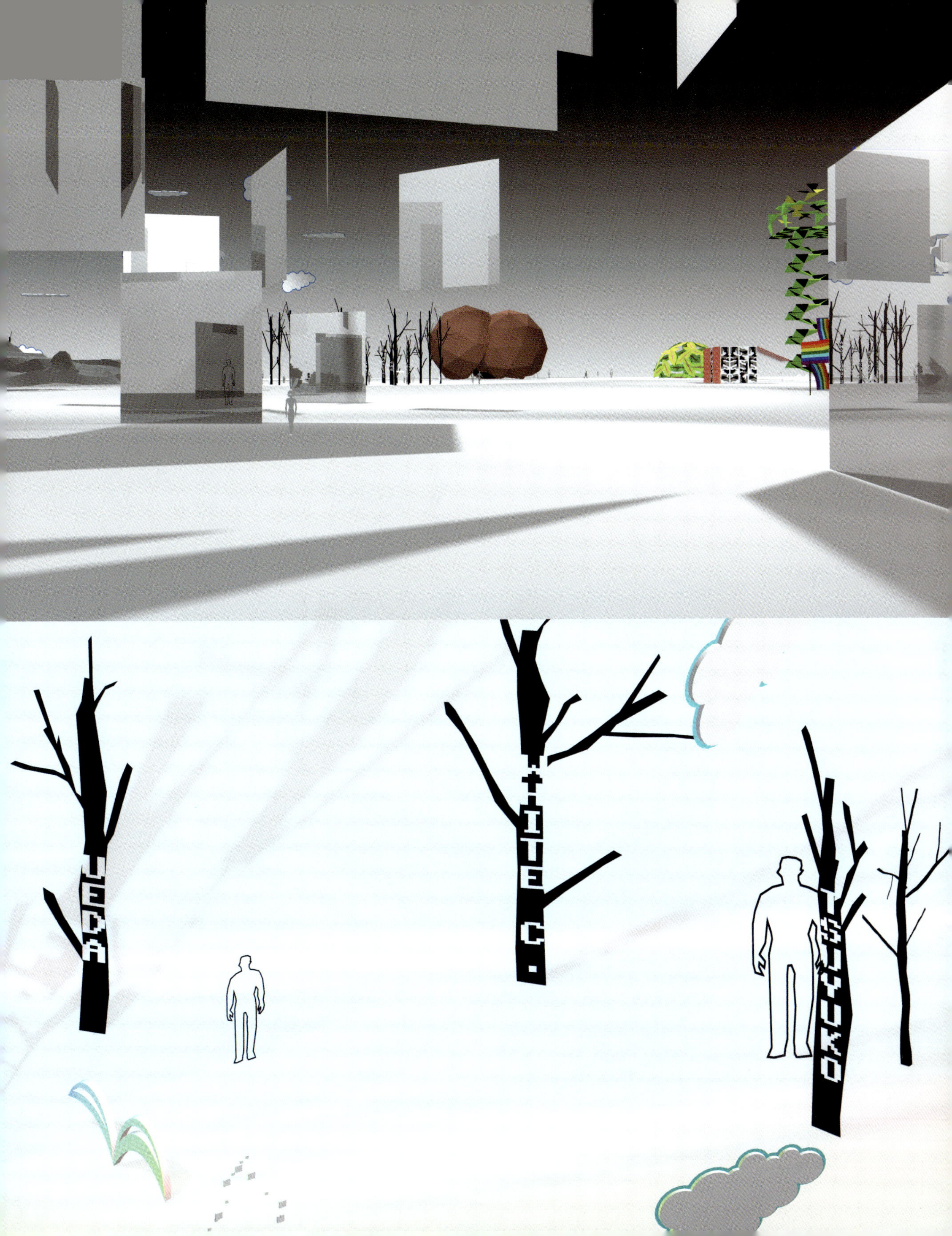
UEDA
TIVE
C.
TSUYUKO

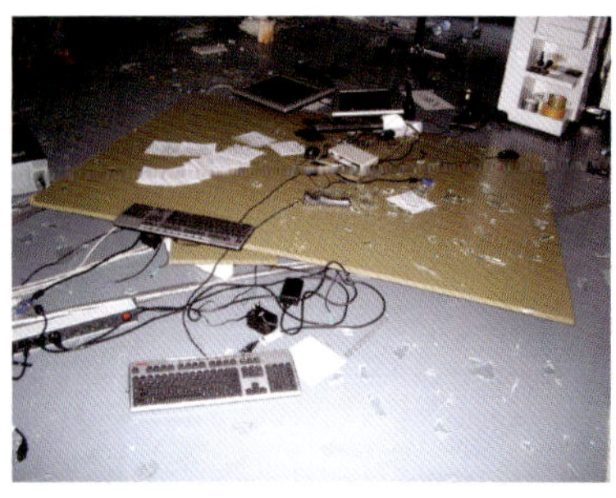 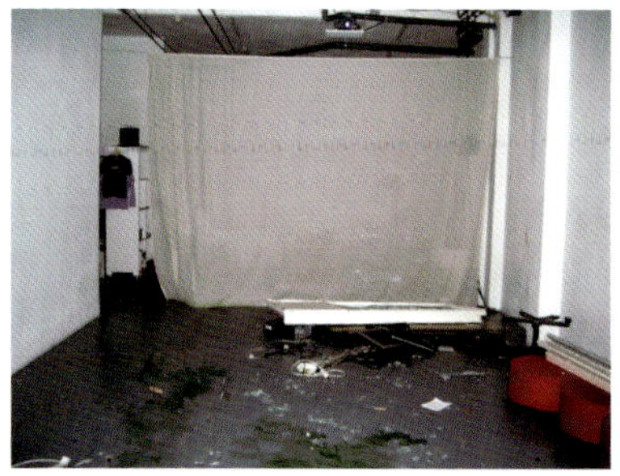 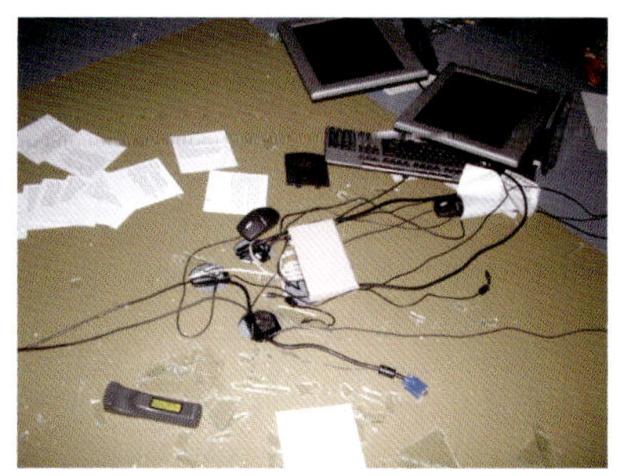

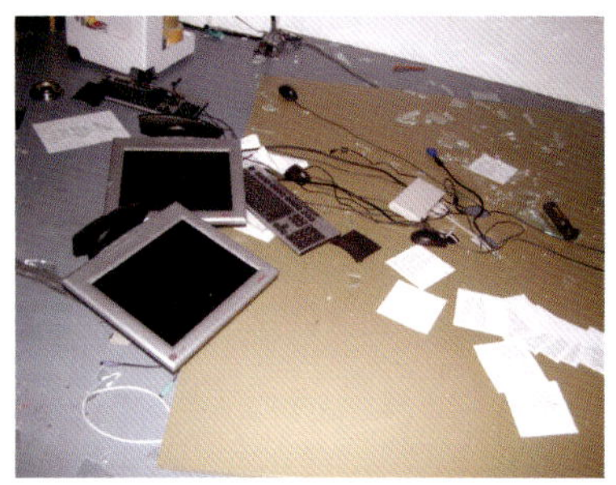 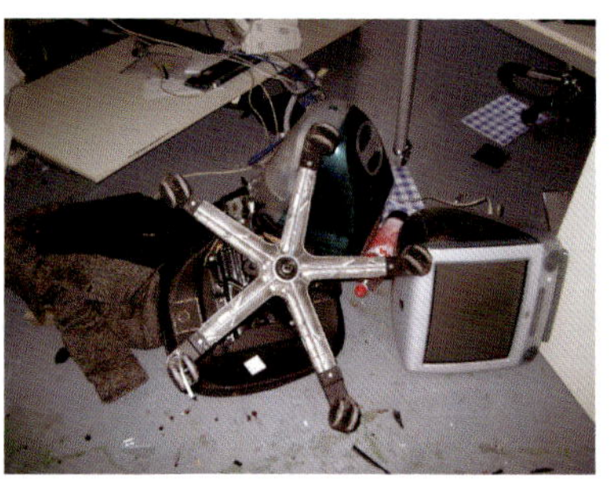 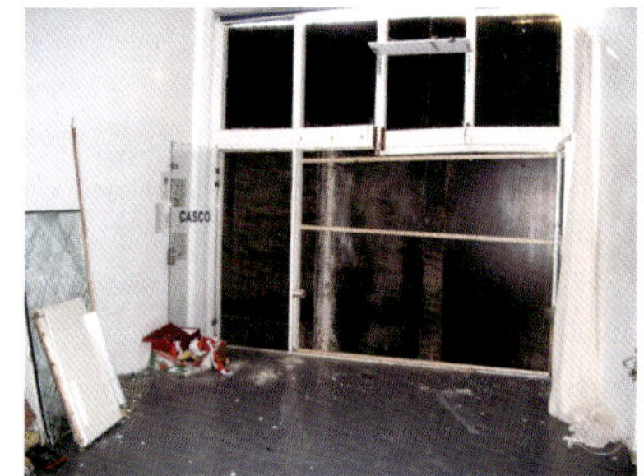

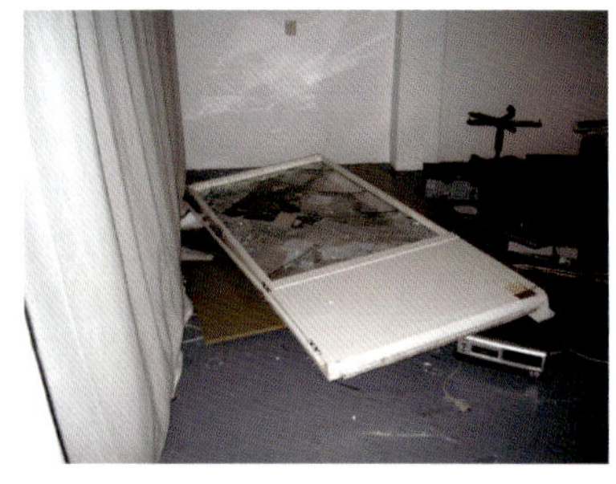 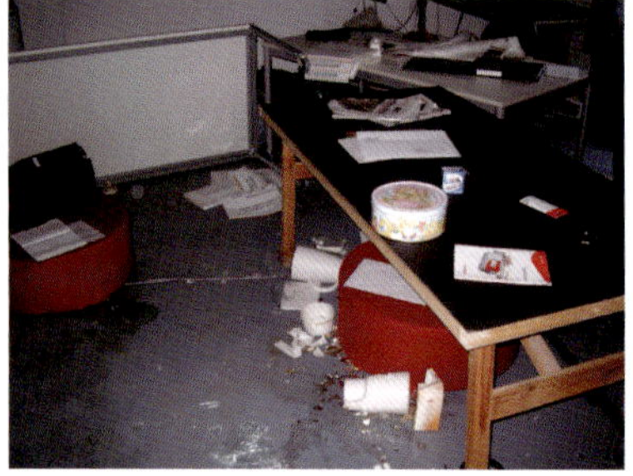 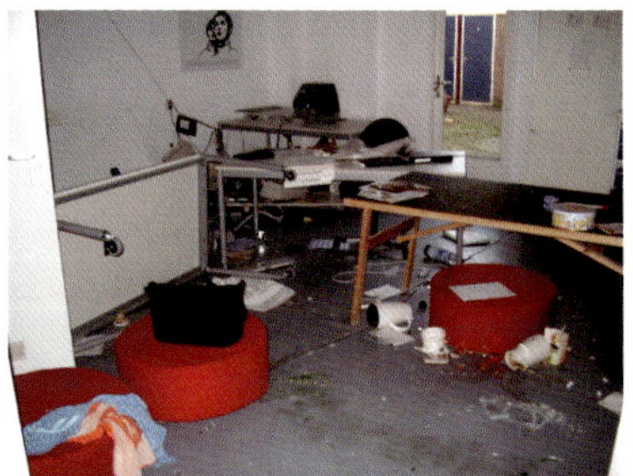

Images taken by the police after the Casco accident

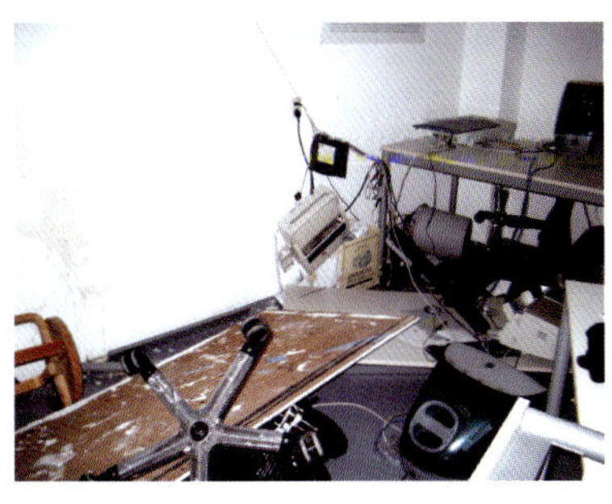 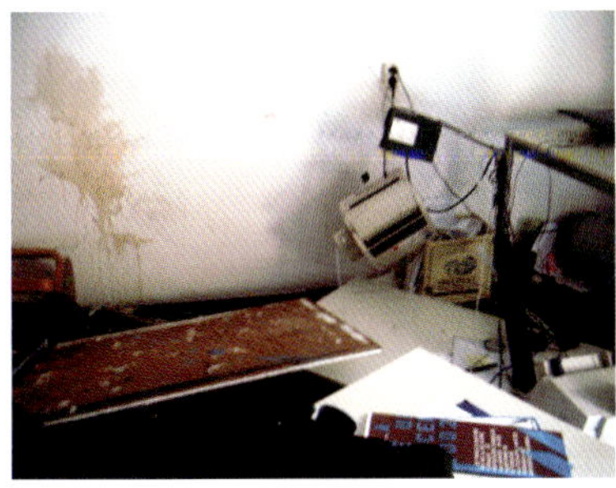 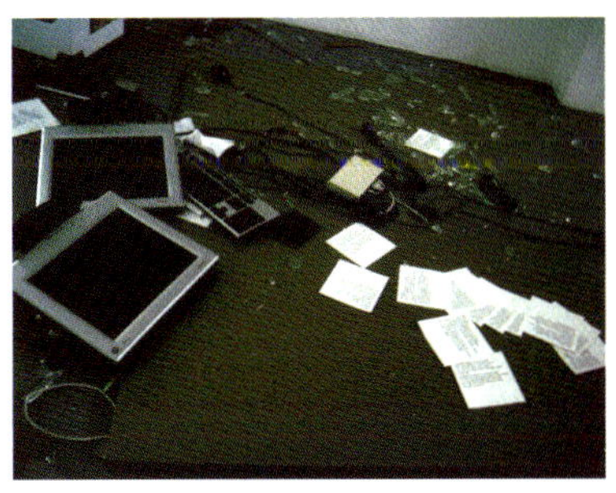

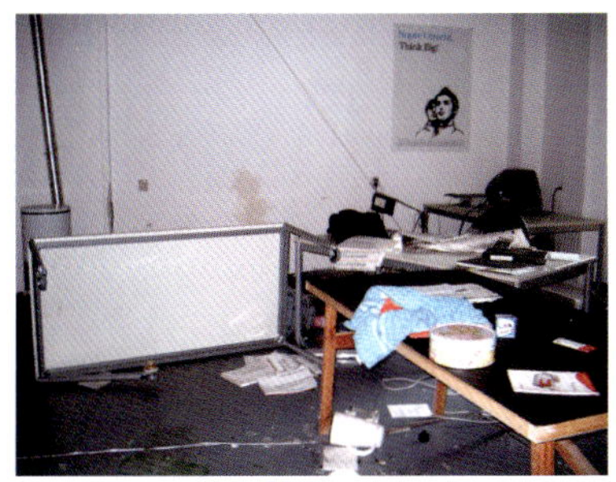 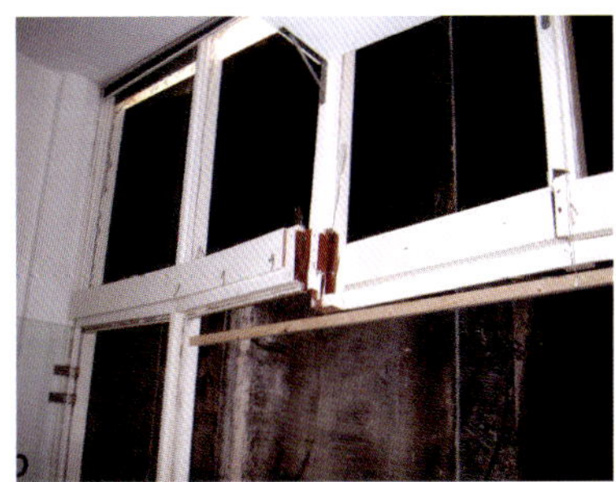 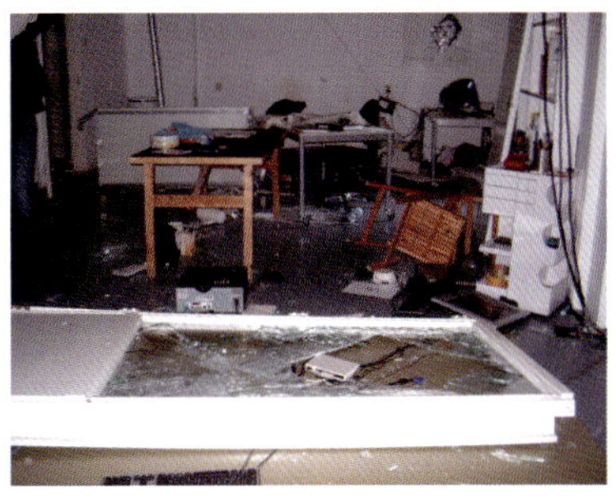

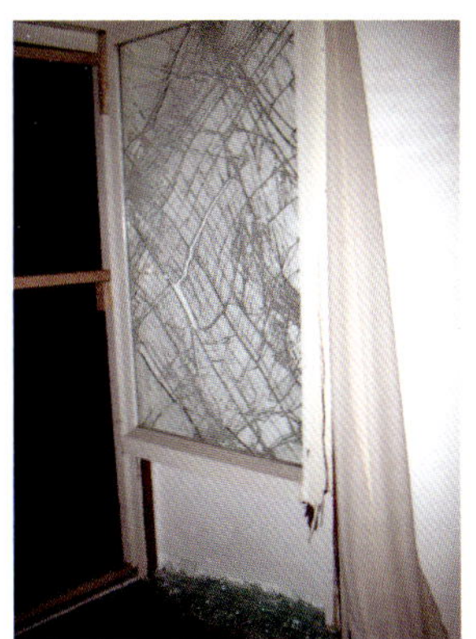 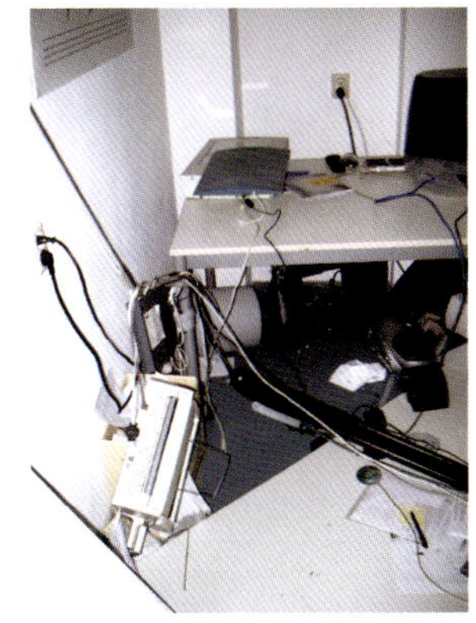 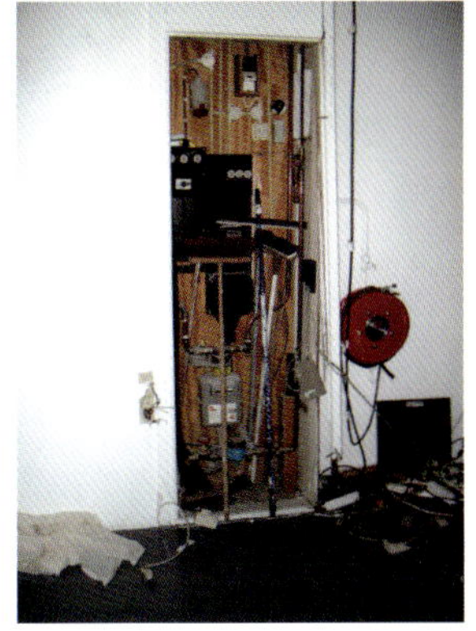

Immagini scattate dalla polizia dopo l'incidente allo spazio Casco

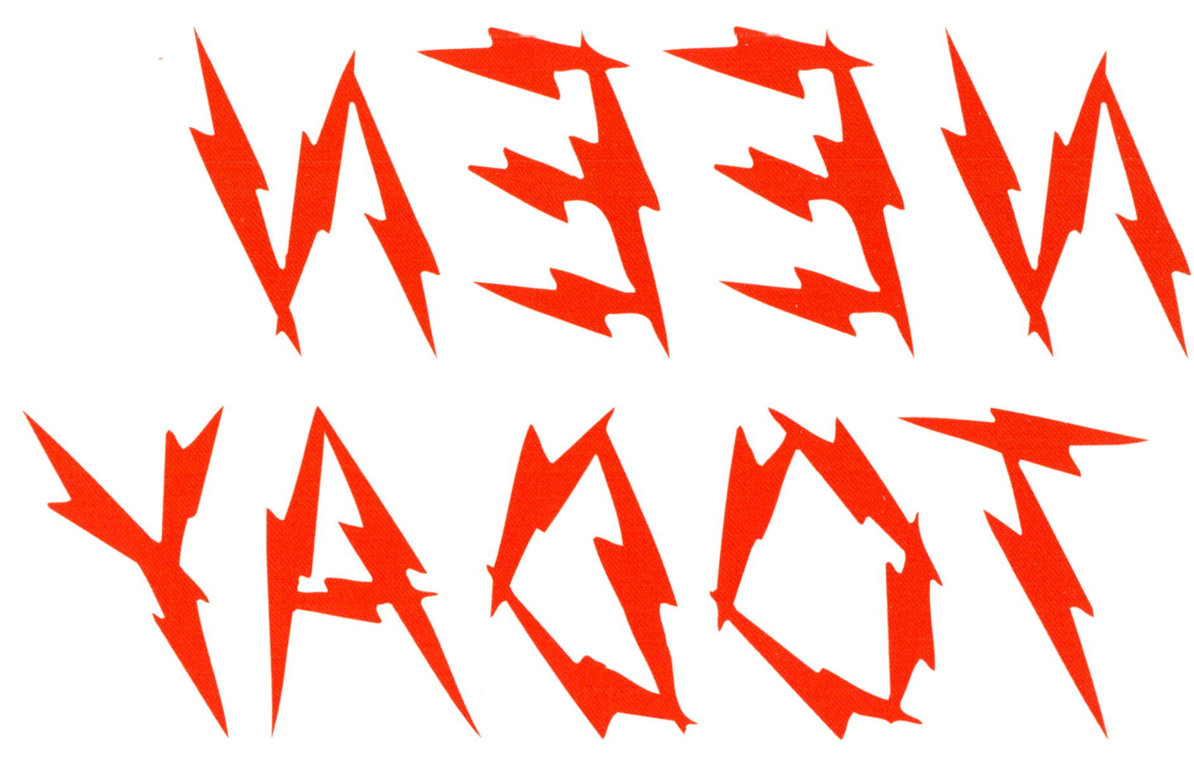

A Neen exhibition is a risky task because whenever Neen is shown in the ordinary and institutionalized context of art, it loses much of its thrill. NeenToday, at the contemporary art space MU in Eindhoven, was curated by Rafaël Rozendaal and was the shortest exhibition ever. A 40,000-Euro production, this show stayed open only for a minute, on April 4, 2004 at 4:44 pm, and closed just 60 seconds later.

The exhibition was commissioned by Ton Van Gool.

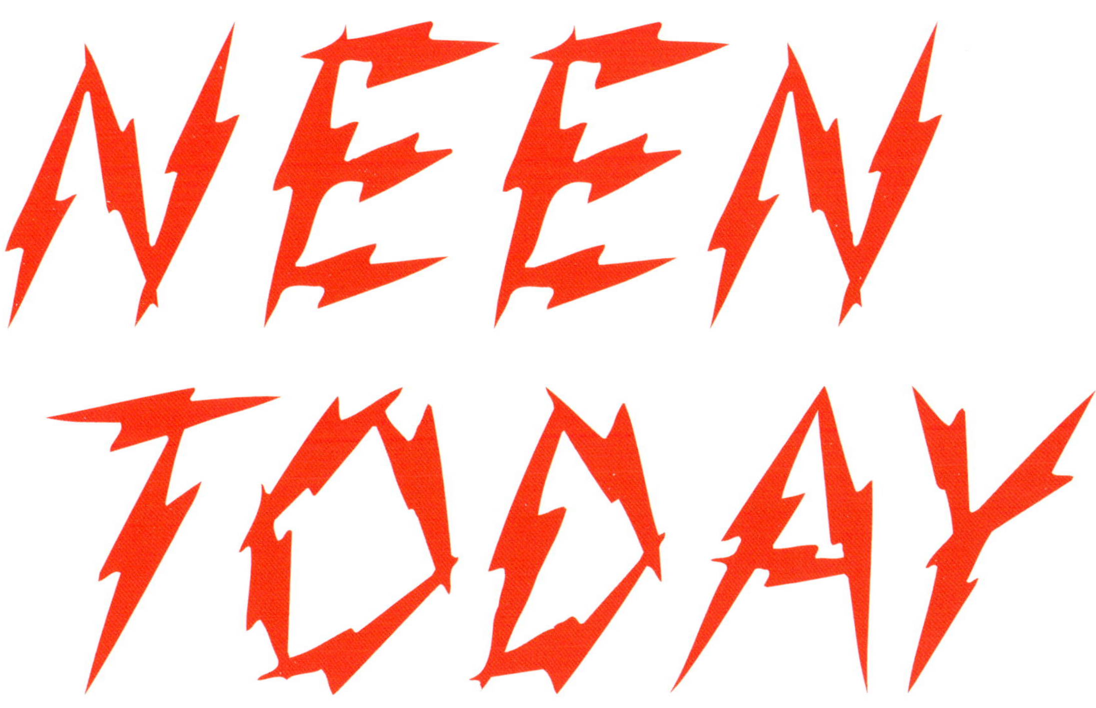

Una mostra Neen è rischiosa perché ogni volta che Neen viene esposto nel contesto ordinario e istituzionalizzato dell'arte, perde buona parte del proprio fascino. *NeenToday*, tenutasi presso lo spazio MU di Eindhoven, curata da Rafaël Rozendaal, è stata la mostra più breve di tutti i tempi.
Costata 40 000 euro, questa mostra è durata solo un minuto: è stata aperta il 4 aprile 2004 alle 16:44 per chiudere 60 secondi dopo.

La mostra è stata commissionata da Ton Van Gool.

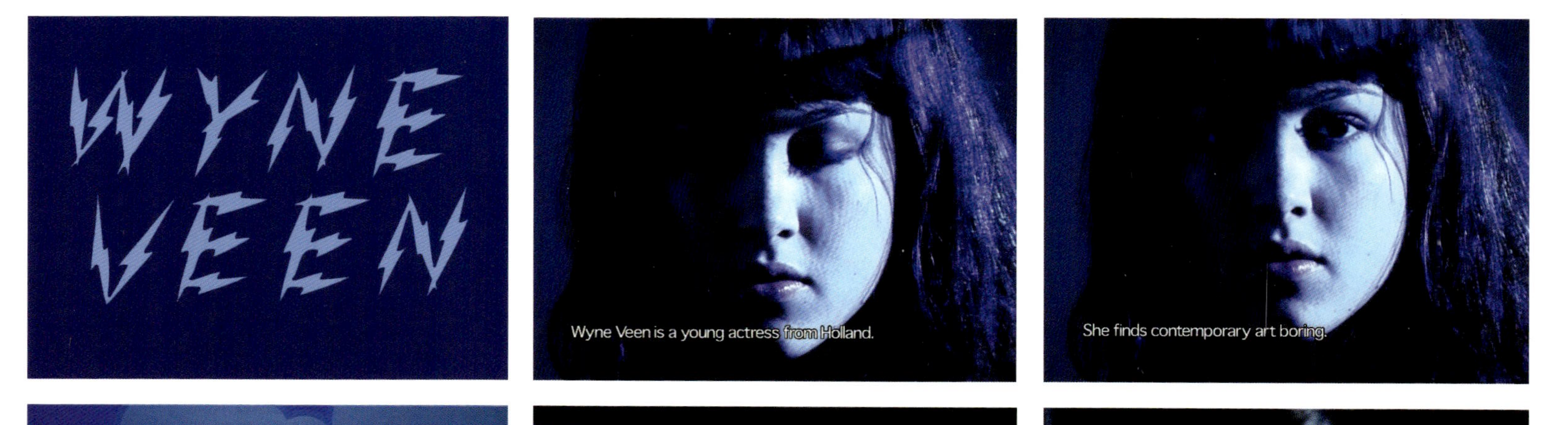

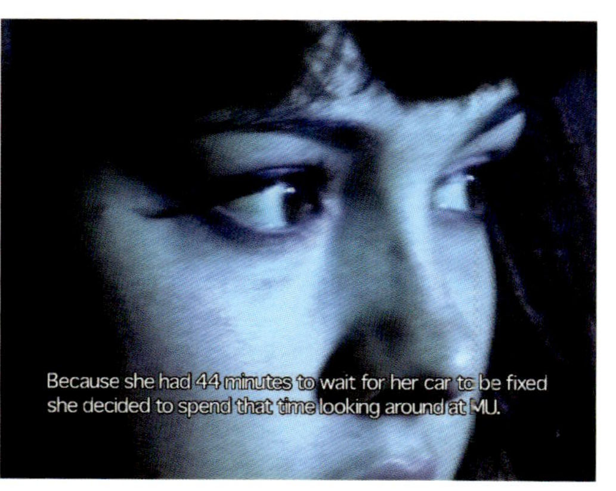
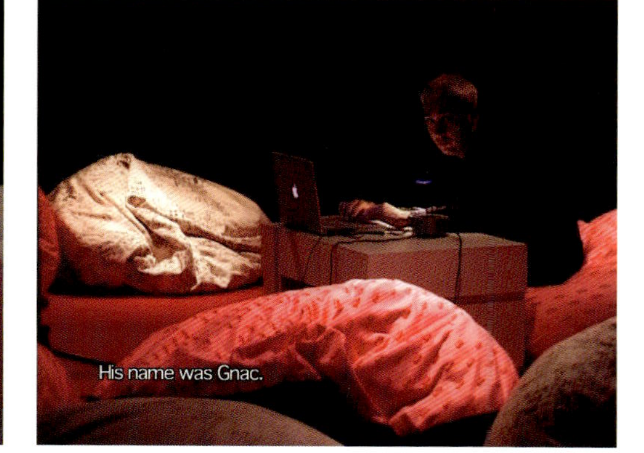
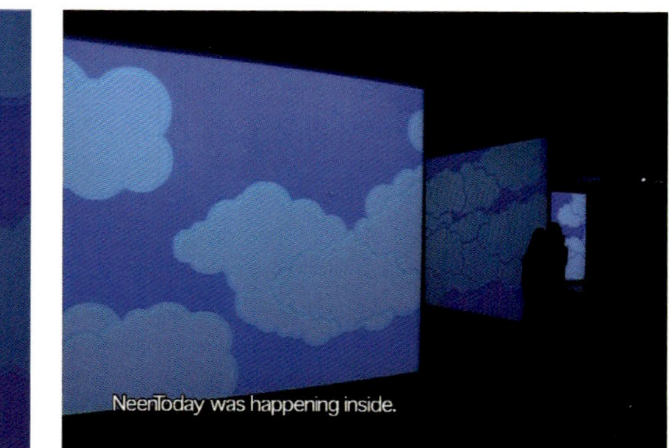

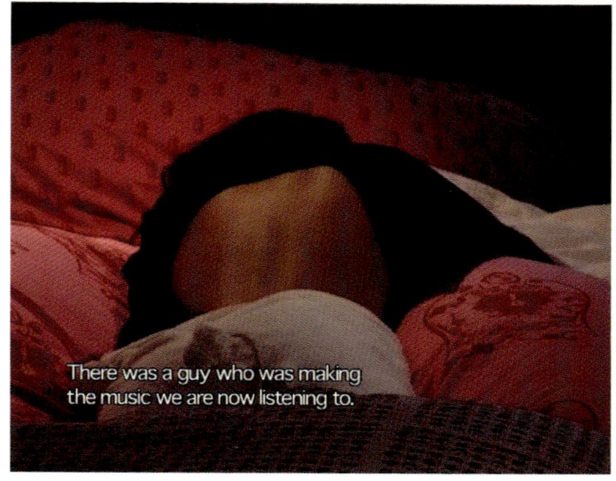
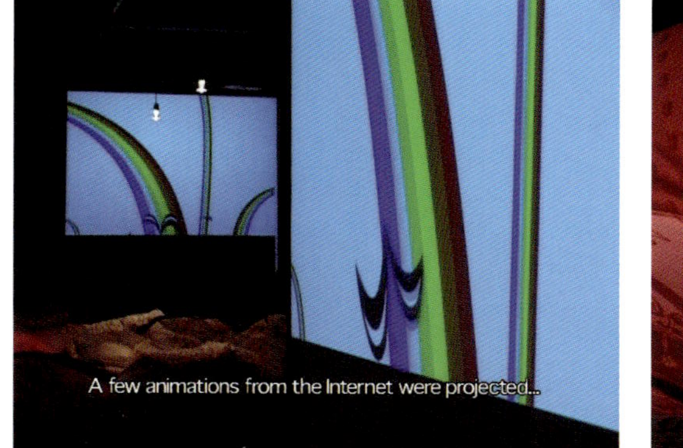

Wyne Veen, a movie by Luuk Bouwman and Miltos Manetas, 2004

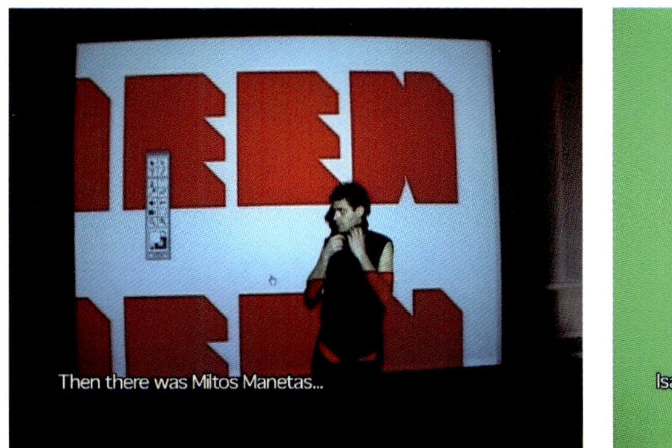

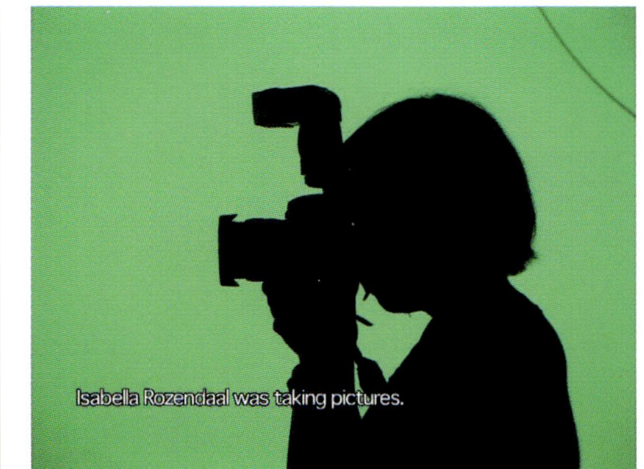

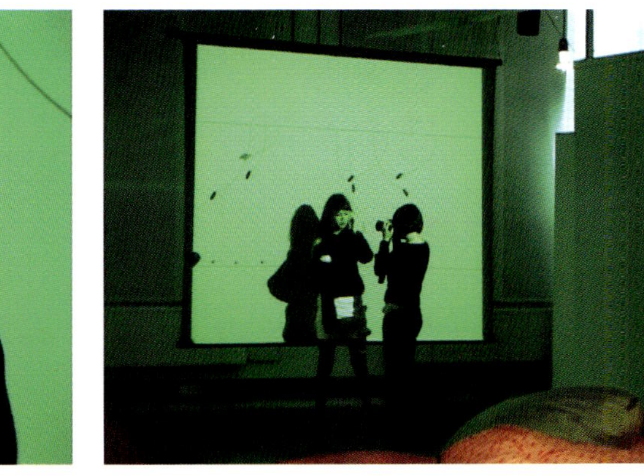

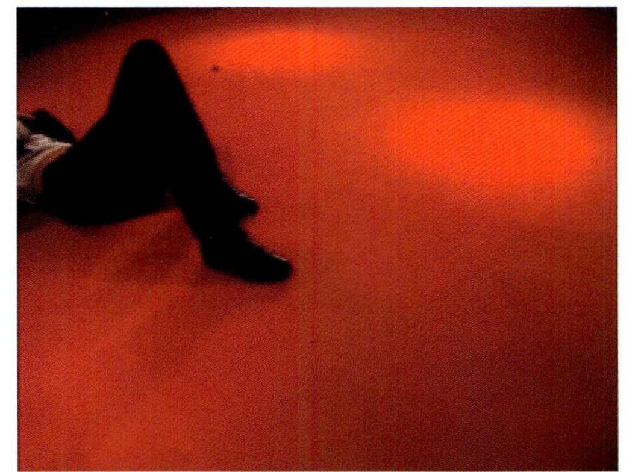

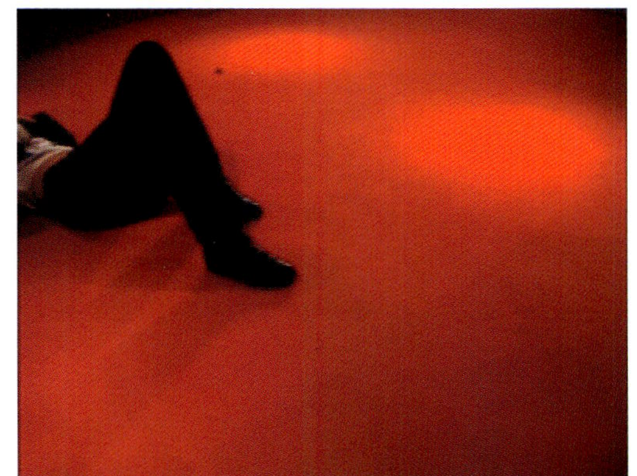

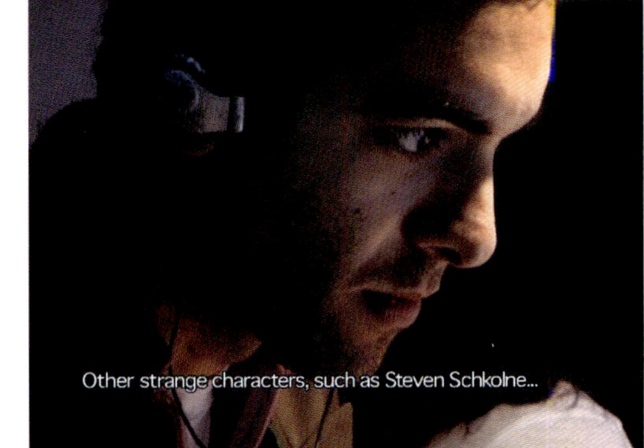

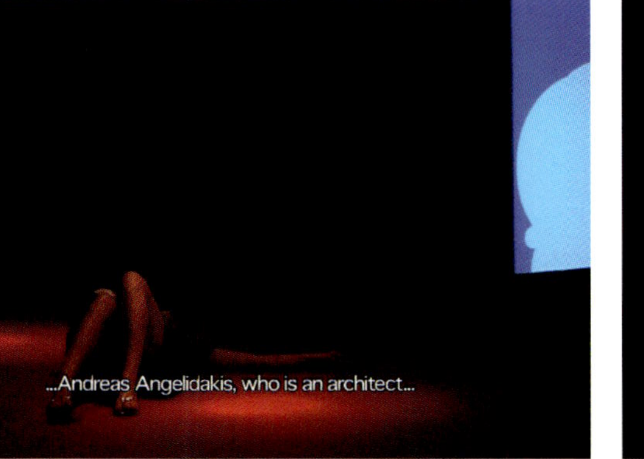

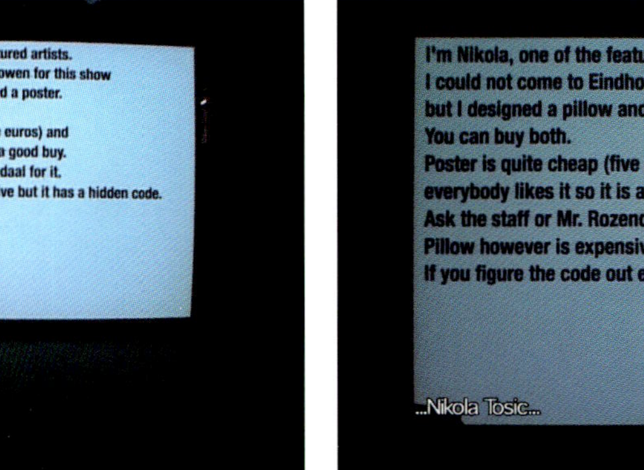

Wyne Veen, un film di Luuk Bouwman e Miltos Manetas, 2004

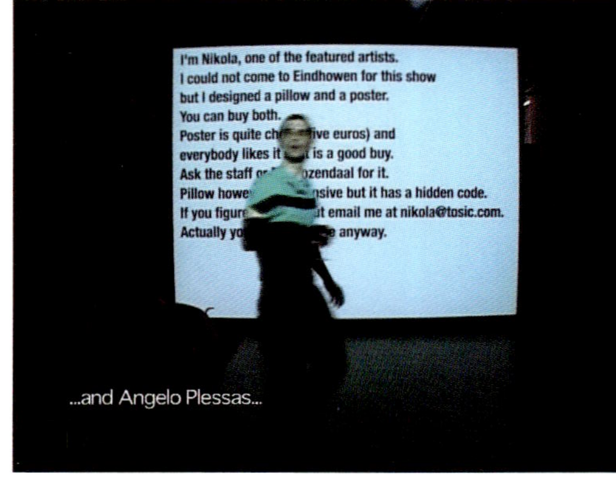
I'm Nikola, one of the featured artists.
I could not come to Eindhowen for this show
but I designed a pillow and a poster.
You can buy both.
Poster is quite ch... (five euros) and
everybody likes it ... is a good buy.
Ask the staff or ... ozendaal for it.
Pillow howev... ...nsive but it has a hidden code.
If you figure ... ut email me at nikola@tosic.com.
Actually yo... ...e anyway.
...and Angelo Plessas...

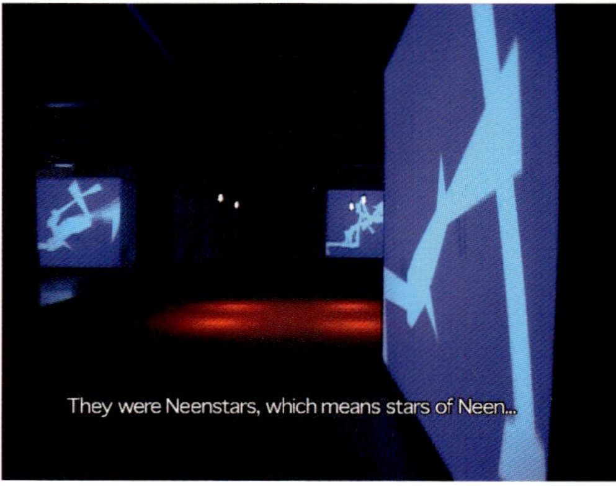
They were Neenstars, which means stars of Neen...

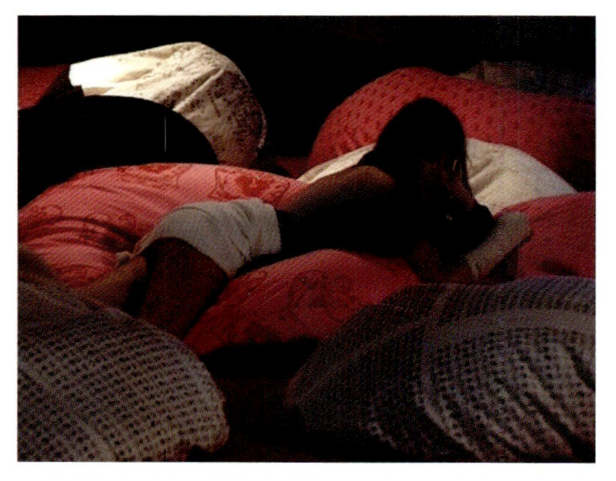

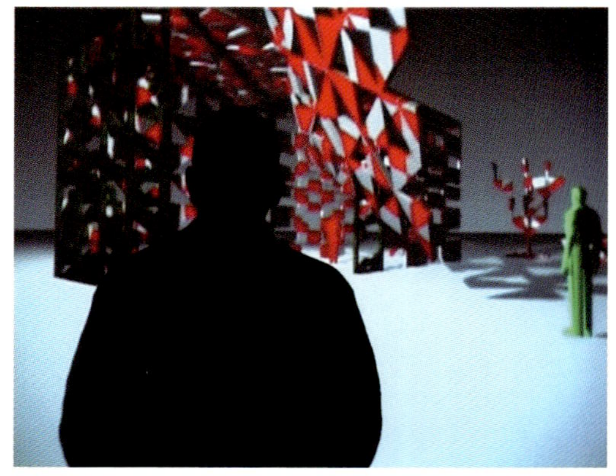

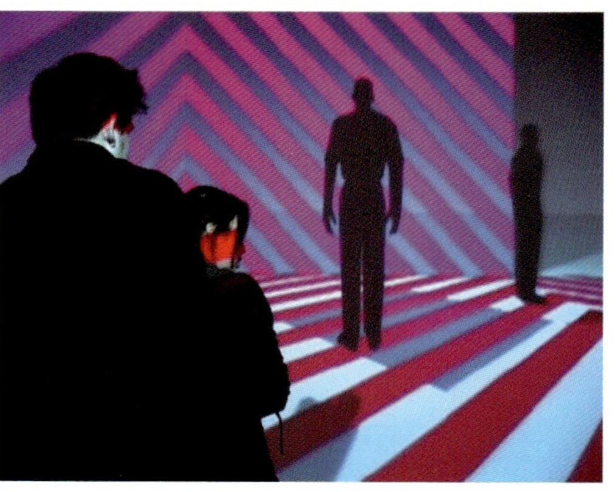

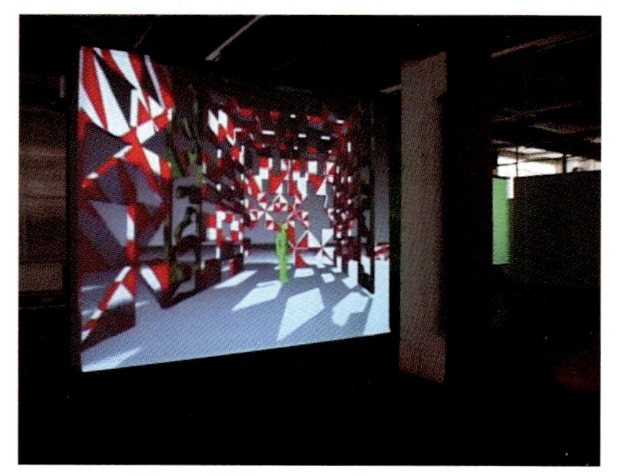

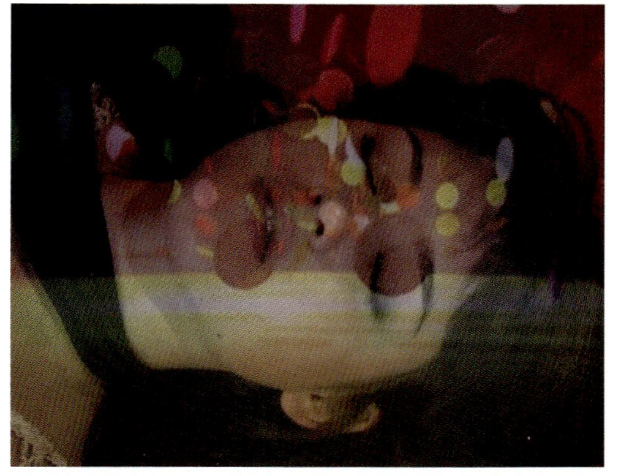

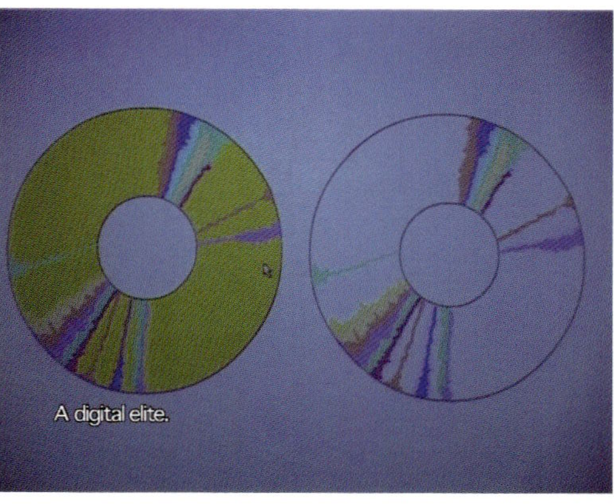
A digital elite.

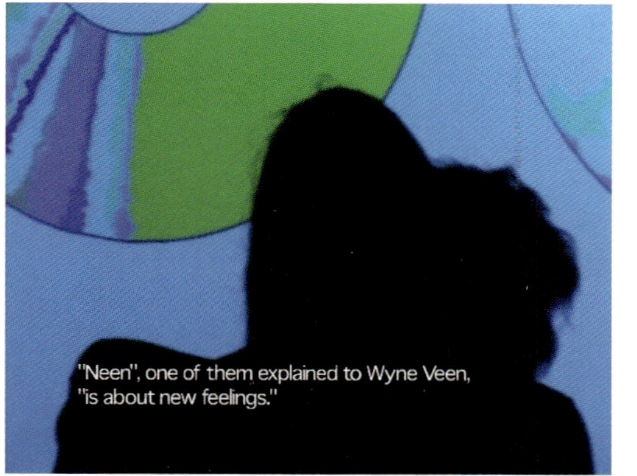
"Neen", one of them explained to Wyne Veen,
"is about new feelings."

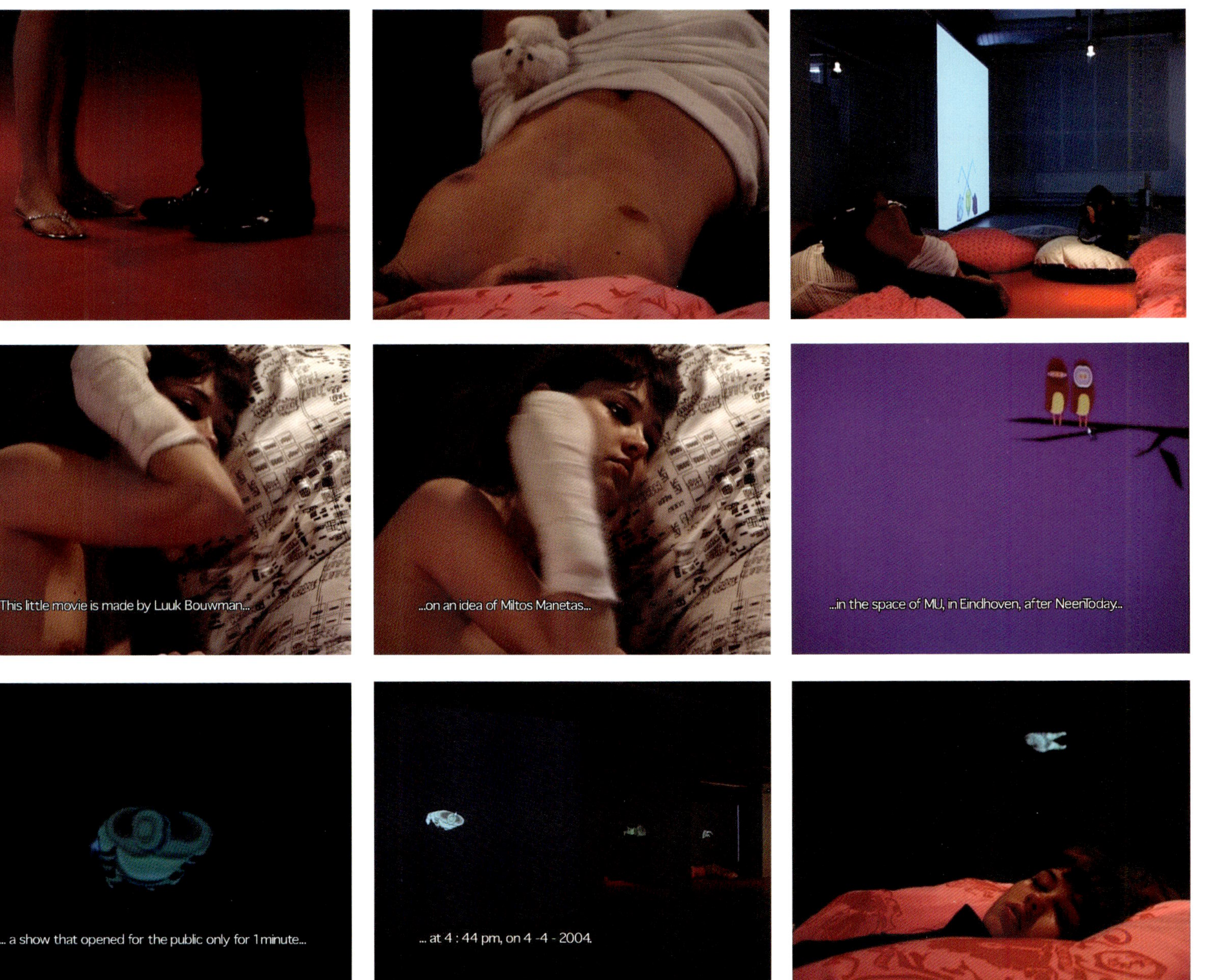
This little movie is made by Luuk Bouwman...
...on an idea of Miltos Manetas...
...in the space of MU, in Eindhoven, after NeenToday...
... a show that opened for the public only for 1 minute...
... at 4 : 44 pm, on 4 -4 - 2004.

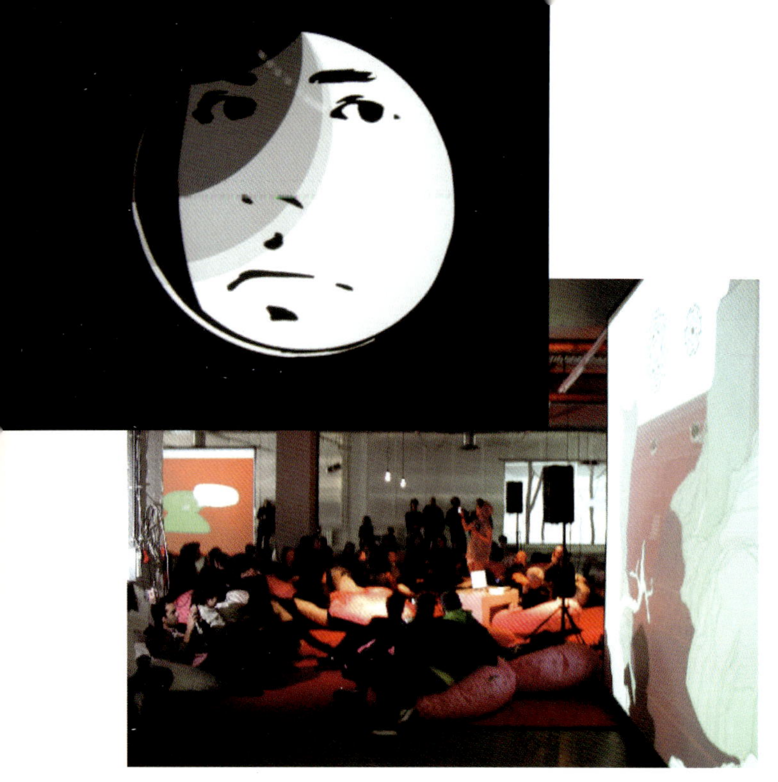

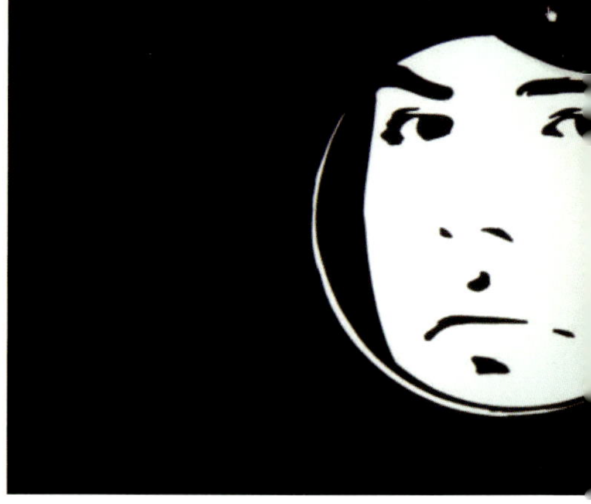

on this page
Rafaël Rozendaal, seethrough.org, 2002

below
Neenstars at the *NeenToday* show

in questa pagina
Rafaël Rozendaal, seethrough.org, 2002

sotto
Neenstars alla mostra *NeenToday*

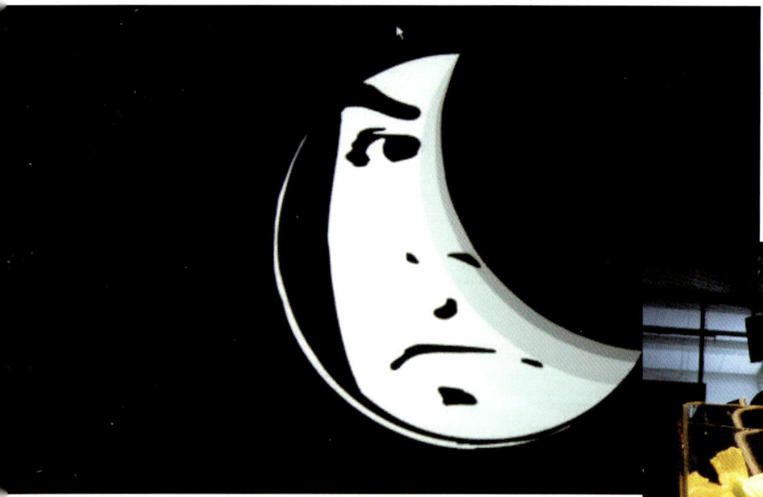

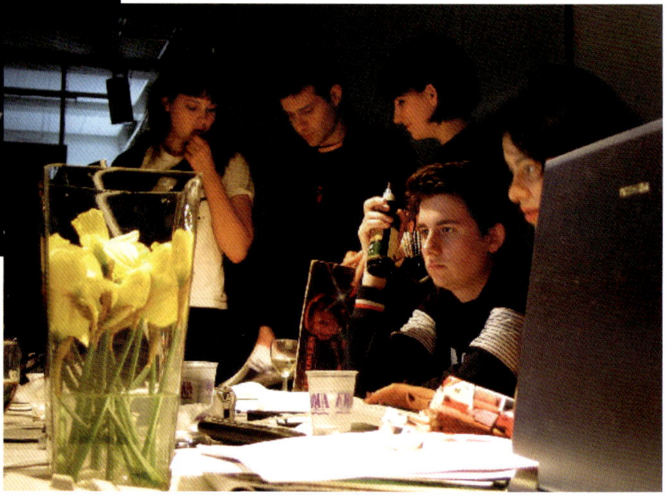

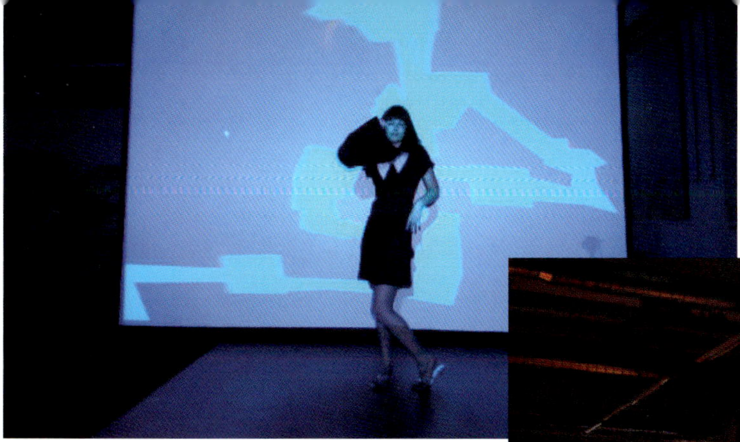

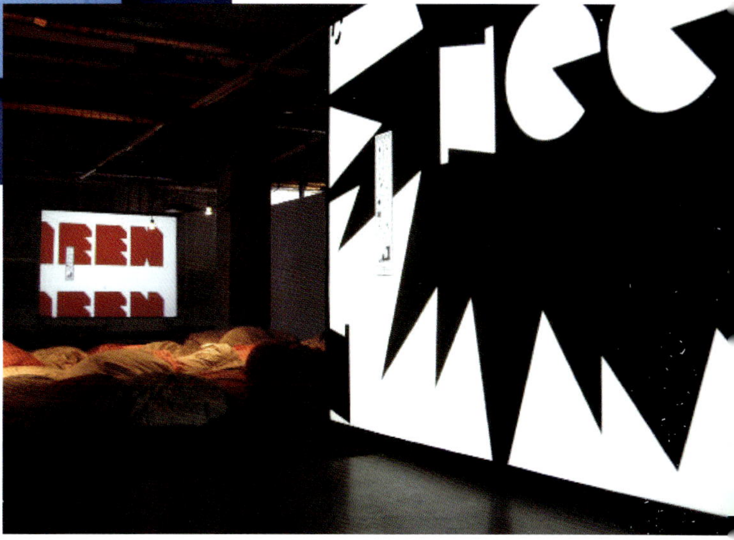

above
Joel Fox, animation, 2002

below
Mai Ueda, philosophyinthebedroom.com, 2002

sopra
Joel Fox, animazione, 2002

sotto
Mai Ueda, philosophyinthebedroom.com, 2002

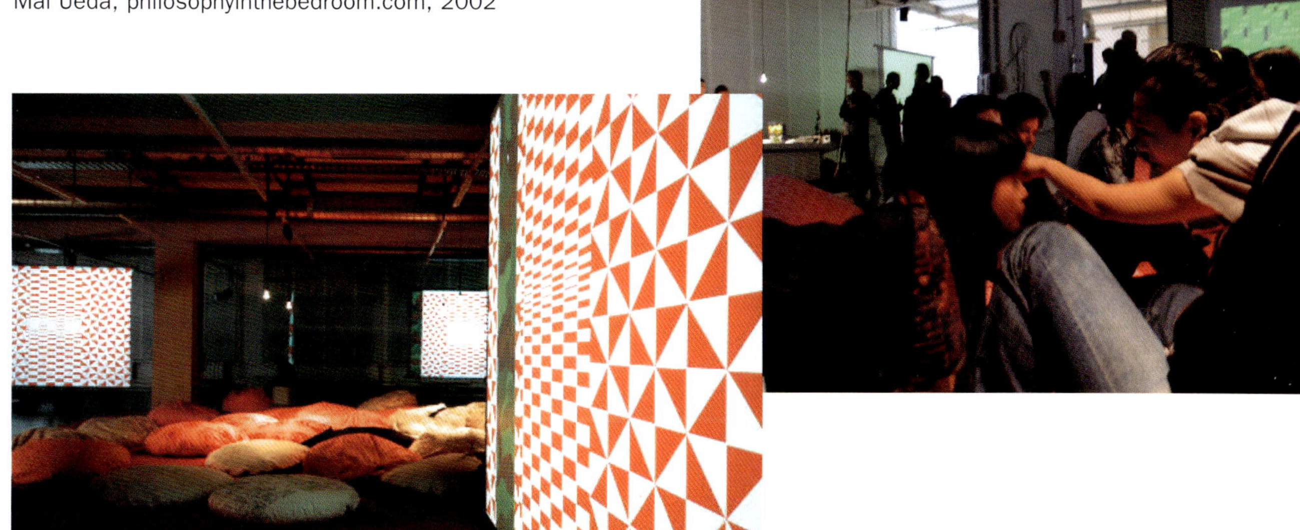

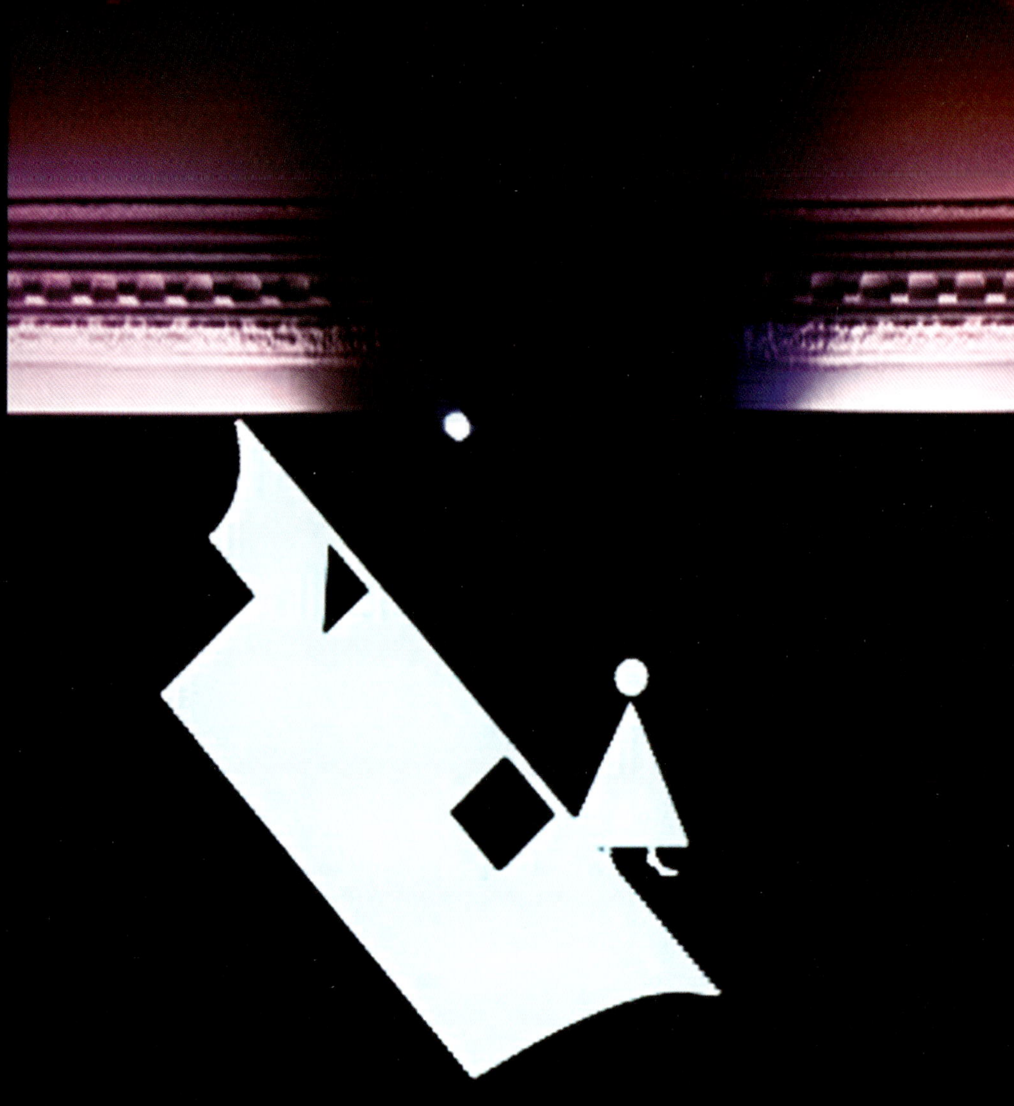

Angelo Plessas, tiptoebehavior.com, 2004

NEEN SEASON

Between January 31 and April 23, 2005, Sketch, the London nightclub
and gallery, dedicated a season to Neen with solo exhibitions of Tobias Burnstump, Mark
Kremers, Miltos Manetas, Angelo Plessas, Rafaël Rozendaal, and Mai Ueda. On Saturday,
April 23 there was a major Neen event called NeenDay. (neen.org/day)

The exhibition was commissioned by Alexandre Pollazon.

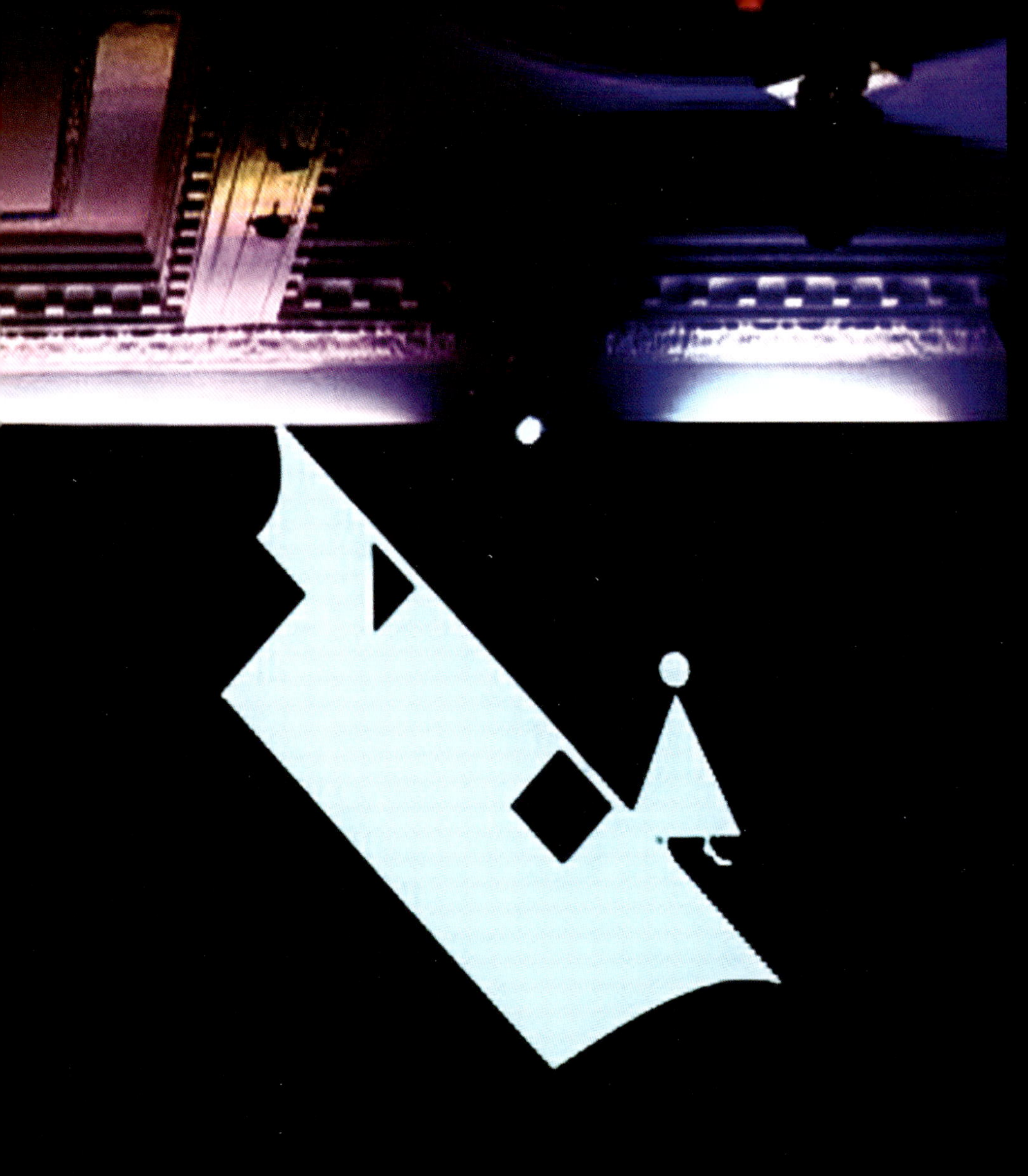

NEEN SEASON

Dal 31 gennaio al 23 aprile 2005, Sketch, nightclub e galleria londinese,
ha dedicato la stagione a Neen, con mostre personali di Tobias Burnstump, Mark
Kremers, Miltos Manetas, Angelo Plessas, Rafaël Rozendaal e Mai Ueda. Sabato,
23 aprile si è tenuto il più importante evento Neen: il NeenDay. neen.org/day

La mostra è stata commissionata da Alexandre Pollazon.

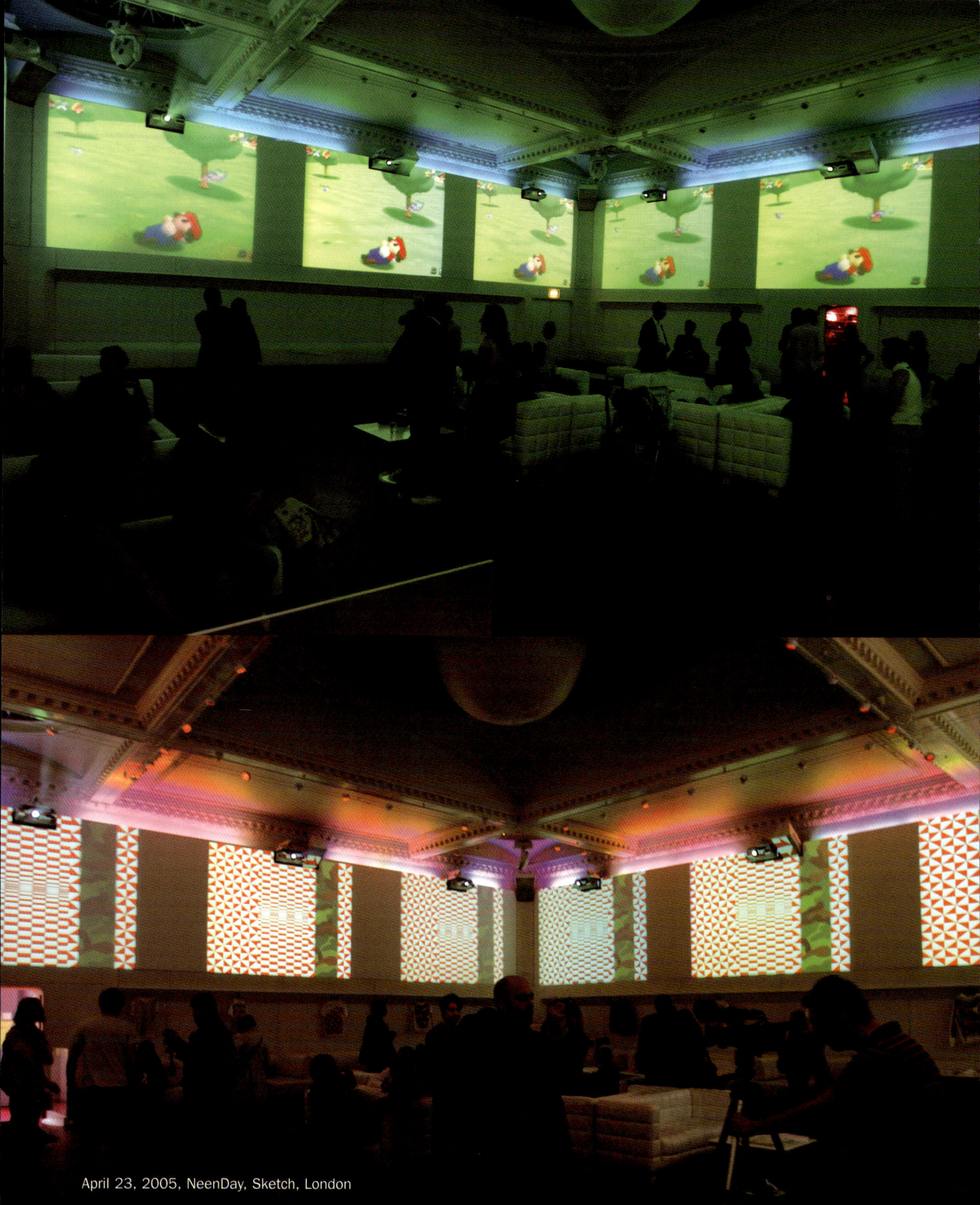

April 23, 2005, NeenDay, Sketch, London

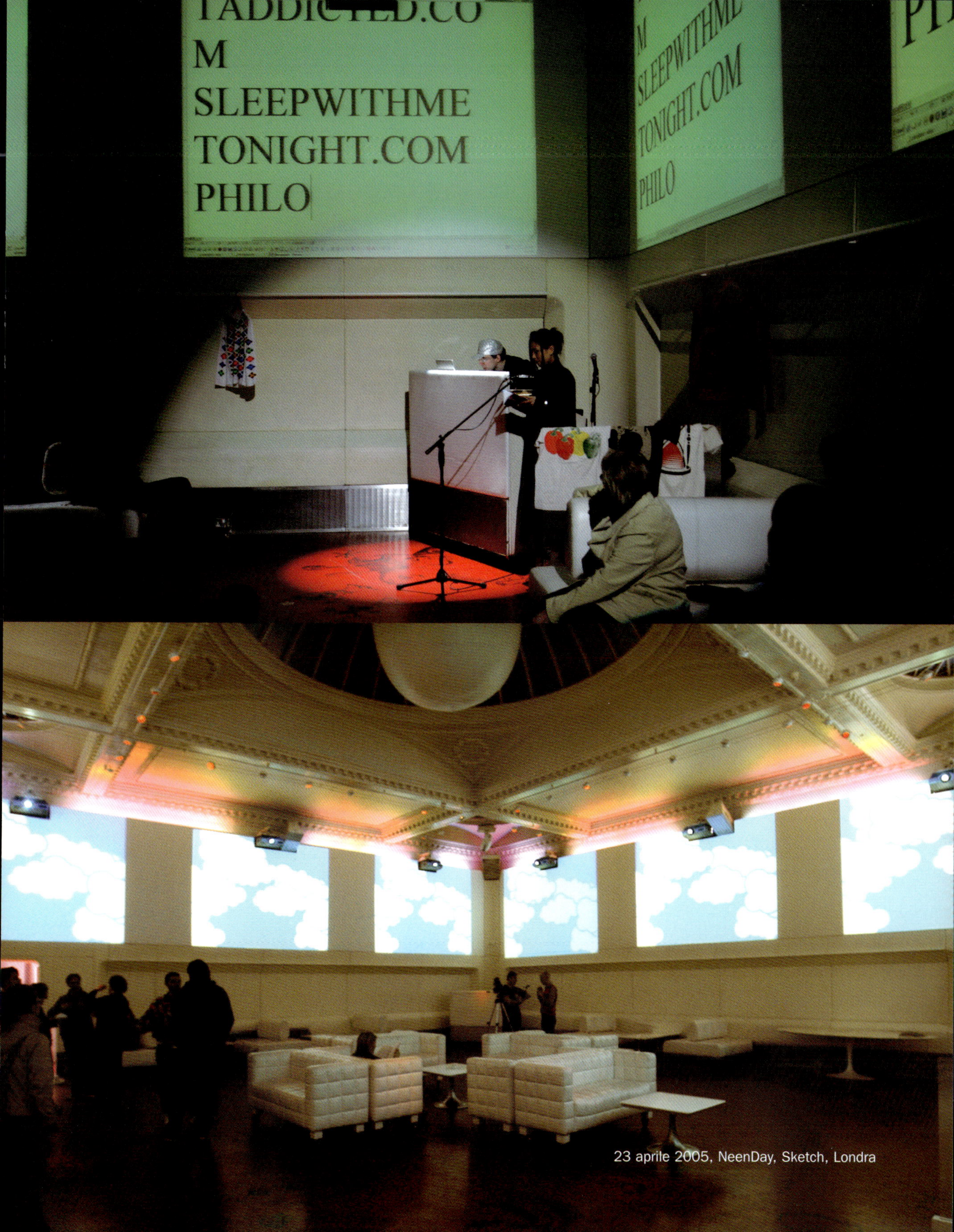

23 aprile 2005, NeenDay, Sketch, Londra

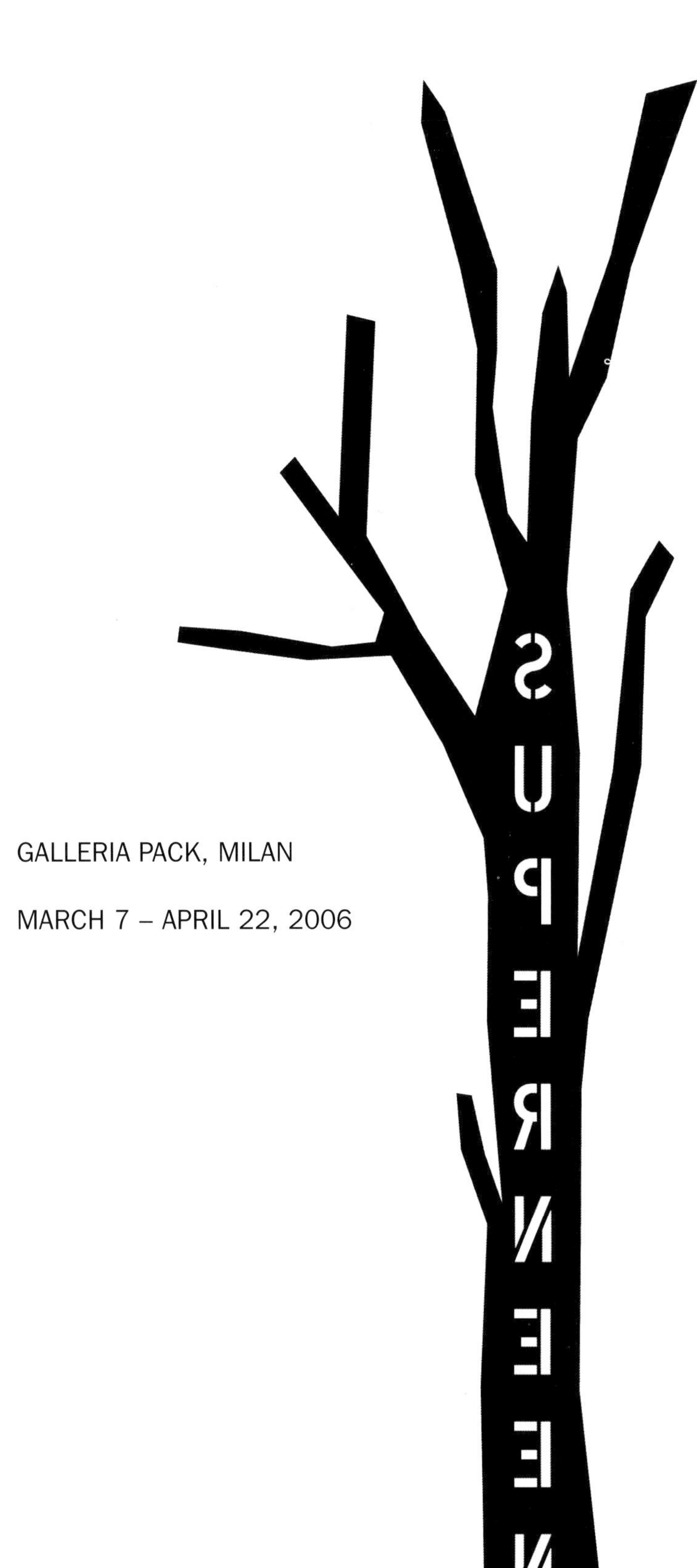

GALLERIA PACK, MILAN

MARCH 7 – APRIL 22, 2006

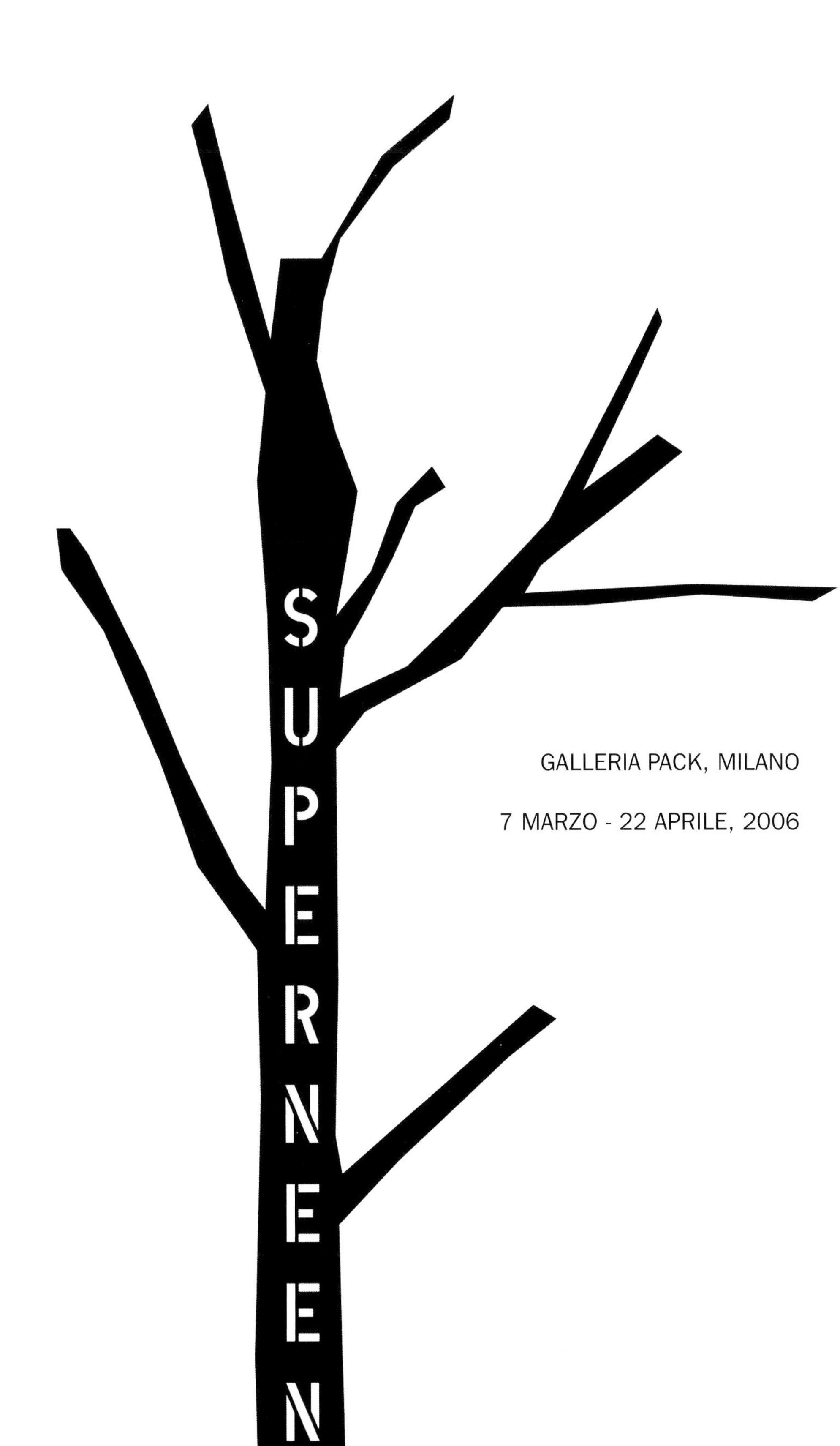

S
U
P
E
R
N
E
E
N
GALLERIA PACK, MILANO
7 MARZO - 22 APRILE, 2006

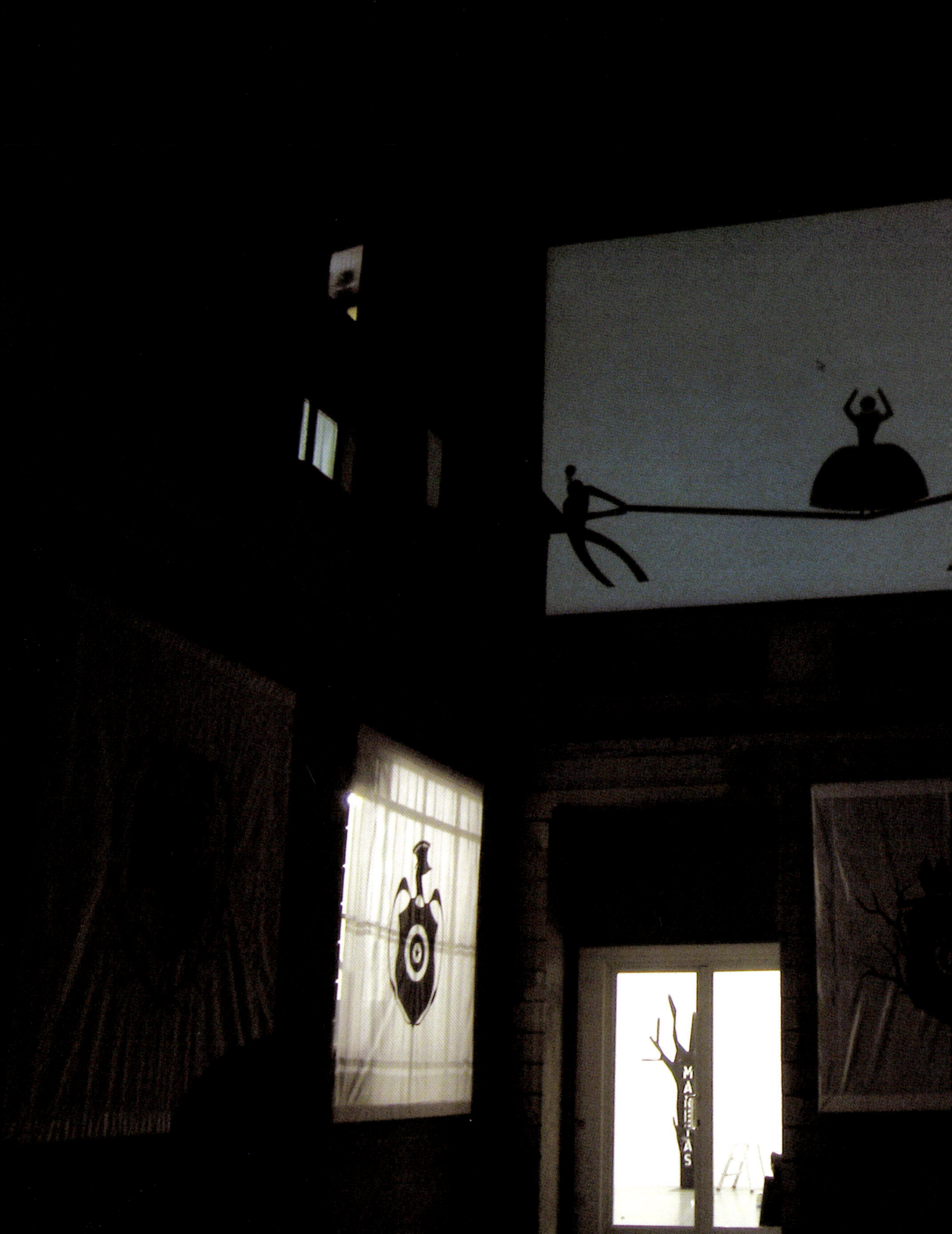
MALETAS

PEOPLE IN SUPERNEEN

architects / architetti
Andreas Angelidakis

visual artists / artisti visivi
Carbonated Jazz, Deconcept, Gabriele
Di Matteo, Dumbo, Joel Fox, Benjamin
Loya, Miltos Manetas, Rob Montgomery,
Angelo Plessas, Rafael Rozëndaal,
Steven Schkolne, Nikola Tosic, Mai Ueda,
Priscilla Vaccari, John White C.

fashion designer
David David, Gaspard Yurkievich, Paolo di
Landro, Bernard Wilhelm

curators / curatori
Nina Vagic

writers / scrittori
Vito Campanelli, Lev Manovich

Internet reporter
Marco Cadioli

music composers / compositori
Mark Tranmer (Gnac), Aki Tsuyuko

magazines / riviste
Boiler Magazine (Massimo Torregiani
and Ivanmaria Vele),
thisisamagazine.com, *Textfield*

guest star
Asia Zahm

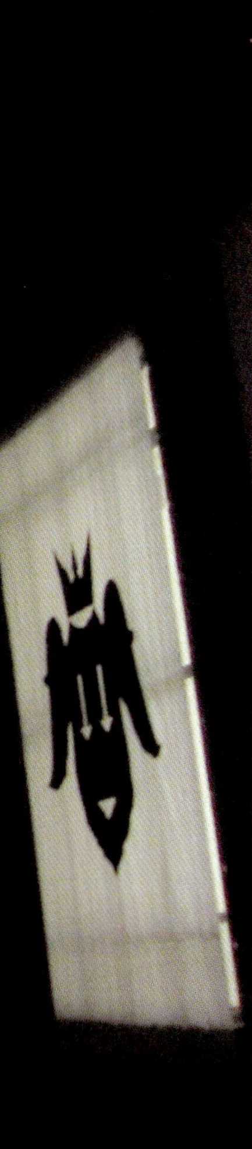

SuperNeen, installation view

above
Angelo Plessas, elasticenthusiastic.com, 2003

SuperNeen, veduta dell'installazione

in alto
Angelo Plessas, elasticenthusiastic.com, 2003

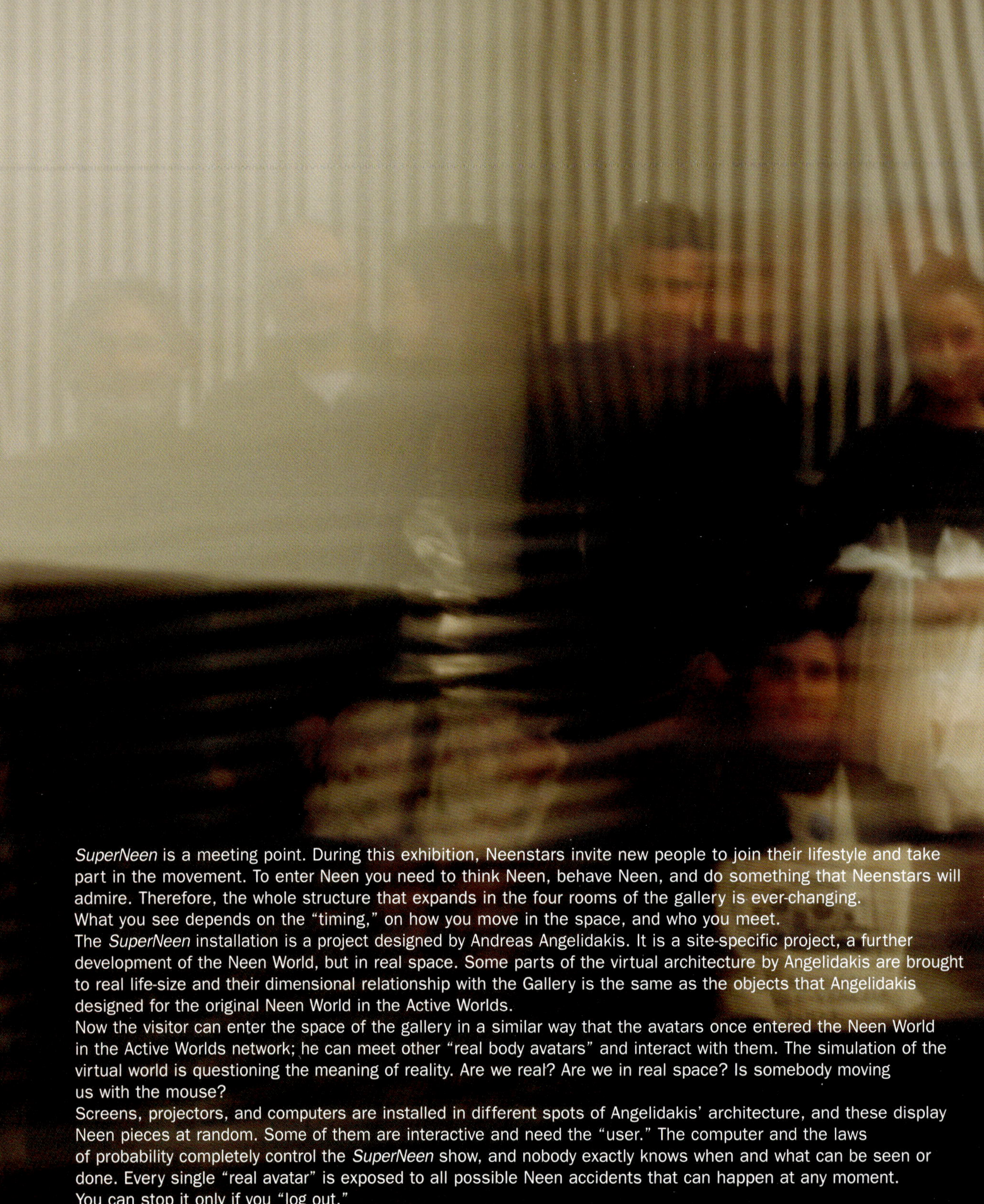

SuperNeen is a meeting point. During this exhibition, Neenstars invite new people to join their lifestyle and take part in the movement. To enter Neen you need to think Neen, behave Neen, and do something that Neenstars will admire. Therefore, the whole structure that expands in the four rooms of the gallery is ever-changing.
What you see depends on the "timing," on how you move in the space, and who you meet.
The *SuperNeen* installation is a project designed by Andreas Angelidakis. It is a site-specific project, a further development of the Neen World, but in real space. Some parts of the virtual architecture by Angelidakis are brought to real life-size and their dimensional relationship with the Gallery is the same as the objects that Angelidakis designed for the original Neen World in the Active Worlds.
Now the visitor can enter the space of the gallery in a similar way that the avatars once entered the Neen World in the Active Worlds network; he can meet other "real body avatars" and interact with them. The simulation of the virtual world is questioning the meaning of reality. Are we real? Are we in real space? Is somebody moving us with the mouse?
Screens, projectors, and computers are installed in different spots of Angelidakis' architecture, and these display Neen pieces at random. Some of them are interactive and need the "user." The computer and the laws of probability completely control the *SuperNeen* show, and nobody exactly knows when and what can be seen or done. Every single "real avatar" is exposed to all possible Neen accidents that can happen at any moment.
You can stop it only if you "log out."

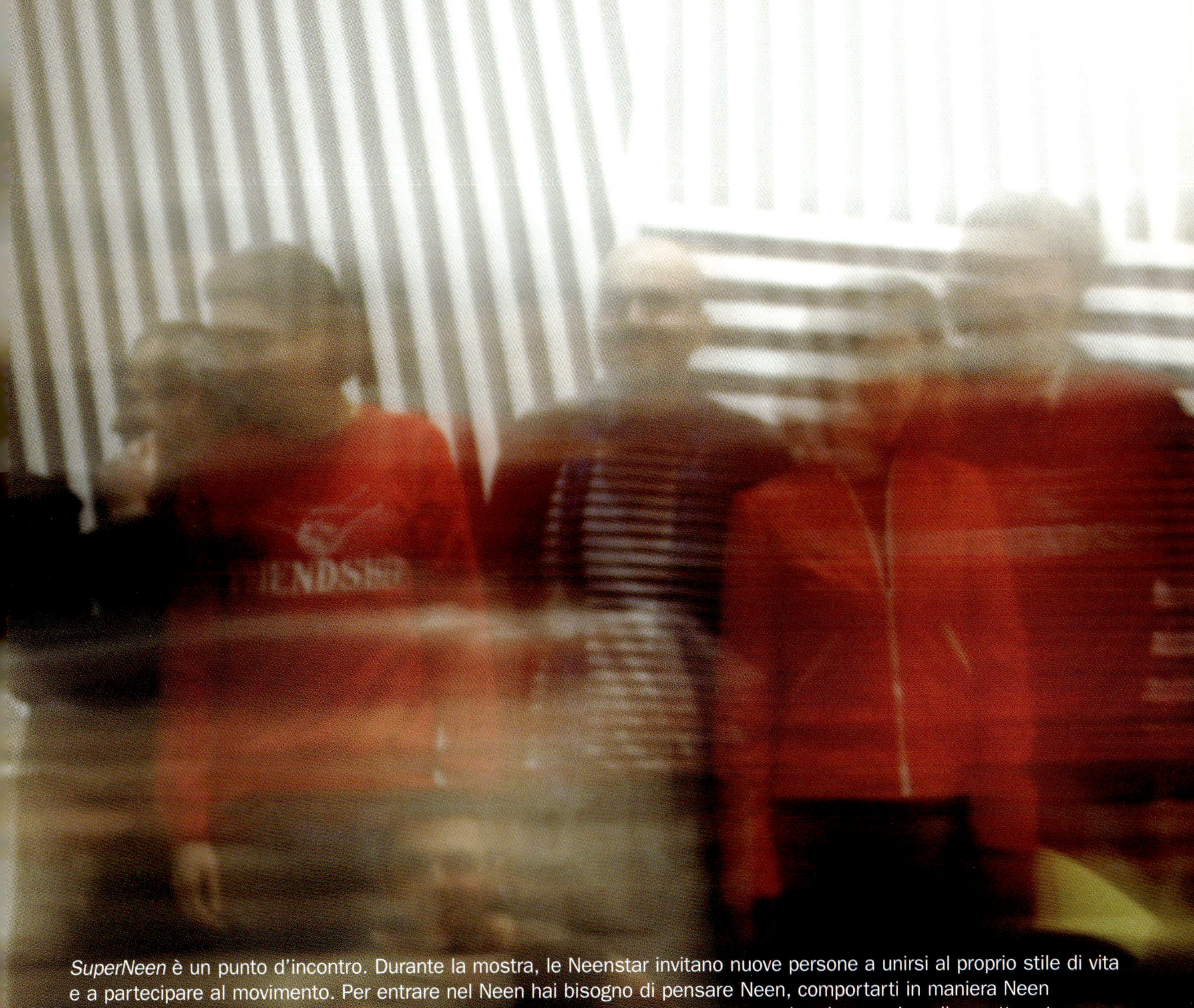

SuperNeen è un punto d'incontro. Durante la mostra, le Neenstar invitano nuove persone a unirsi al proprio stile di vita
e a partecipare al movimento. Per entrare nel Neen hai bisogno di pensare Neen, comportarti in maniera Neen
e fare qualcosa che le Neenstar possano ammirare. Pertanto, l'intera struttura, che si espande nelle quattro stanze
della galleria, cambia incessantemente.
Quello che vedi dipende dalla "tempistica", dipende da come ti muovi nello spazio e da chi incontri.
L'istallazione *SuperNeen* è un progetto realizzato da Andreas Angelidakis. È un progetto site-specific,
uno sviluppo ulteriore del Neen World, ma realizzato in uno spazio reale. Alcune parti dell'architettura virtuale
di Angelidakis sono riportate in scala reale e le loro relazioni dimensionali con la galleria sono le stesse degli oggetti
che Angelidakis ha disegnato per l'originale Neen World, all'interno di Active Worlds.
Ora, il visitatore può entrare negli spazi della galleria nello stesso modo in cui gli avatar entrano in Neen World,
nel network Active Worlds. Può incontrare altri "avatar in carne e ossa" e interagire con loro.
La simulazione del mondo virtuale sta mettendo in discussione il significato della realtà: siamo reali?
Viviamo in uno spazio reale? C'è qualcuno che ci sta muovendo con un mouse?
Monitor, proiettori e computer, istallati in differenti punti dell'architettura di Angelidakis, mostrano opere Neen
con una successione affidata al caso. Alcune di queste opere sono interattive, hanno dunque bisogno di utenti.
Il computer e le leggi della probabilità controllano completamente la mostra *SuperNeen* e nessuno sa esattamente
dove e cosa potrà essere visto o fatto. Ogni singolo "avatar in carne e ossa" è esposto a ogni possibile incidente Neen,
che può accadere in qualsiasi momento. Puoi fermarlo solo se ti disconnetti…

Nina Vagic

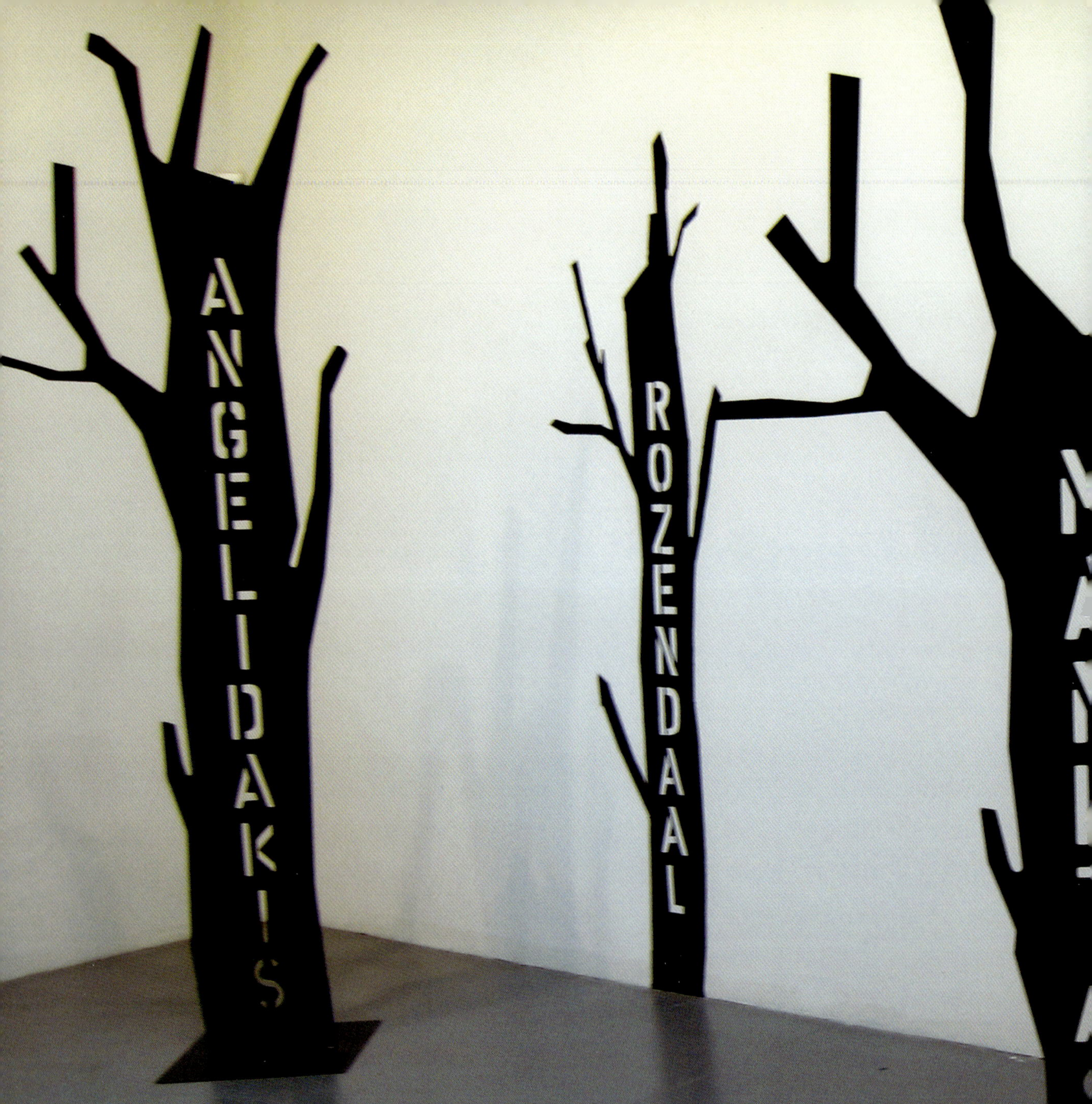

If there is a beautiful thing in art, it is that there is truly no system, because it is about objects that are not art, so the very moment that they are the most like art, they are not art. Because if they were really art, we would already know it, and it would seem banal.
There does not exist any system in art. There are no gallerists, there are no artists, there are no curators, and there are no museums. There are people that play with these illusory things. It is not a system; it is a mess; it is like fog, a fog where things appear and then disappear. It is something almost metaphysical.

Miltos Manetas, in Vito Campanelli, *L'arte della Rete, l'arte in Rete. Il Neen, la rivoluzione estetica di Miltos Manetas*. Aracne editrice, Rome, 2005

Se c'è una cosa bella dell'arte è che veramente non ha nessun sistema, perché si tratta di oggetti
che non sono arte, cioè, proprio nel momento in cui sono nel loro proprio massimo essere arte, non sono arte.
Perché se fossero veramente arte, lo sapremmo già e sarebbe una banalità.
Non esiste nessun sistema dell'arte, non ci sono galleristi, non ci sono artisti, non ci sono curatori
e non ci sono musei. C'è gente che gioca con queste cose illusorie. Non è un sistema, è un casino,
è una specie di nuvola, una nuvola dove le cose appaiono e poi scompaiono.
È una cosa quasi metafisica.

Miltos Manetas, in Vito Campanelli, *L'arte della Rete, l'arte in Rete. Il Neen, la rivoluzione estetica di Miltos
Manetas*. Aracne editrice, Roma, 2005

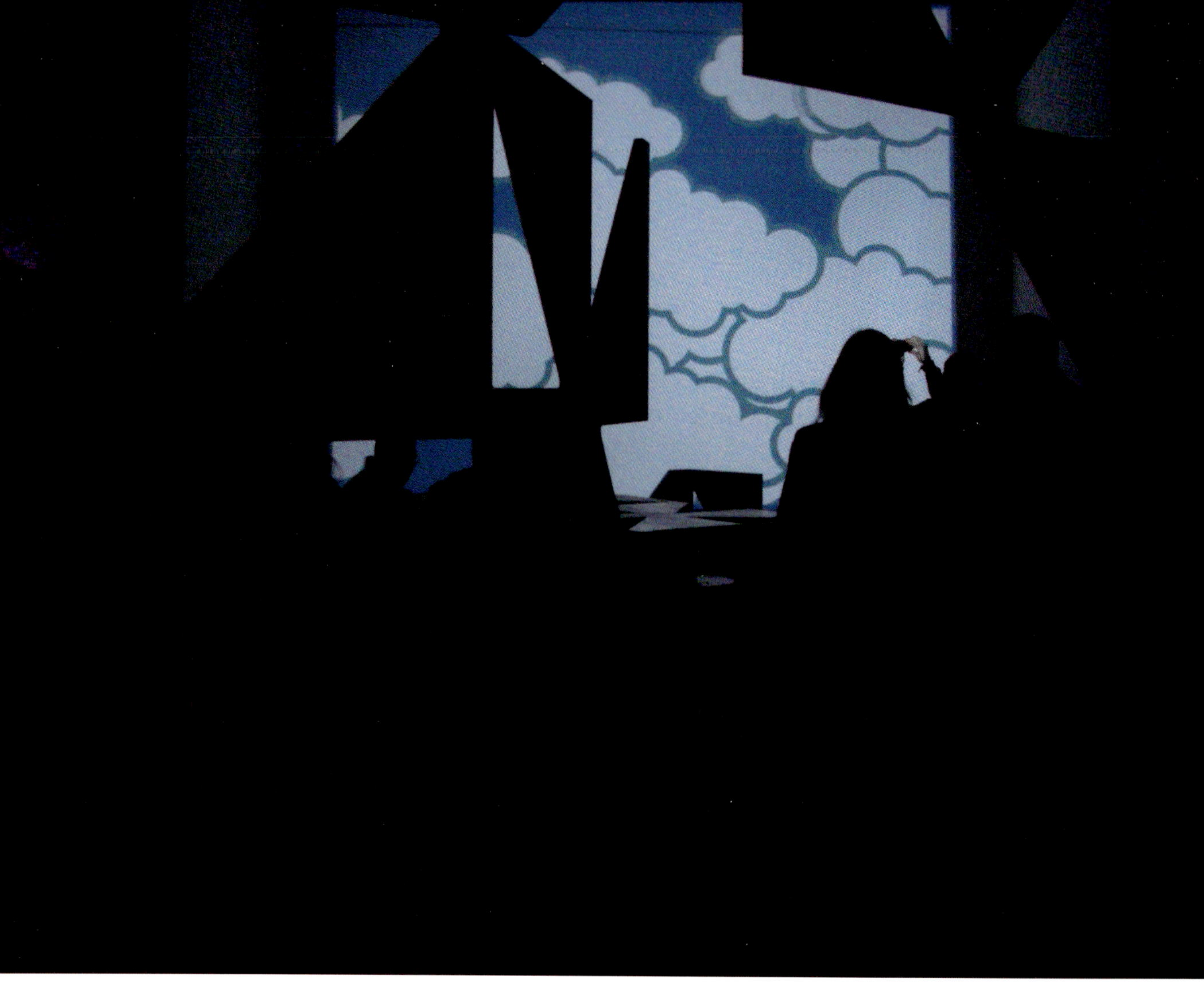

The Web is nothing more or less than what the World has always been. Unvisited and unfriendly territories that one after the other change to interior landscape. From the Alps to the Japanese garden: this is the scenario. However, what in a Japanese garden may look like rocks and sand in a well-arranged composition is, for a better-trained intellect, black holes and chaos. The Web came from this chaos, in a certain way, directly out of the Trojan Horse, described in Homer's *Iliad*. And now we are all again Ulysses lost in the ocean.

Miltos Manetas, in Emma Reves (ed.), "Beyond Borders," *Another Magazine*, no. 6, spring–summer 2004

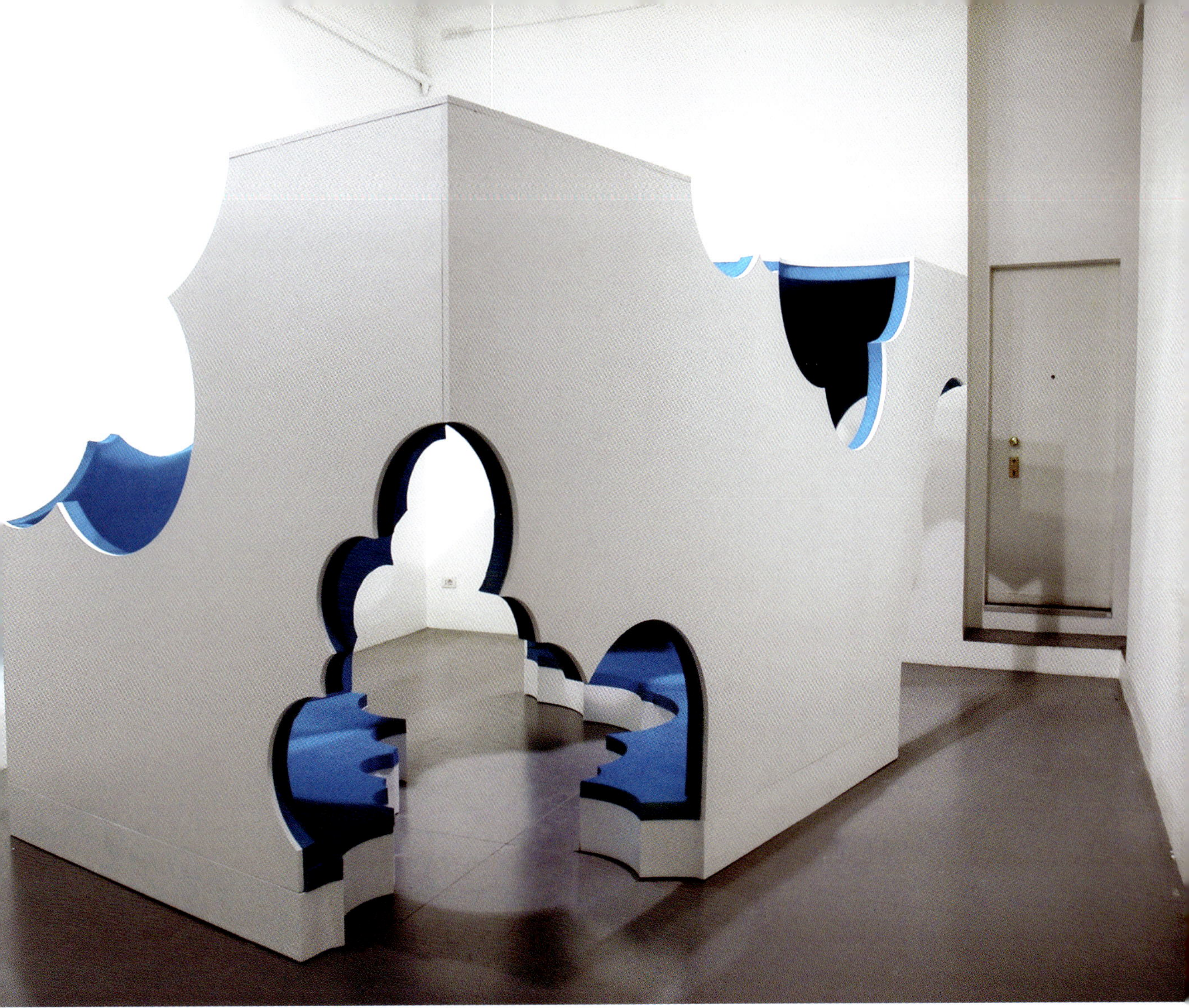

Il Web è, né più né meno, ciò che il mondo è sempre stato: territori sconosciuti e inospitali che si sono
gradualmente trasformati in un paesaggio domestico. Dalle Alpi ai giardini giapponesi lo scenario è questo:
l'illusoria promessa di ordine e sistema. Tuttavia, ancora oggi, le semplici rocce e la sabbia ben distesa
dei giardini giapponesi sono, per un intelletto meglio allenato, buchi neri e caos. Il Web si origina da tale caos.
In qualche modo deriva direttamente dal cavallo di Troia descritto nell'*Iliade* di Omero, e ora noi siamo
tanti Ulisse persi di nuovo nel mare.

Miltos Manetas, in Emma Reves (a cura di), "Beyond Borders", *Another Magazine*, n. 6, primavera-estate 2004

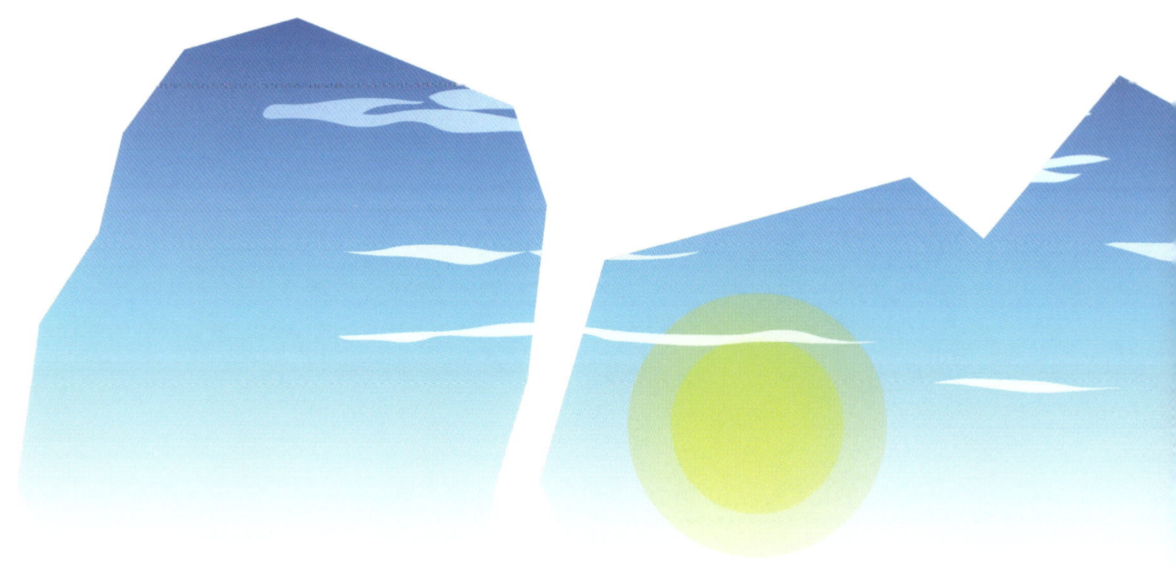

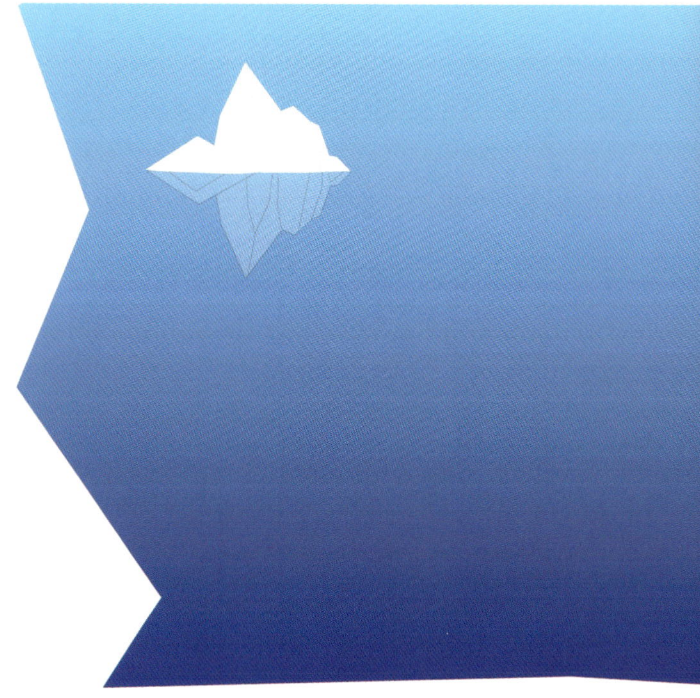

The soundtrack of the *SuperNeen* show included music by Gnac (Mark Tranmer), Essetesse, Sawako, and Aki Tsuyuko

La colonna sonora di *SuperNeen* comprende pezzi di Gnac (Mark Tranmer), Essetesse, Sawako e Aki Tsuyuko

Gnac, marktranmer.com, design Angelo Plessas, 2003

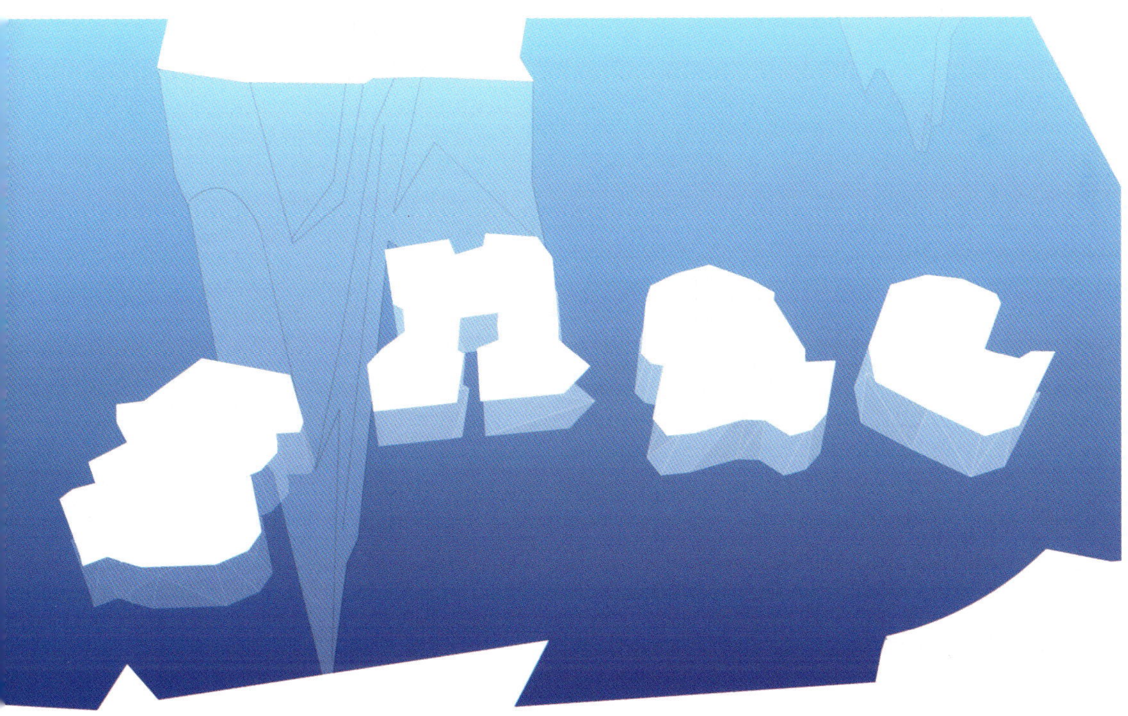

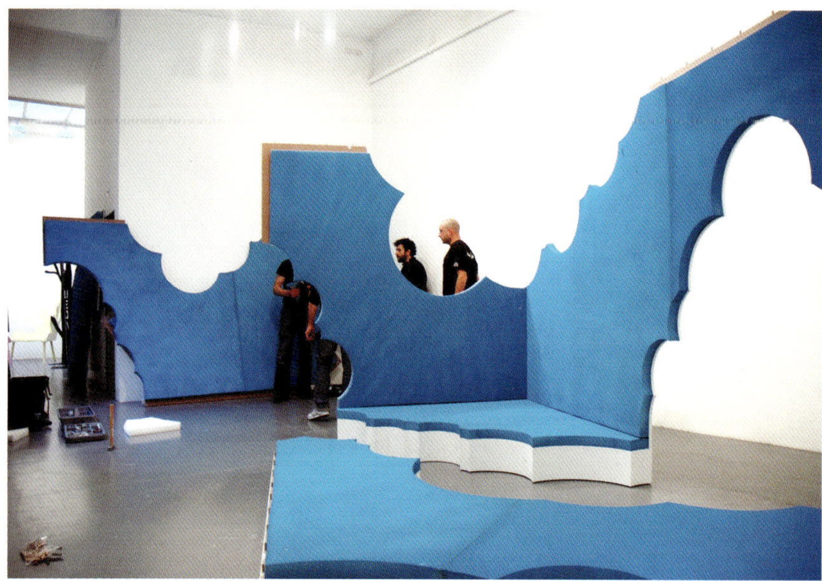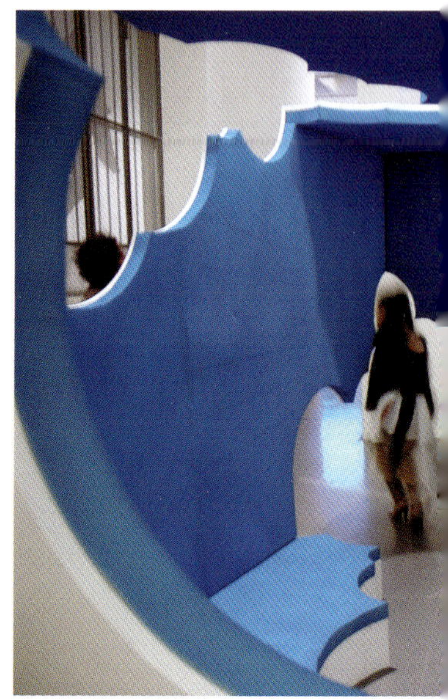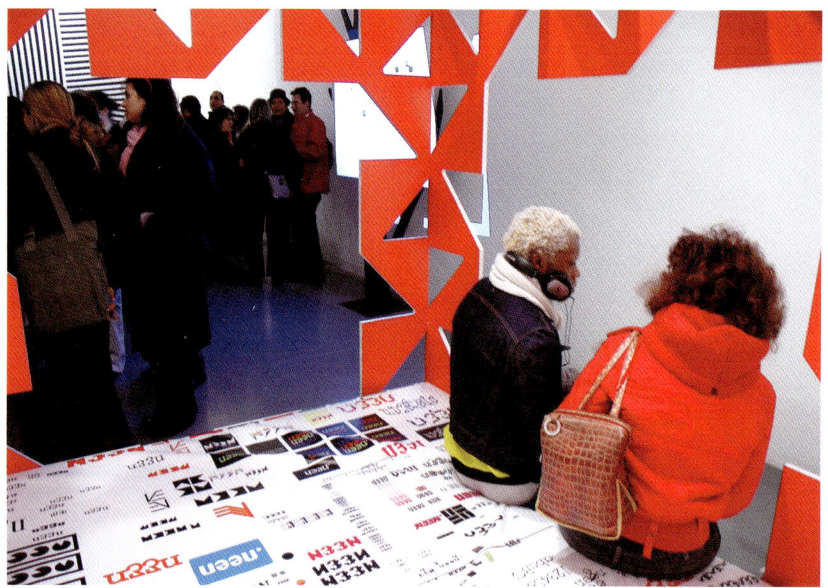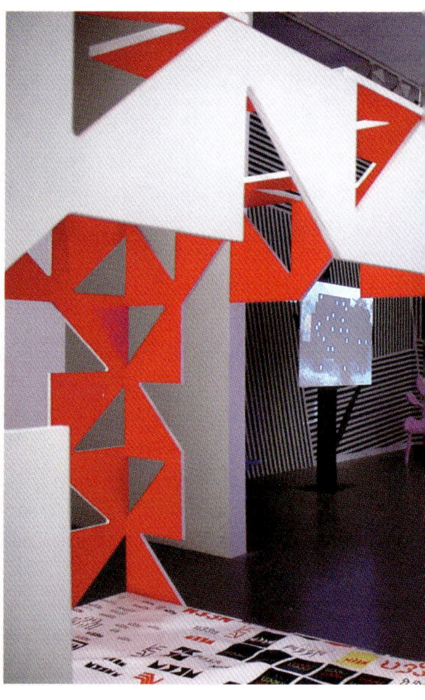

Q: What is the meaning for you to create for the Internet?
A: It is just the only place. It's like being in the jungle, and you
try to create a civilization. You find a script, you test to see if you can start a fire.

from an interview by Isabelle Arvers with Angelo Plessas, fluctuat.net, Paris, August 2002
http://www.fluctuat.net/1253-Miltos-Manetas-Andreas-Angelidakis

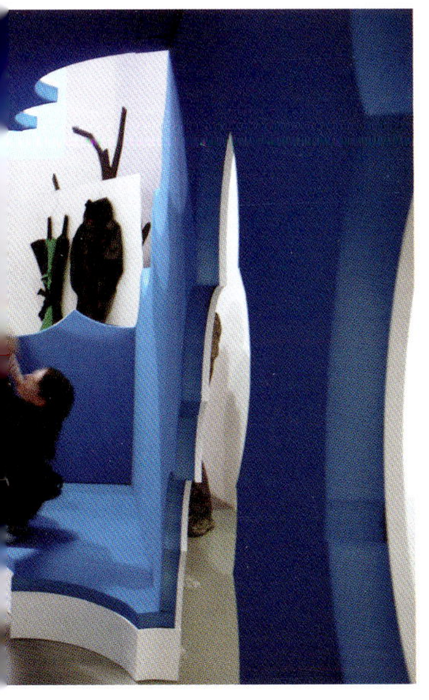

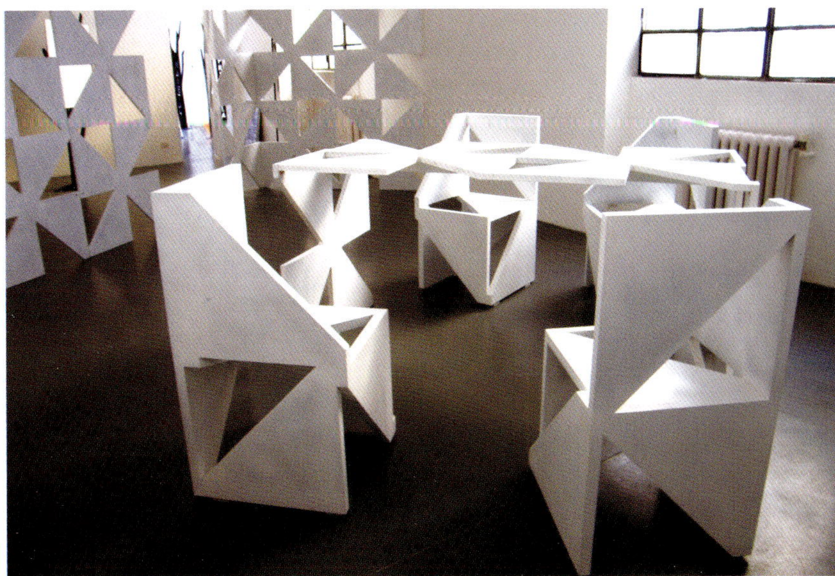

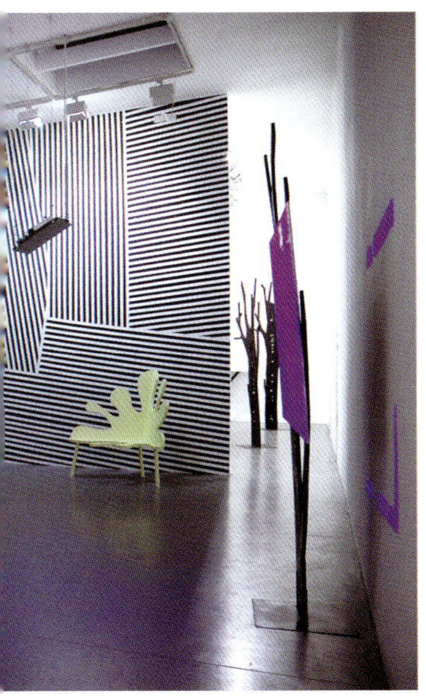

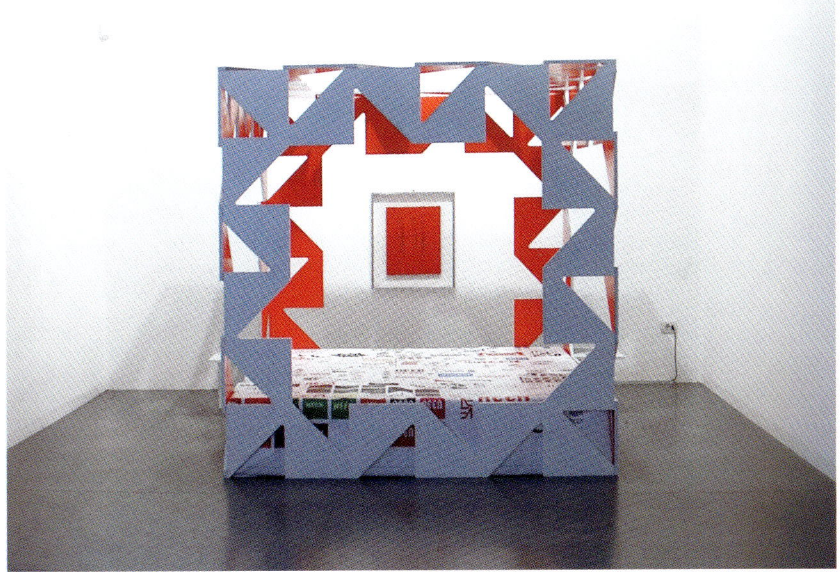

D: Qual è per te il significato di creare per Internet?
R: È per me l'unico spazio possibile. È come essere nella giungla e provare a creare una civiltà. Trovi uno script, lo provi per vedere se riesci ad accendere un fuoco.

da un'intervista di Isabelle Arvers a Angelo Plessas, fluctuat.net, Parigi, agosto 2002
http://www.fluctuat.net/1253-Miltos-Manetas-Andreas-Angelidakis

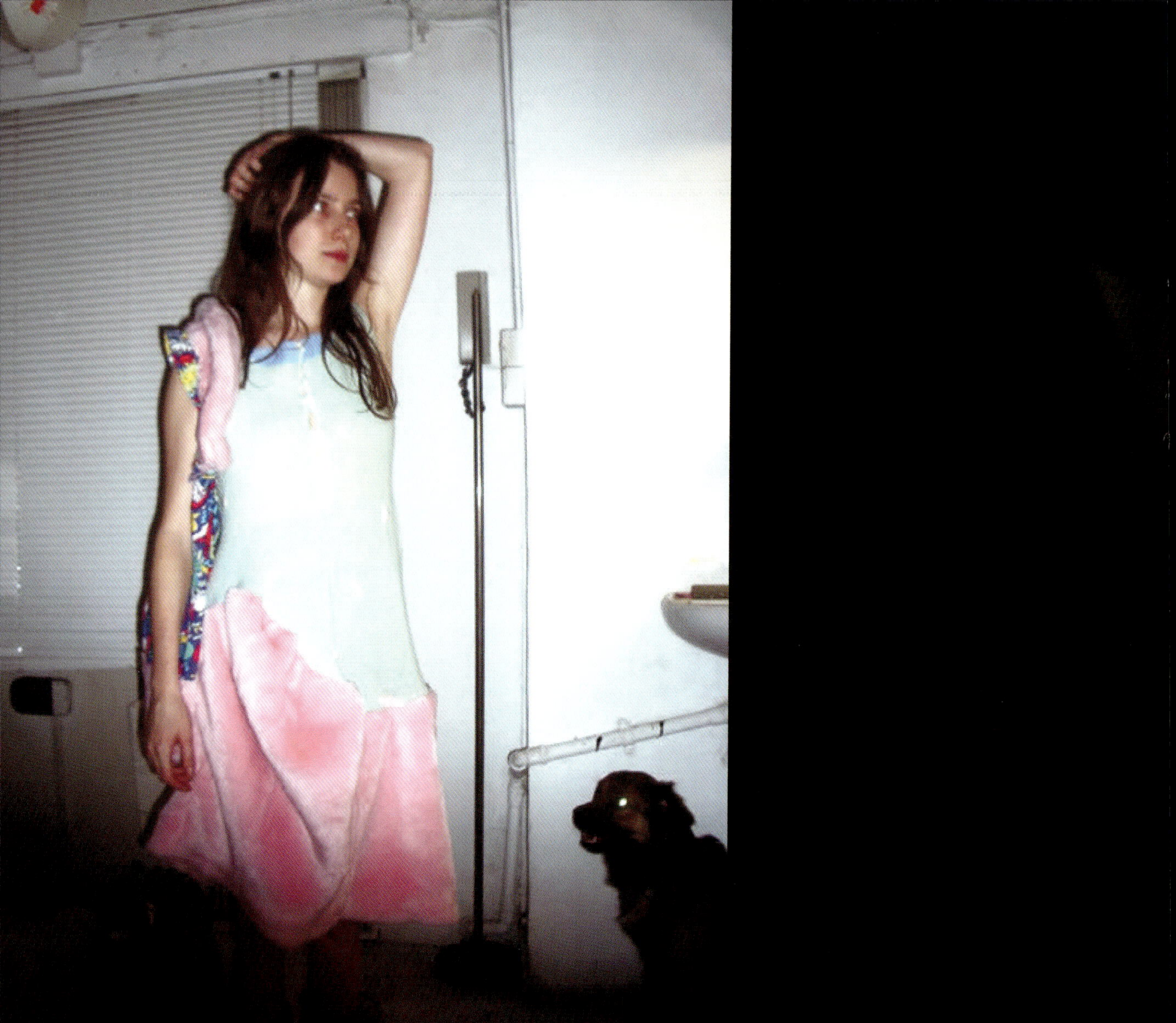

Priscilla Vaccari dressed by Paolo di Landro

Priscilla Vaccari vestita da Paolo di Landro

To come to an agreement without being able to explain why: this is the only guarantee
that what we do is worth doing.

Miltos Manetas, interviewed by Vito Campanelli, boilermag.it, 2003
http://www.boilermag.it/article.php?sid=173

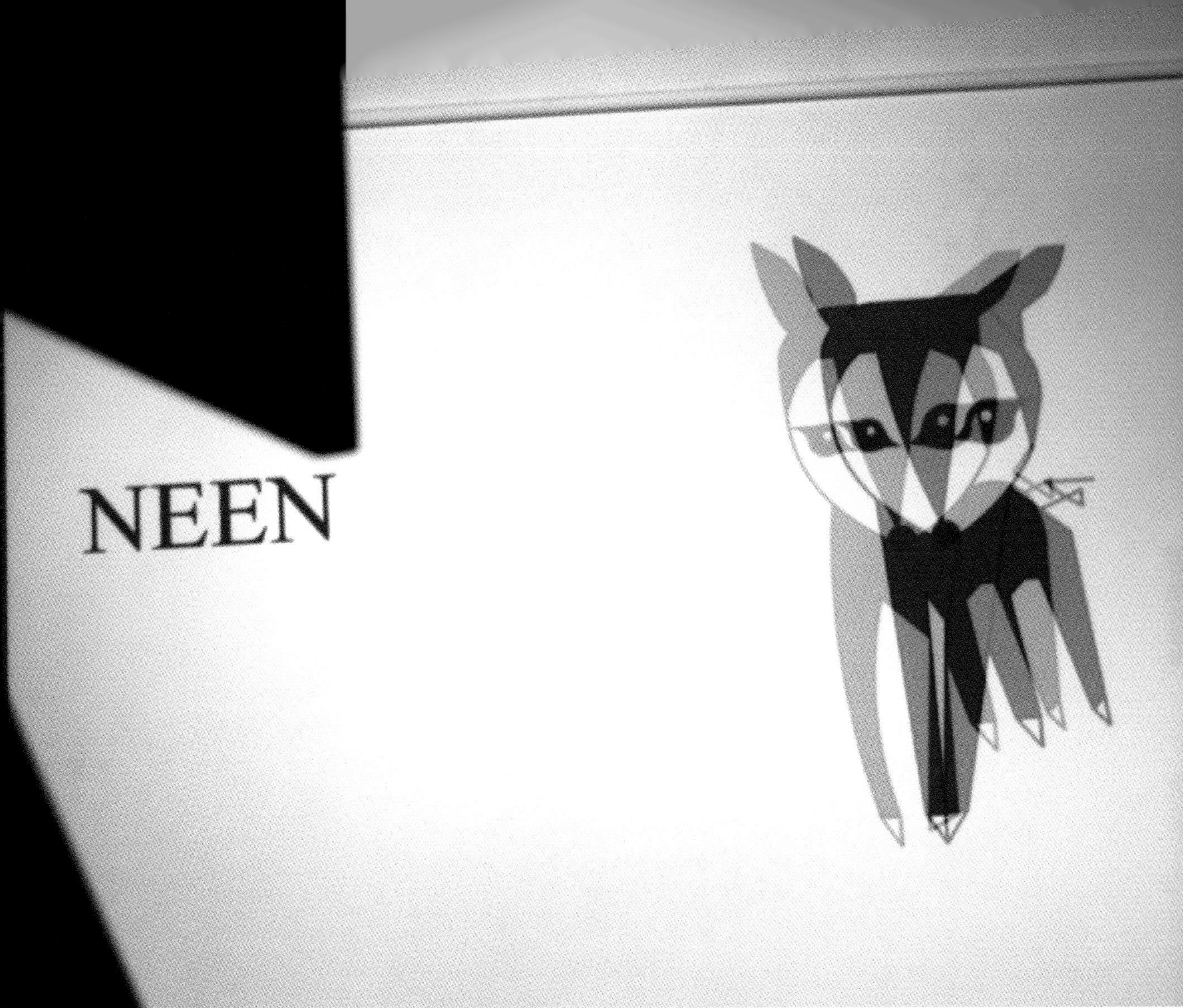

Mai Ueda, animation, 2002

Mettersi d'accordo senza riuscire a spiegarsi il perché: ecco, questa è l'unica garanzia che ciò che facciamo, vale la pena di essere realizzato.

Miltos Manetas, intervistato da Vito Campanelli, boilermag.it, 2003
http://www.boilermag.it/article.php?sid=173

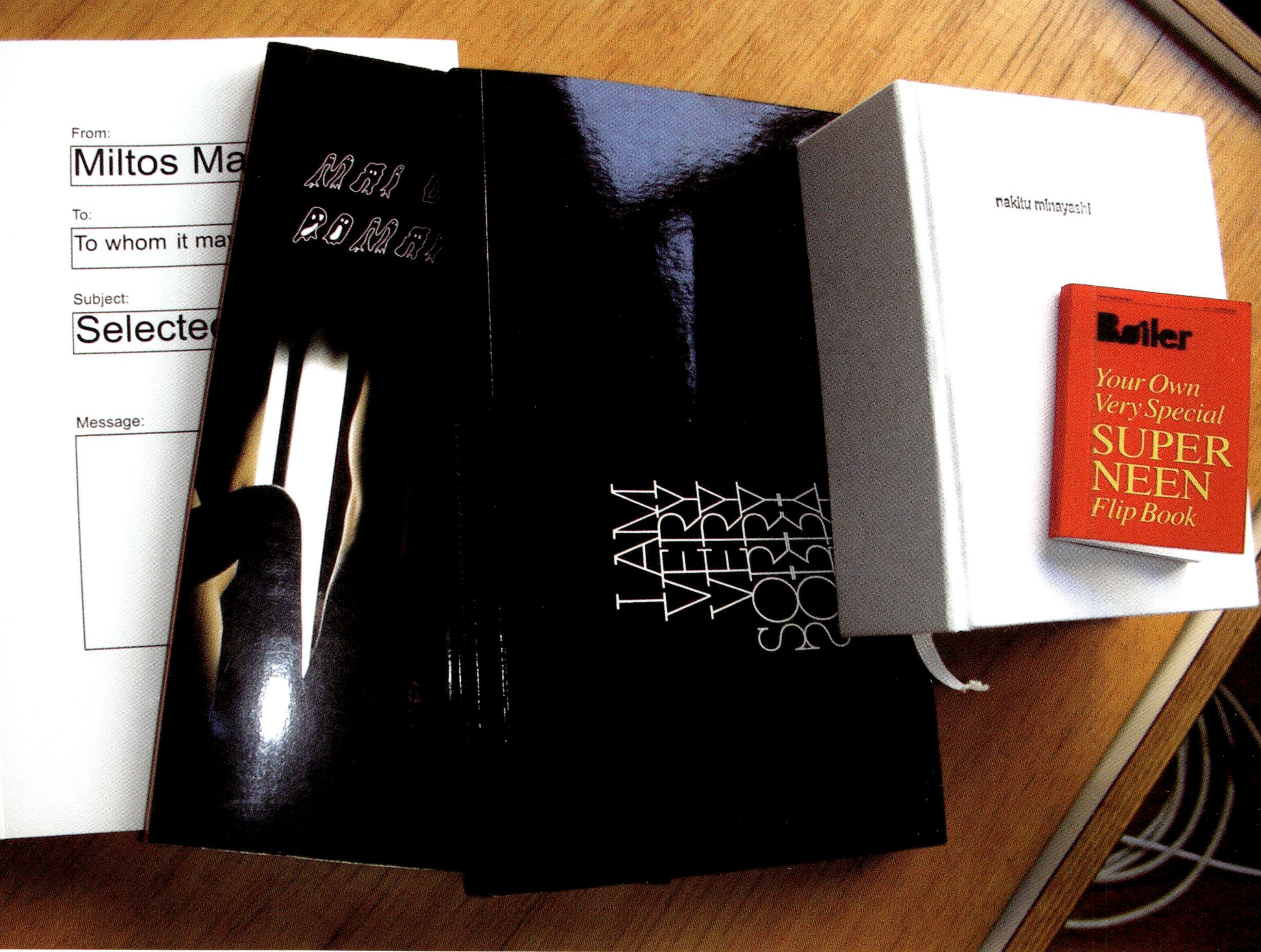
From:
Miltos Ma
To:
To whom it may
Subject:
Selected
Message:
nakitu minayashi
Butler
Your Own
Very Special
SUPER
NEEN
Flip Book
I AM VERY VERY SORRY

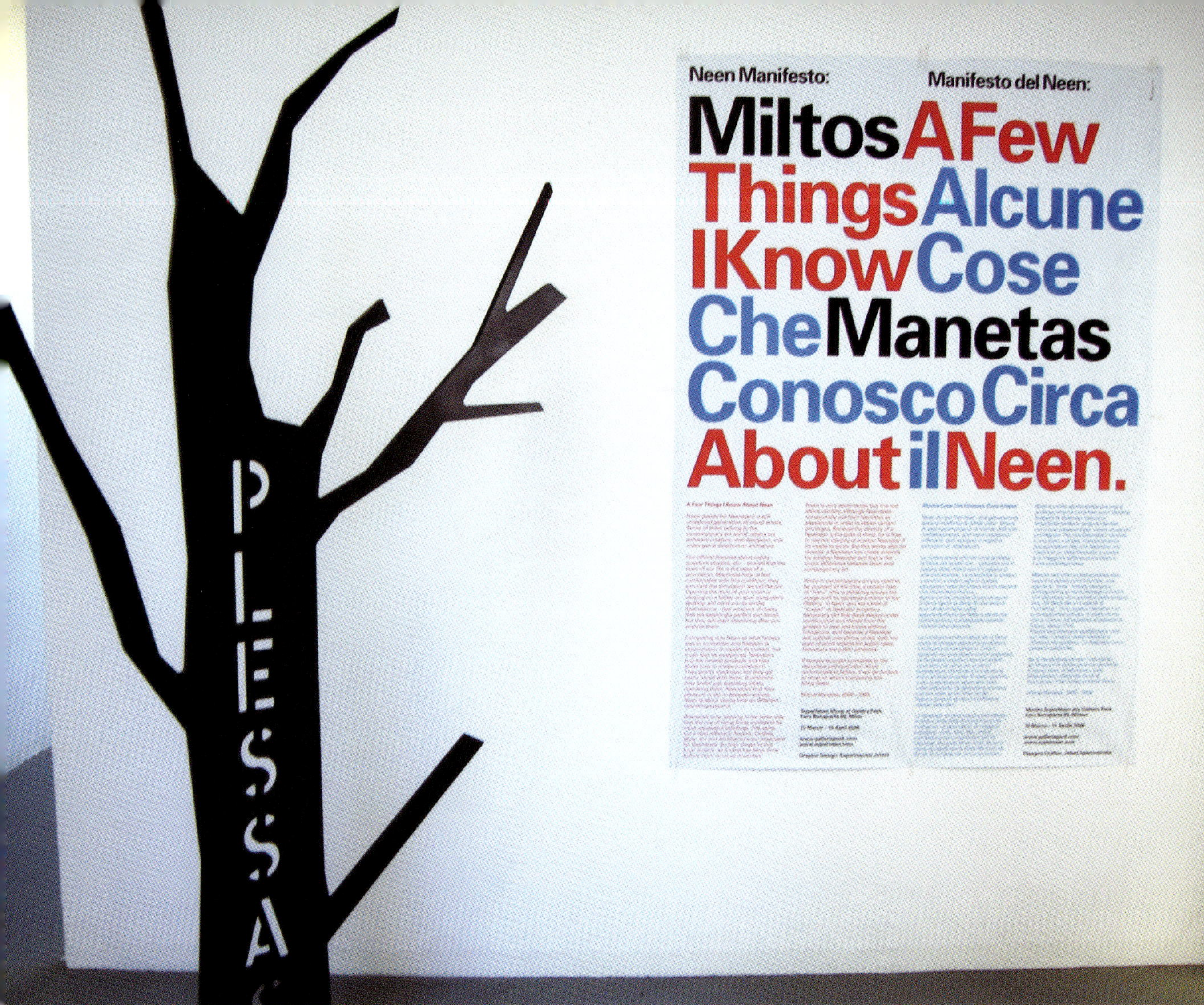

Neen poster by Experimental Jetset

Manifesto Neen di Experimental Jetset

opposite
Neen books and a *Boiler* issue printed in 300 copies,
published on the occasion of the *SuperNeen* show

a sinistra
Libri Neen e un'edizione speciale di *Boiler,* stampata in 300
copie, in occasione della mostra *SuperNeen*

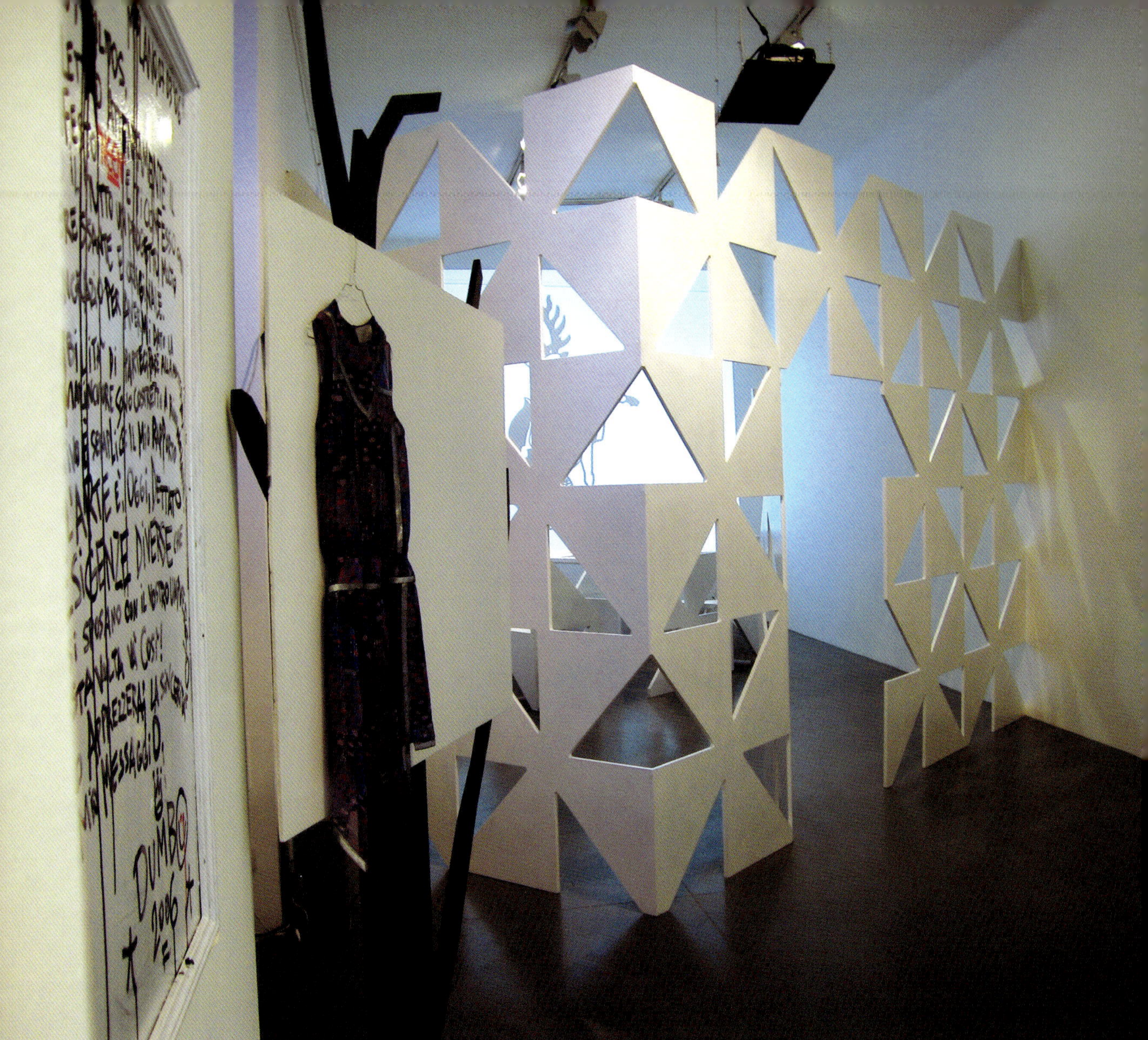

For Neen, the computer is the last thing on which we should place our attention. Neen is not for the digital
or for the computer. Computers do not exist anymore because we have become computers. I am not
Miltos Manetas, but I am Miltos Manetas plus manetas.com, and you are a person plus your e-mail that cannot return
to being a person without a computer. There no longer exists real space and digital space. Right now, you are meeting
me here, but at the same time, someone is clicking on my Web page and meeting the other Miltos Manetas.
So what are we doing? We are not making art, we are making a new style, charming, beautiful,
and intelligent, in order to dress our other body that is found on the Internet.

Miltos Manetas, in Vito Campanelli, *L'arte della Rete, l'arte in Rete. Il Neen, la rivoluzione estetica di Miltos Manetas*. Aracne editrice, Rome, 2005

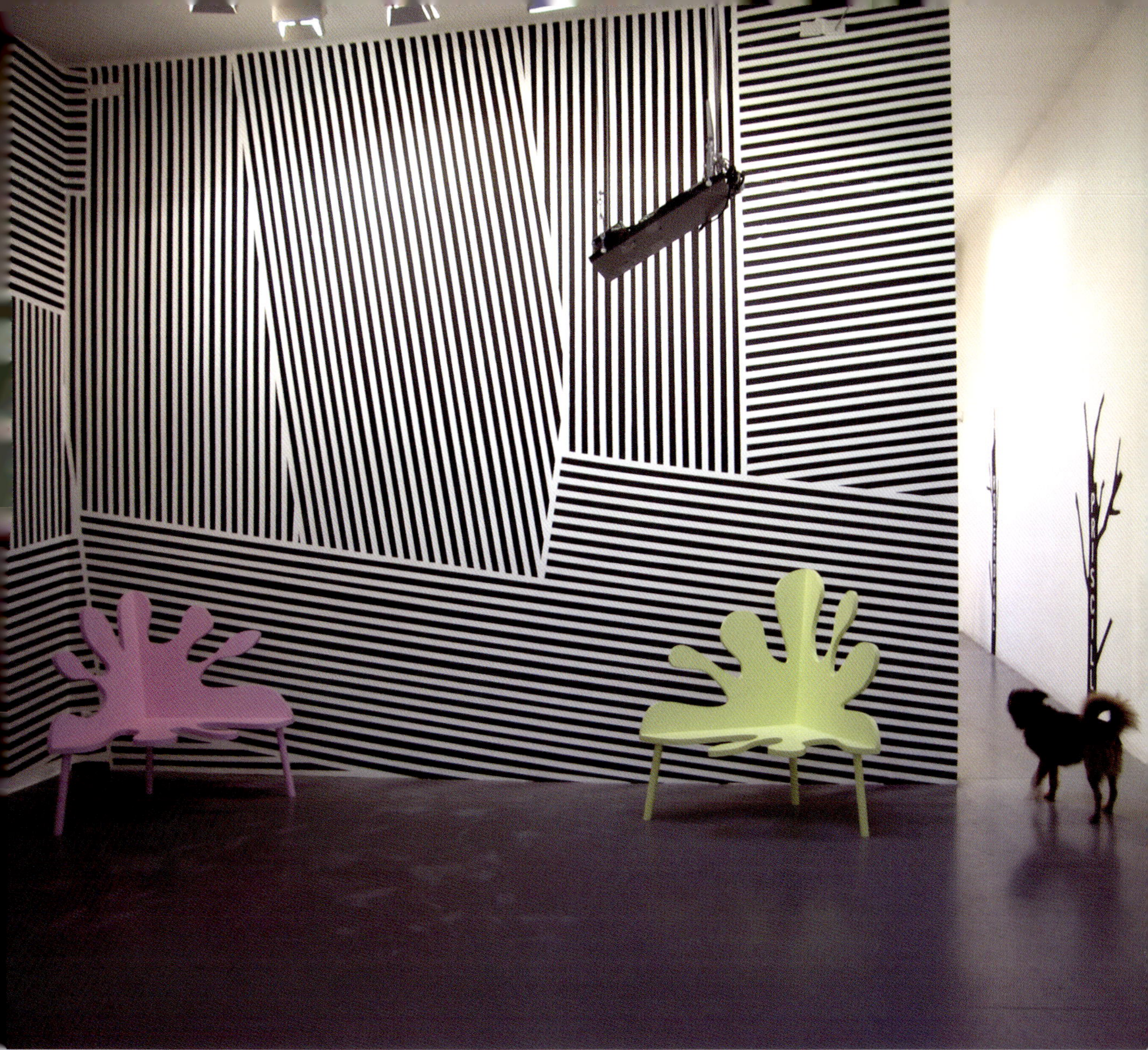

Per il Neen il computer è l'ultima cosa sulla quale fermare l'attenzione. Neen non è per il digitale e non è per il computer. I computer non esistono più perché noi siamo diventati dei computer. Io non sono Miltos Manetas, ma sono Miltos Manetas più manetas.com, e tu sei una persona più la tua e-mail, non potrai più tornare a essere una persona senza computer. Non esiste più uno spazio reale e uno spazio digitale. Ora voi mi incontrate qui, ma nello stesso momento qualcuno sta cliccando sulla mia pagina Web e sta incontrando quell'altro Miltos Manetas. Allora noi cosa facciamo? Noi non facciamo arte, facciamo un nuovo tipo di stile, carino, bello e intelligente per vestire quest'altro nostro corpo che si trova in Internet.

Miltos Manetas, in Vito Campanelli, *L'arte della Rete, l'arte in Rete. Il Neen, la rivoluzione estetica di Miltos Manetas.* Aracne editrice, Roma, 2005

VIDEO GAMES

Pierluigi: Surfing on the Web, I found a nice
project. It comes from a group of designers, called
Brave Space, that makes interesting experiments
somewhere between video games and design.
Their latest project is *Tetris Shelves*, a sort of interior
design project inspired by the arcade game Tetris.
Maybe it's not very new, but I think it's cool. Design
is changing. Young designers draw their inspiration from
virtual worlds and video games. The living room is going
to become a simulation space as Andreas shows in his
works. In fact, the *SuperNeen* show transforms
the Galleria Pack into a simulation environment.
It looks like the mushroom world of Super Mario Bros.
There are trees, images, bonuses, hyper-textual links . . .

Andreas: The *SuperNeen* show is as you describe—a
simulation environment. I think it is so, conceptually.
In reality, it looks like the drawings, a space with some
strange furniture in it. But with animations and all the
Neen material the space is further transformed.

Pierluigi: It seems that video games are very important
for Neen.

Angelo: Video games for me have always represented
a safe "territory" especially now that Hollywood is going
bad. I spend a lot of time playing with video games to
distract myself, but I don't get inspiration for my work.
Video games for me are the epitome of Telicness. Telic
stuff is admirable and makes us confident, but it easily
gets boring.
An interesting field of video games is the new online
multi-player games. I use them for socializing. You can
find some cool places to hang out on there and create
a certain behavior as in real-life situations. It is very
interesting to see how easily social relations are
changing there, too. If you get the chance to play with
famous online players, then it feels like being in a V.I.P.
Hollywood party. These stars, as in every kind of
society, have their ups and downs. The death of an
online player in a role-playing game can be a bigger
headline on *Google News* than, for example, if Tom
Cruise is gay or not. I don't know if these societies are
better places, but we can surely give it a try.

CRESTS

Pierluigi: Angelo, I looked at your crests. It is a very
nice project. Could you explain more?

Angelo: The idea of the crests is to visualize every
Neenstar with a crest. This time we made six, after the
main Neen artists.

Pierluigi: The crests look like old coats-of-arms, but in
a sort of digital version . . . tradition and innovation
and vice versa.

Angelo: Tradition in simulation is always innovation.
I started this idea with the crests a few years ago for
a show we did in Sweden. I did as many as twenty
crests. One for every person involved with Neen.
To create these crests I got inspiration from the
personality and work of each person. So if you look
carefully on every crest, you will see a lot of Neen and
maybe can decipher each person. Since then, these
crests have become one of the most characteristic
Neen works. So maybe yes, you can call them the heart
of Neen aesthetic.
It is an ongoing thing. I will continue doing them as long as
more and new people are involved with Neen.

Pierluigi: So they are portraits. But I don't
understand how you make them. I mean, do they
resemble visually the people represented or are they
symbolic representations?

Angelo: They are portraits of each Neenstar. They are
symbolic representations. Let's take how I thought of
Miltos' emblem. Miltos is a woman-driven machine.
He loves to maneuver and be maneuvered by women
and in exchange he gets their tenderness and
freshness. At the same time Manetas is a fighter
(represented by swords here) and he has somehow
a "thorny" personality (represented by thorns and a
sharp-edged crown).

Blog excerpts: superneen.com/blog
Project by Pierluigi Casolari

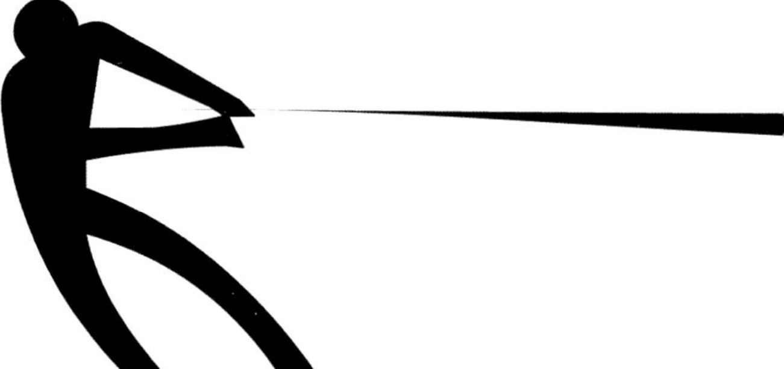

VIDEOGIOCHI

Pierluigi: Andando in giro per il Web, ho trovato
un bel progetto. Provienc da un gruppo di designer
chiamati Brave Space, che realizzano interessanti
sperimentazioni a cavallo tra i videogiochi e il design.
Il loro ultimo progetto è *Tetris Shelves*, una sorta di
progetto di design d'interni ispirato a Tetris, un classico
da sala giochi. Forse non è nuovissimo, ma penso sia figo.
Il design sta cambiando. I giovani designer hanno mutato
la propria ispirazione dal mondo virtuale e dai videogiochi.
Le sale da pranzo diventeranno uno spazio simulato come
Andreas dimostra nei suoi lavori. Infatti, la mostra
SuperNeen trasforma la Galleria Pack in un ambiente
simulato. Sembra il mondo dei funghi di Super Mario Bros.
Ci sono alberi, immagini, bonus e link ipertestuali.

Andreas: La mostra *SuperNeen* è, come tu la descrivi,
un ambiente simulato. Io penso sia così, concettualmente.
In realtà, appare come nei disegni, uno spazio con
qualche strano mobile. Ma con le animazioni e tutto
il materiale Neen lo spazio è ulteriormente trasformato.

Pierluigi: Sembra che i videogiochi siano molto
importanti per Neen.

Angelo: I videogiochi rappresentano sempre per me un
territorio sicuro, specialmente ora che Hollywood sta
andando male. Passo un sacco di tempo a giocare ai
videogiochi per distrarmi ma non ne ricavo ispirazioni
per il mio lavoro. I videogiochi per me sono l'epitome
dell'essere Telic. La roba Telic è ammirevole e ci dà
fiducia, ma facilmente diventa noiosa. Un campo
interessante dei videogiochi sono i nuovi giochi on line
in modalità *multiplayer*. Li uso per socializzare. Puoi
trovare alcuni posti fighi da bazzicare nei quali puoi
dare vita a comportamenti simili alle situazioni della vita
reale. È molto interessante osservare la facilità con la
quale anche le relazioni sociali stanno cambiando.
Se ne hai la possibilità, giocare con famosi giocatori
on line, è come essere in un party per V.I.P. di
Hollywood. Queste stelle, come in ogni tipo di società,
hanno i propri momenti alti e bassi. La morte di un
giocatore on line in un gioco di ruolo può dare vita a un
articolo su *Google News* più importante di quello
dedicato, per esempio, a stabilire se Tom Cruise è gay
o meno. Non so se queste società siano posti migliori,
ma sicuramente possiamo provarle.

STEMMI

Pierluigi: Angelo, ho dato un'occhiata ai tuoi stemmi.
È un progetto molto carino. Puoi darmi qualche ulteriore
spiegazione?

Angelo: L'idea degli stemmi araldici è di visualizzare
ciascuna Neenstar attraverso un simbolo. Questa volta
ne abbiamo realizzati sei, degli artisti principali del
Neen.

Pierluigi: Gli stemmi sembrano vecchi cappotti di eserciti,
ma in una sorta di versione digitale... tradizione
e innovazione e viceversa.

Angelo: La tradizione nella simulazione è sempre
innovazione. Ho dato inizio a questa idea degli stemmi
araldici, qualche anno fa per una mostra che abbiamo
fatto in Svezia. Realizzai ben venti emblemi, uno per
ogni persona coinvolta nel Neen.
Per crearli ho preso ispirazione dalla personalità e dal
lavoro di ciascuno. Dunque, se guardi ogni stemma,
ci vedrai un sacco di Neen e probabilmente potrai
decifrare ciascuna persona. Sin da quel momento gli
stemmi sono diventati uno dei lavori Neen più caratteristici,
forse possono essere definiti come il cuore dell'estetica
Neen. È una cosa in divenire. Continuerò a farli finché
nuove persone saranno coinvolte nel Neen...

Pierluigi: Quindi sono ritratti. Ma non ho capito come li
fai, voglio dire: riassumono visivamente le persone
rappresentate o sono rappresentazioni simboliche?

Angelo: Sono ritratti di ciascuna Neenstar. Sono
rappresentazioni simboliche. Per esempio, ecco come
ho pensato all'emblema di Miltos: Miltos è una macchina
guidata da una donna, ama manovrare ed essere
manovrato dalle donne e, in cambio, prende da loro
tenerezza e freschezza. Allo stesso tempo, Manetas
è un lottatore (ciò è rappresentato dalle spade) e ha,
in qualche maniera, una personalità spinosa
(rappresentata dalle spine e dalla corona dai bordi affilati).

tratto dal Blog superneen.com/blog
Progetto a cura di Pierluigi Casolari

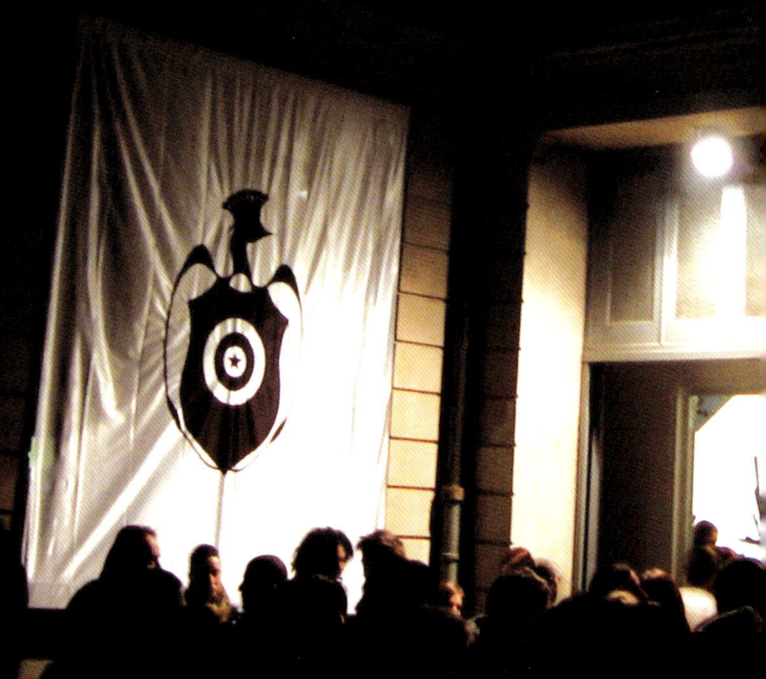

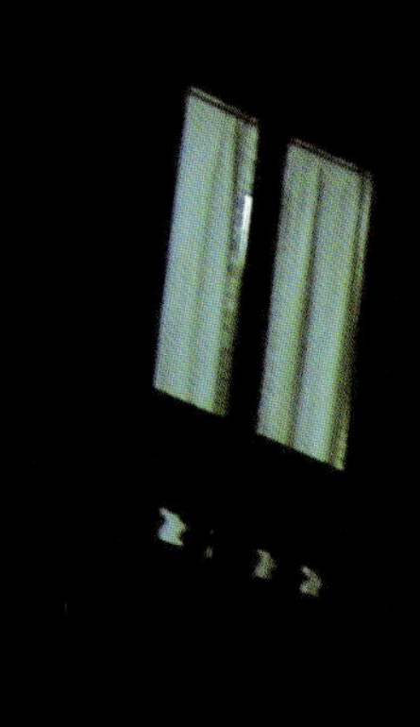

To come to an agreement without being able to explain why: this is the only guarantee that what we do is worth doing.

Miltos Manetas, boilermag.it, 2003

Neen: as you understand from the name, it doesn't mean anything that you know. So we have to create what it means from scratch.

Mai Ueda, *Mai Ueda Times*, 2006

Many Neen things happen to me by chance. I cannot clearly explain . . .

Angelo Plessas, 2005

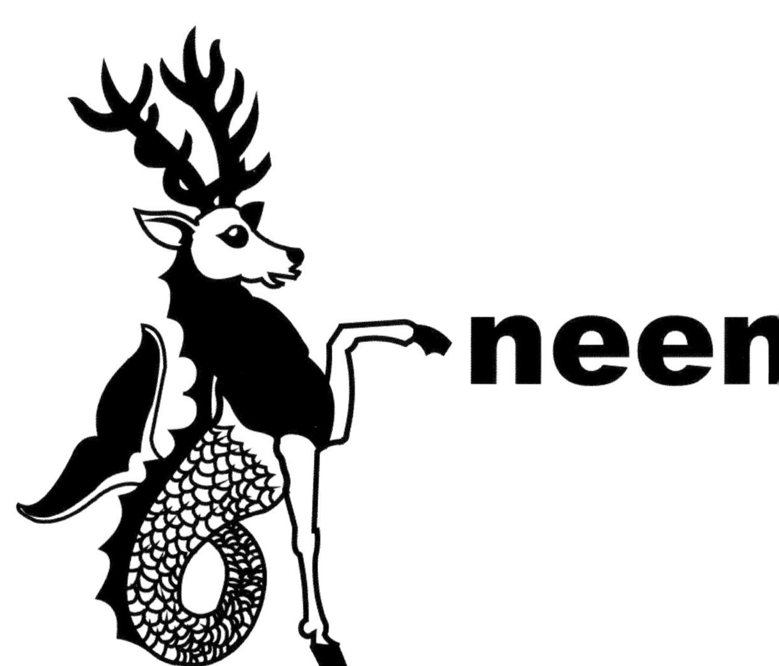

Angelo Plessas, Neen mascot, 2004

Neen   (n-e-n) describes an art movement that uses or abuses technology, in particular computers, to create unexpected and delightful artistic results.

wikipedia.org/wiki/Neen

Essere d'accordo senza saper spiegare il perché: ecco, questa è l'unica garanzia che ciò che facciamo,
vale la pena di essere realizzato.

Miltos Manetas, boilermag.it, 2003

Neen: come puoi capire dal nome, non significa niente che tu possa conoscere.
Così dobbiamo costruire il suo significato dal nulla.

Mai Ueda, *Mai Ueda Times*, 2006

Molte cose Neen mi sono accadute per caso. Non posso spiegarle in maniera chiara…

Angelo Plessas, 2005

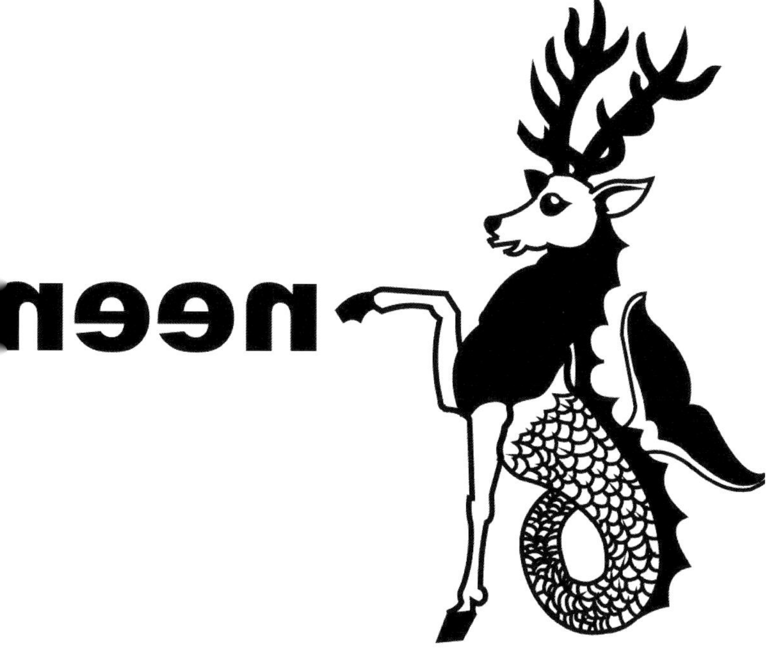

Neen (n-i-n) descrive un movimento artistico che usa o abusa della tecnologia, particolarmente dei computer per
creare risultati artistici piacevoli e imprevisti.

wikipedia.org/wiki/Neen

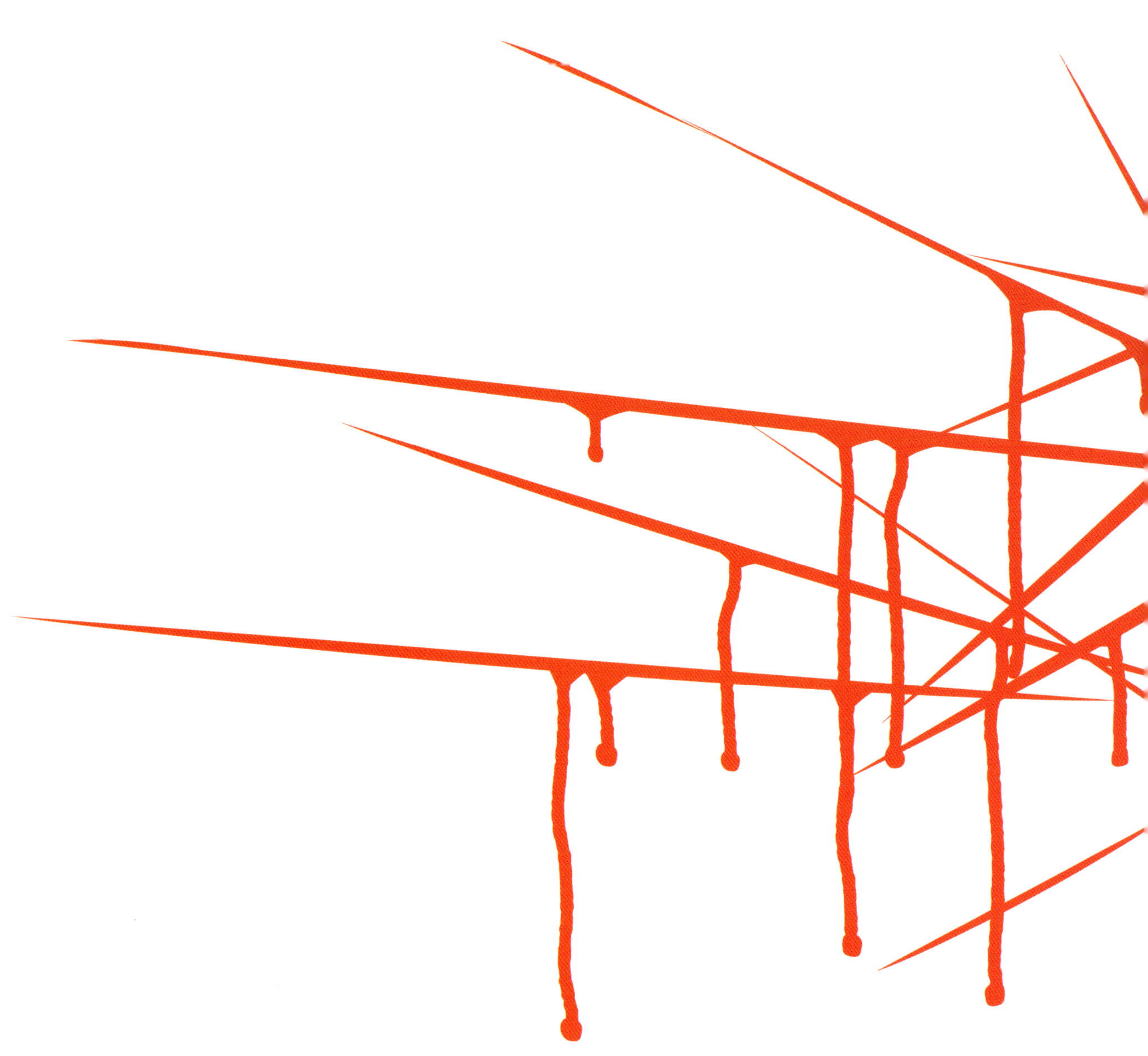

Rafaël Rozendaal, fataltotheflesh.com, 2004

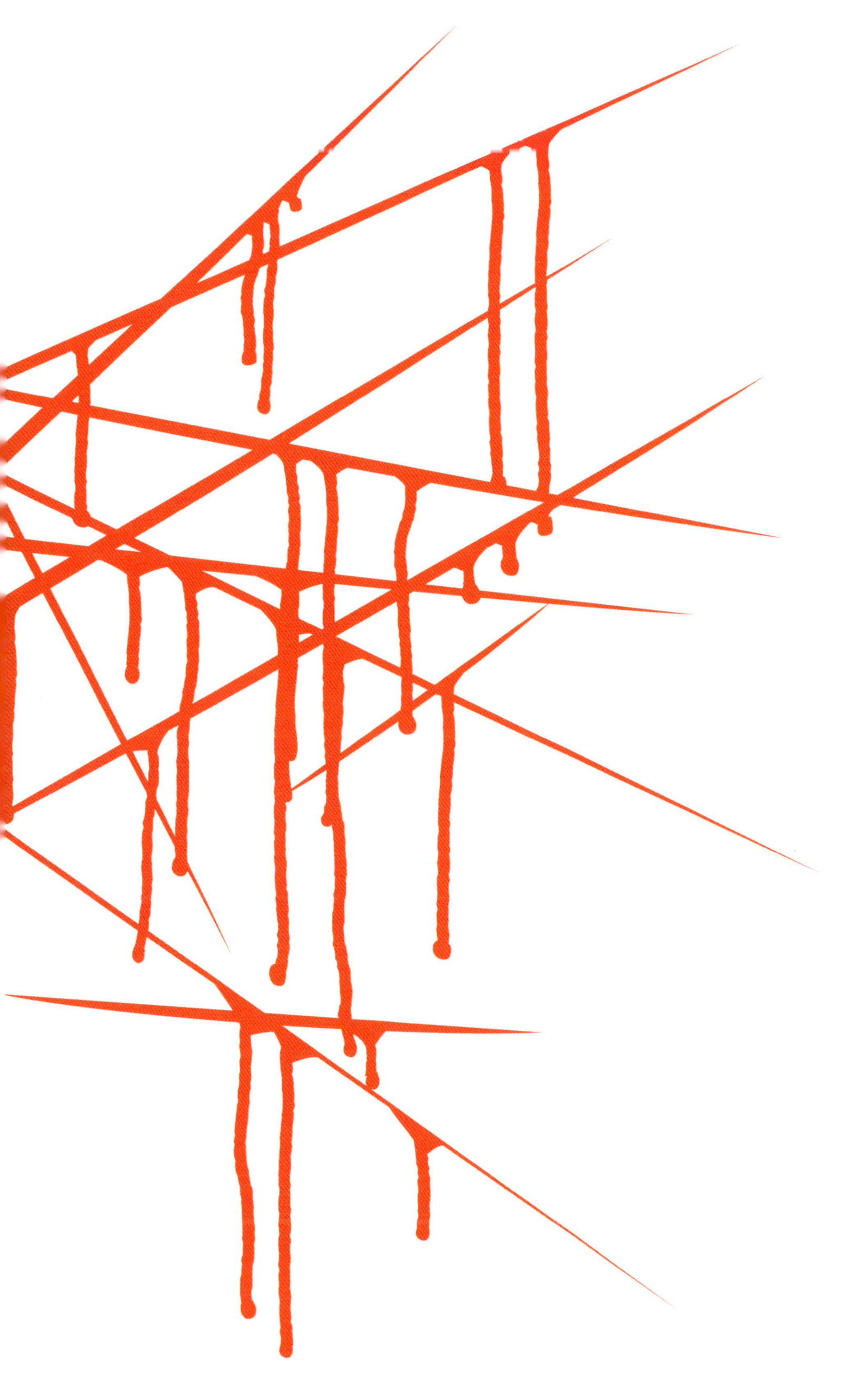

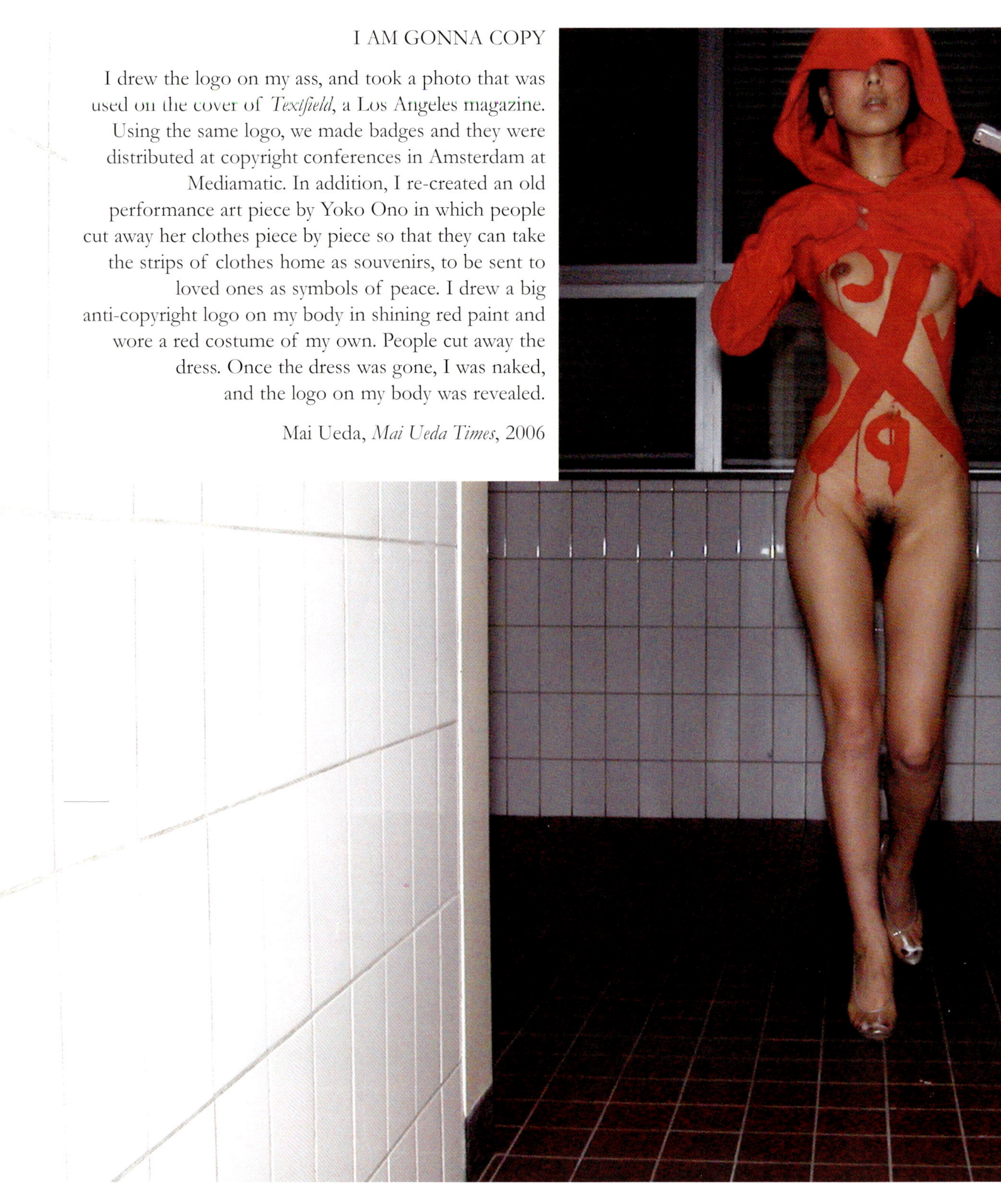

I AM GONNA COPY

I drew the logo on my ass, and took a photo that was used on the cover of *Textfield*, a Los Angeles magazine. Using the same logo, we made badges and they were distributed at copyright conferences in Amsterdam at Mediamatic. In addition, I re-created an old performance art piece by Yoko Ono in which people cut away her clothes piece by piece so that they can take the strips of clothes home as souvenirs, to be sent to loved ones as symbols of peace. I drew a big anti-copyright logo on my body in shining red paint and wore a red costume of my own. People cut away the dress. Once the dress was gone, I was naked, and the logo on my body was revealed.

Mai Ueda, *Mai Ueda Times*, 2006

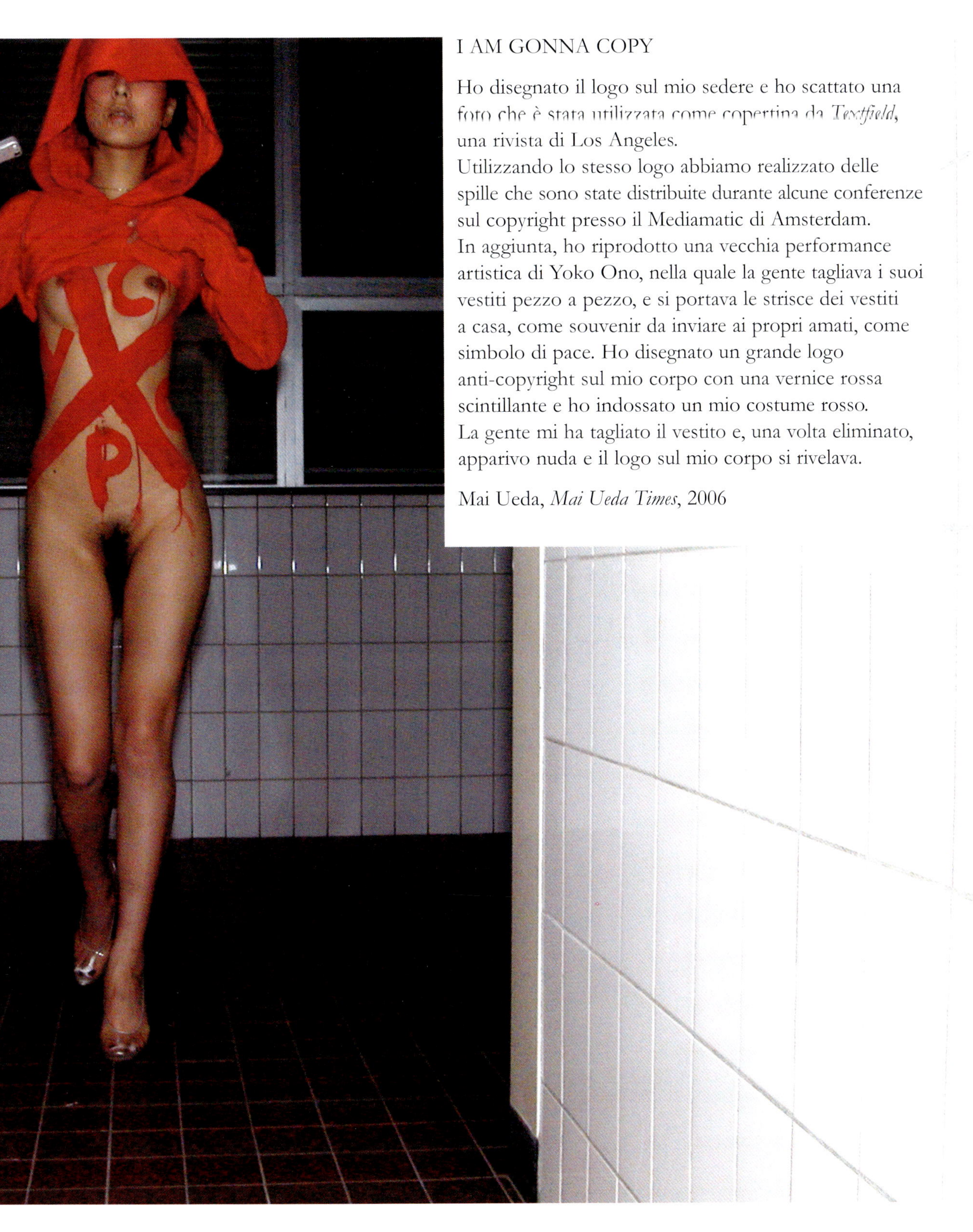

I AM GONNA COPY

Ho disegnato il logo sul mio sedere e ho scattato una foto che è stata utilizzata come copertina da *Textfield*, una rivista di Los Angeles.
Utilizzando lo stesso logo abbiamo realizzato delle spille che sono state distribuite durante alcune conferenze sul copyright presso il Mediamatic di Amsterdam.
In aggiunta, ho riprodotto una vecchia performance artistica di Yoko Ono, nella quale la gente tagliava i suoi vestiti pezzo a pezzo, e si portava le strisce dei vestiti a casa, come souvenir da inviare ai propri amati, come simbolo di pace. Ho disegnato un grande logo anti-copyright sul mio corpo con una vernice rossa scintillante e ho indossato un mio costume rosso.
La gente mi ha tagliato il vestito e, una volta eliminato, apparivo nuda e il logo sul mio corpo si rivelava.

Mai Ueda, *Mai Ueda Times*, 2006

DON'T CALL ME ELEPHANT
PRONTO PRONTO DOMANI COME STAI
PONY WHERE ARE YOU,
ARE YOU IN THE BATHROOM?

Songs can be just one line; other parts are decoration made to go with music, so we can just say "lalala" or "fufufu" for the other parts instead. The essence has to be strong enough, so while you sing the "lalala" part people can meditate on the lyrics of the essence part and make their own fantasy while they hear the whole song. We can play with the same idea with existing songs. For example, "Yesterday" of the Beatles would be "Yesterday, lalalalalalalalala, la lalalala lalala lala lala la Yesterday." So you make your own version of "Yesterday." Or it also works with languages you don't understand, for example "lalalalalalalala Emanuelle lalalalala lala . . ."

Mai Ueda, *Mai Ueda Times*, 2006

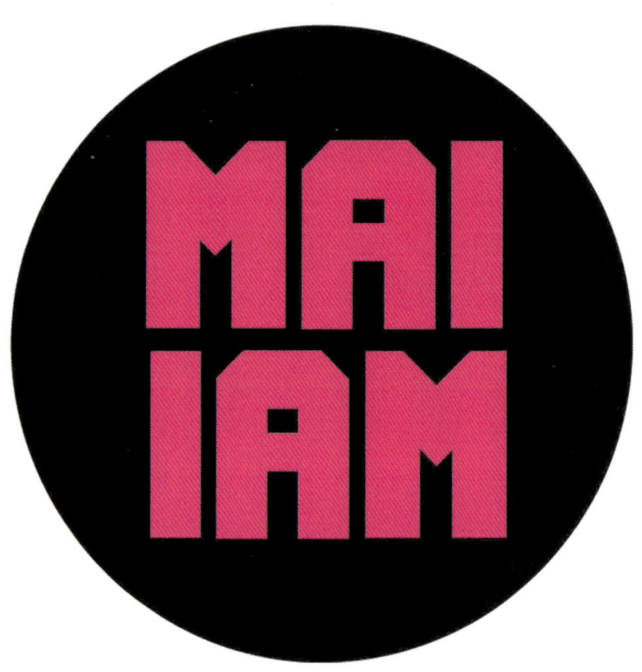

alldaydoingnothing.com
wefollowthesun.com
talkingandwalking.com
itwassummertime.com

from Mai Ueda, *Domain Poem*, Onestar Press, 2005

Domain names are new poems, giving a special award to a word by putting ".com" at the end. Poems having a new rule. It is playing with a limitation to expand the effect, as we did in the old days with the haiku. *Domain Poem* is a collection of sentimental and emotional poems that are presented as dancing domain names in a 150 page book.

Mai Ueda, *Mai Ueda Times*, 2006

Le canzoni possono essere di un solo verso; altre parti sono decorazioni realizzate per accompagnare la musica, così possiamo limitarci a cantare lalala o fufufu in luogo delle altre parti. La parte essenziale deve essere abbastanza forte, così mentre canti la parte lalala, altre persone possono meditare sulle parole della parte essenziale e dare spazio alle proprie fantasie, mentre ascoltano l'intera canzone. Per esempio "Yesterday" dei Beatles fa: "Yesterday, lalalalalalalalala, la lalalala lalala lala lala la Yesterday", così puoi realizzare la tua versione di "Yesterday".
Funziona anche con le lingue che non capisci, per esempio: "lalalalalalalalala Emanuelle lalalalala lala…".

Mai Ueda, *Mai Ueda Times*, 2006

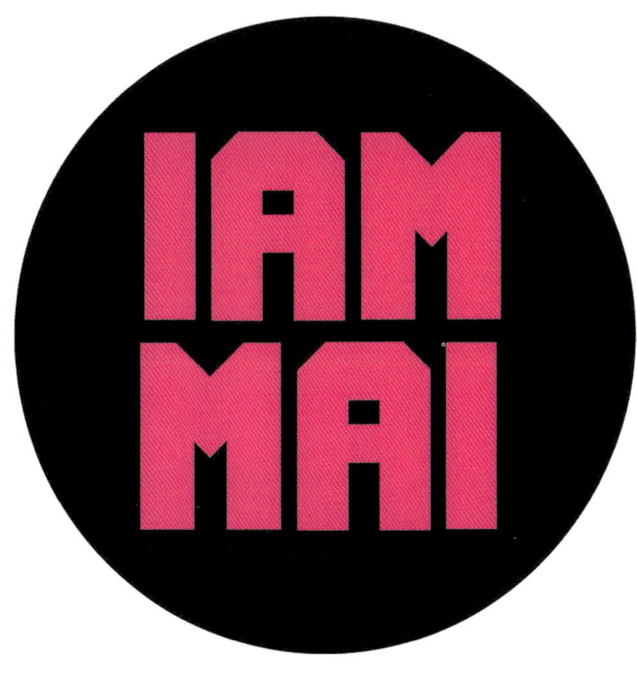

alldaydoingnothing.com
wefollowthesun.com
talkingandwalking.com
itwassummertime.com

da Mai Ueda, *Domain Poem*, Onestar Press, 2005

Il nomi a dominio sono nuove poesie che conferiscono un premio speciale a una parola aggiungendovi un .com alla fine. Una poesia con un nuovo ruolo: è giocare con una limitazione per espanderne l'effetto, come abbiamo fatto in passato con l'haiku. *Domain Poem* è una collezione di poesie sentimentali ed emotive che sono presentate come nomi a dominio, danzanti nelle 150 pagine del libro.

Mai Ueda, *Mai Ueda Times*, 2006

Naming is a major art: it builds the future.
Namingway is the state of mind of a Neenstar, the moment
he comes up with an original name for a Web site or for a concept.
Neen is built on words as much as it is built on aesthetics:
if something sounds nice, it has to be nice;
therefore, it has to be done.

Miltos Manetas

Miltos Manetas, namingway.com, design Rafaël Rozendaal, 2000

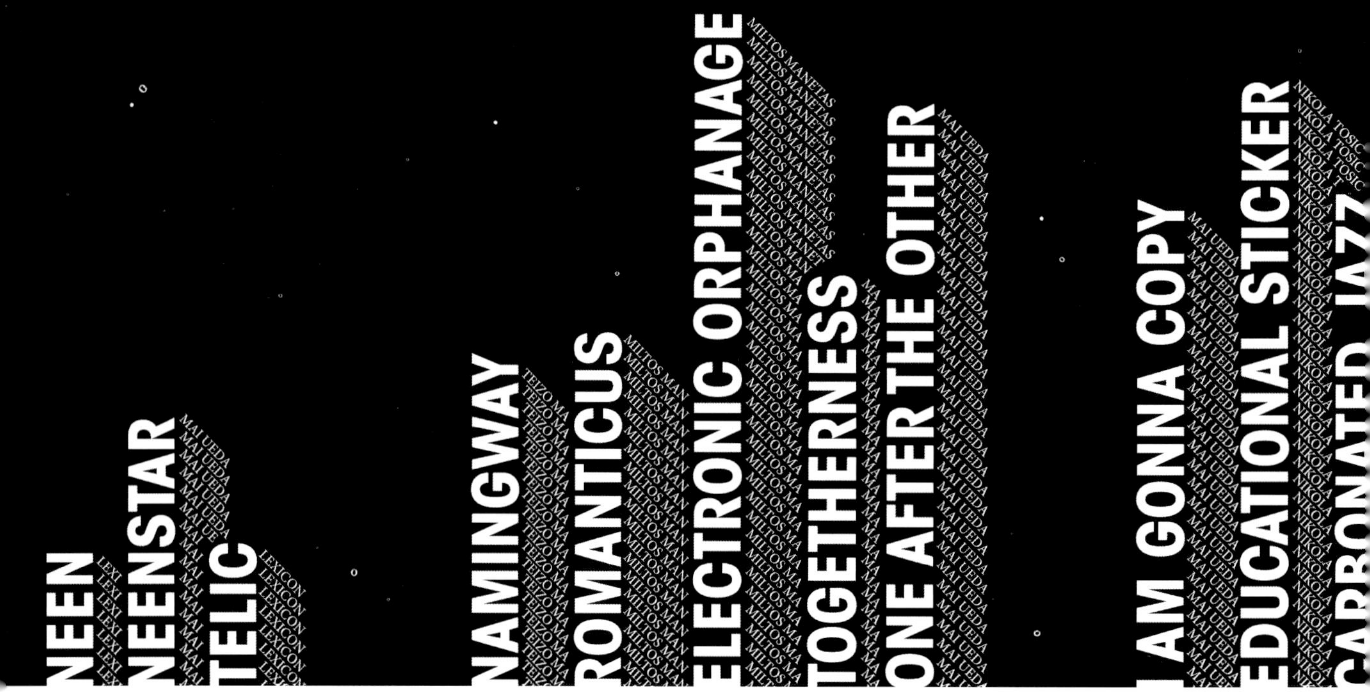

NEEN

NEENSTAR

TELIC

NAMINGWAY

ROMANTICUS

ELECTRONIC ORPHANAGE

TOGETHERNESS

ONE AFTER THE OTHER

AM GONNA COPY

EDUCATIONAL STICKER

CARBONATED JAZZ

BEFORE THE WAR

BROTHER OF VELVET

JURIBOT

AROUND MYSELF

FOURFORTYFOUR MOMENT

AFTERNEEN

BOY IN STATIC

WORLD PLUS PLUS

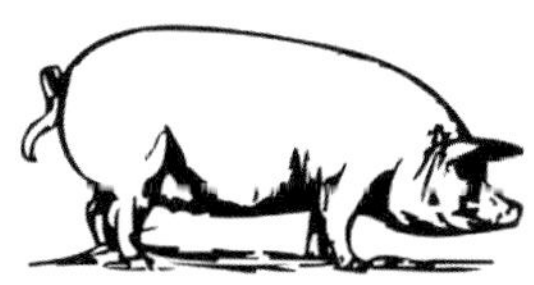

HISTORY OF NEEN

I met Rafael when I came to Rotterdam for a lecture, I was very sick and we did not talk much but he seemed to be very patient about it. We met because we were both neen, as Miltos said. Now Rafael is having this show and he asked me and many of the other neen people to contribute. First I was thinking of writing a whole book because I had some essays I liked and I wanted to write a few more to complete it as a book, but it just did not go well, luckily then a hand of God touched me and I decided to write a short history of neen, short enough to distribute it as a poster.

In order to tell the story of neen, or as much as I know about it, I have to start with 1998 when I enlisted in the Serbian army in Kosovo. Not many people know, but at this point the war in Kosovo was already very alive and there was lots of fighting in the deep woods. Many people from my generation were enlisted in the army and fighting. Of course there was plenty of fighting to be done, but just as in any army - we were mostly snorting cocaine, getting drunk and watching movies on VHS. Sometime we would walk around the woods, and we would hear a noise and fire about several thousand bullets and bombs at it and then run away. And sometimes we would have sex with local girls for money (we would pay them), but since their parents wanted them to marry as virgins - only anal and oral sex was allowed.

One day I got so messed up on drugs and drinks that I fucked this sixteen year from a local village, but in her pussy, and then I got very paranoid that she would get pregnant and that her father would want to kill me, so I ran to the deep woods in the middle of the night alone.

I spent the whole night getting more and more lost and at some point I just fell over and looked at the stars which started moving slowly in circles... I was sure I was losing it, but I liked it, and when I though back about how I got there - I liked it all. I liked everything or, better said, I loved everything: the girl, the drugs, the father, the war, the stars, the whole mess and everything that was good and bad. Everything was loved by me.

But than I heard this horrible noise in the back of my head and in the beginning it was very fuzzy but slowly it became more and more understandable until I realized it was a repeating word. I never heard this word before but it was so powerful yet so simple. It was like a little cute child that had its finger on a button which can destroy the world. I was both terrified and drawn to it.

I never told this story to anyone and most of my friends don't even know I was in the war and that I murdered and raped fellow humans. I was afraid to tell them, and I do not know why, but now I am happy there is a poster about it.

After the war was over I went to live in Milano which is where I met Miltos and Mike and later I met everybody else and that is about when Miltos started saying I am neen. Since than everybody fucked, betrayed, loved and hated everybody else - and it is all just fine.

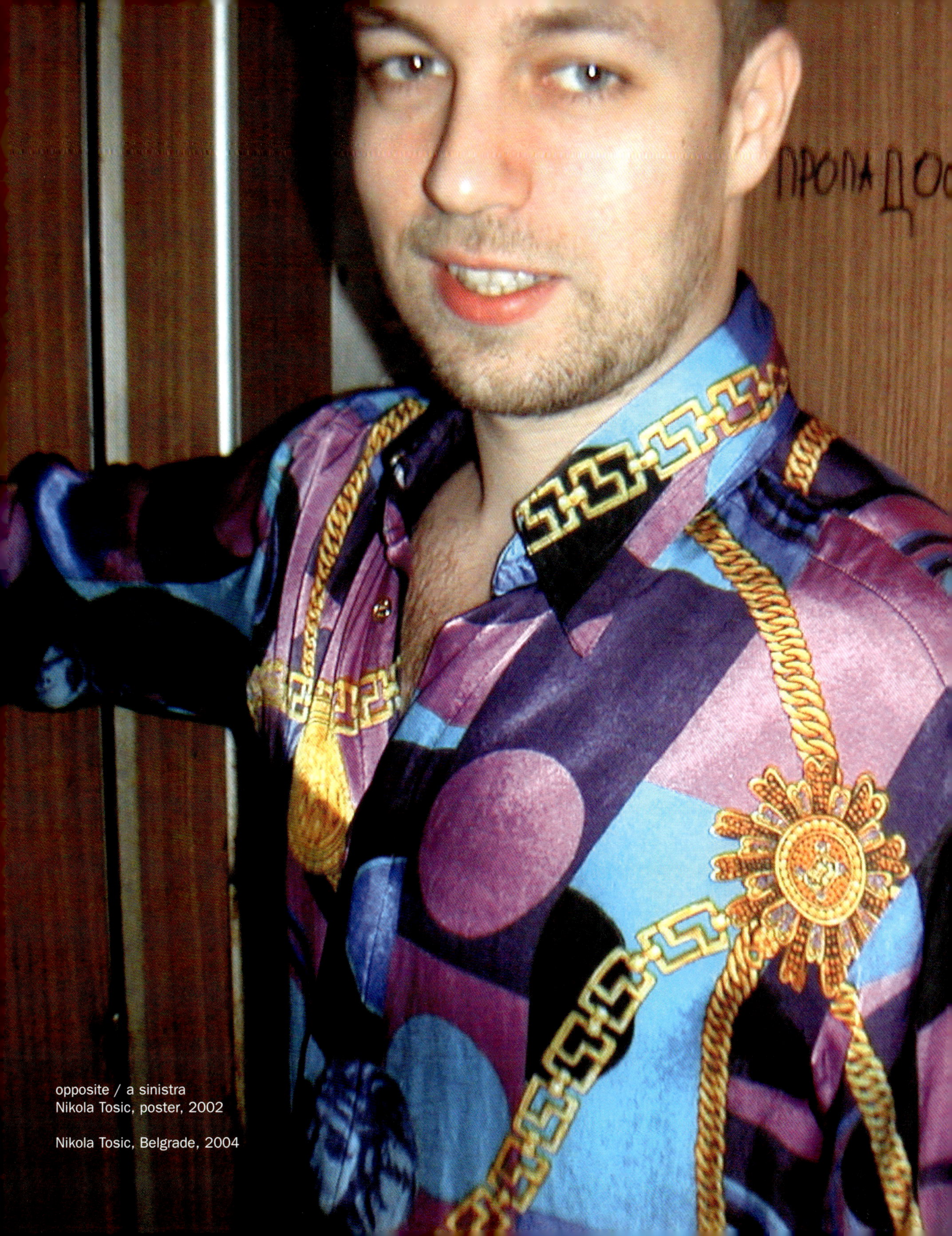

opposite / a sinistra
Nikola Tosic, poster, 2002

Nikola Tosic, Belgrade, 2004

Googlism for: **neen**

neen is not interested about identity

neen is an allen f

neen is a name to evoke a movement

neen is not copyrighted? and i can do anything i want with it? yes

neen is the town that you originally start out in and

neen is one of those initiated

neen is an outgrowth of the northeast energy education network

neen is the first town that you will visit when you reach morrowind

neen is lovely

neen is a state of mind. neen stands for neensters

neen is a connection

neen is the crazy little brother

neen is ein klein gehuchtje

neen is one person who definitely "walks her talk"

neen is in shape in that she has to try to get into the wetsuit by herself

neen is located in kalsnava parish in madona district in the village of aiviekste in a site built at the end of the thirties

neen is fontana

neen is sprake van waarnemingen die duiden op mogelijke bodemverontreiniging?

neen is in de toekomstige situatie de woonfunctie rechtstreeks vanaf de openbare weg toegankelijk? ja/neen

neen is the starting city

neen is a voluntary network that aims to raise awareness of environmental issues and particularly issues around education for sustainable development through

neen is profoundly integrated

neen is profoundly integrated with the chapter sequence of isaiah

neen is de tegenpool van het ja of van de waarheid

neen is a style of art branded by lexicon

neen is a state of mind in a digital world

neen is a good friend and has a very informative site

neen is like "seen"

neen is part of the atlanta krewe

neen is playing the clarinet

neen is a reader, thank you very much

neen is de hygiene van de handen perfect?

neen is telic

neen is under construction; we are collecting theories and samples

neen is a fort in morrowind

neen is hij

neen is daarbij iets bijzonders gebleken? 9b

neen is rallying

neen is encouraging me not to end on this downer of a note

neen is a volunteer run

neen is the partnership of diane and steve camarda

neen is het vooropgestelde onderzoek onderworpen aan de bioveiligheidsnormen maw wordt er gebruik gemaakt van genetisch gemodificeerde

neen is ga dan naar vraag 2

neen is de hond wedstrijdklaar ja/neen is de handler ervaren ja

neen is to promote environmental education at university level

neen is just about

neen is just about the best in the world

neen is

neen is uw strafregister blanco? ja/neen zo niet

neen is aangewezen

neen is gehuurd is mijn

neen is neen

Neen is not a static thing, we cannot really put it down in words. When we will be able to do so,
it will probably become Telic. Like the old miracle of Jesus walking on water: if he came back today
and he did it again, it would be a sort of "déjà vu," "Jesus as usual." Instead, if he started swimming,
most people would refuse to believe that he is actually Jesus.

Miltos Manetas, 2004

Miltos Manetas, jesusswimming.com, 2001
site projected onto a canvas of the same size as the paintings on display, Yvon Lambert Gallery, New York, January 2006

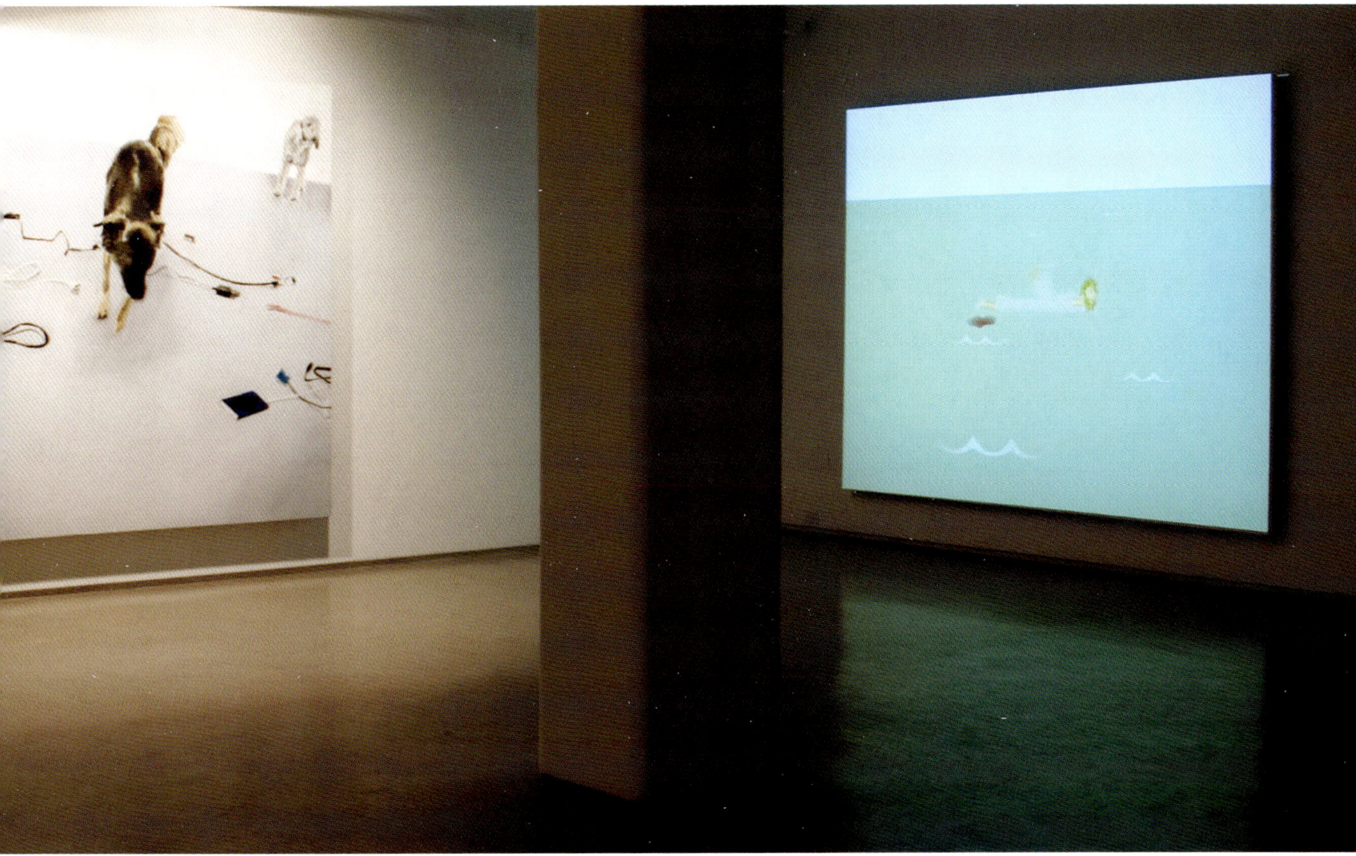

Miltos Manetas, jesusswimming.com, 2001
sito proiettato su una tela delle stesse dimensioni dei dipinti in mostra, Yvon Lambert Gallery, New York, gennaio 2006

Neen non è una cosa statica, non possiamo veramente spiegarlo attraverso le parole. Quando
ne saremo capaci, probabilmente si trasformerà in Telic. Come il vecchio miracolo di Gesù che
cammina sulle acque: se oggi tornasse indietro e lo rifacesse, sarebbe una sorta di già visto,
"il solito Gesù". Se invece cominciasse a nuotare, la maggior parte rifiuterebbe di credere
che si tratta veramente di Gesù.

Miltos Manetas, 2004

NEEN DOGMA OF PAINTING

There was a time when paintings were pretty and fresh things to create, in the same way that Flash animations and Web sites are today. But maybe there is still a way to paint amazing pictures.
Here are the rules of the "Neen Dogma of Painting."

1. To paint a large canvas, buy large brushes. Buy many of them, because you will need clean brushes to smooth the line where the different colors meet. Only oil on canvas is allowed. Never mix the colors with anything else than linseed oil. That should give to your paintings the "glossiness" of a computer screen.

2. Use a projector to display the picture you want to paint on the canvas.
If you know how to draw, do not make paintings: make Flash animations instead.

3. Abstract paintings are prohibited unless you invent an "automatic system," such as that of Jackson Pollock or Lucio Fontana. That is always cool because anybody can use their systems and successfully produce Fontana and Pollock pictures. Abstract art is interesting only when it originates from a machine or from a person who emulates a machine.

4. Use the most expensive material so you will feel the urgency to make something valuable in order to get your money back.

5. Composition, colors, and the size of the painting should always be copied from other paintings in museums.

6. Deal with the brushstroke as if you were a hairdresser.

7. You should use assistants as much as possible. They should have no experience or any interest in painting. Just hire the people whose features match the characters you want to paint and ask them to fill your canvas as if they were painting a wall: without any passion. Command your assistants to use the wrong color so you will feel the urgency of taking over and saving the work from them.

8. Paint many pictures at the same time and let them dry before you apply new layers of color. Sometimes, you'll notice that the color you have prepared for a painting should go to another painting instead. A picture may take many years until it is completed, and actually, it's not even your job to finish it. If people want to buy it before it's done, just sell it to them.

9. Make copies of your most important paintings and permit others to copy them. The most important painters of the past were making copies and that's why their work has survived today.

10. The most important instruction: try to discover and represent something that has never been painted before. If you find such a subject, you will produce a masterpiece, whatever the manner you may use to paint it.

The "Neen Dogma of Painting" was written by Miltos Manetas, on the occasion of the 50. Venice Biennale, curated by Francesco Bonami in 2003.

Published on francescobonami.com

IL DOGMA NEEN DELLA PITTURA

C'era un tempo nel quale i dipinti erano cose fresche e carine da creare, alla stessa maniera
in cui lo sono oggi le animazioni in Flash e i siti Web. Ma forse si possono ancora dipingere quadri
sorprendenti. Ecco le regole del "dogma neen della pittura".

1. Per dipingere una grossa tela, compra grossi pennelli. Comprane molti perché avrai bisogno
di pennelli puliti per smussare le linee dove si incontrano i differenti colori.
Solo i colori a olio sono consentiti sulla tela. Non mischiare mai i colori con qualcosa di differente
dall'olio di semi di lino. Questo dovrebbe dare ai tuoi dipinti la patinatura dello schermo di un computer.

2. Usa un proiettore per visualizzare il quadro che vuoi dipingere sulla tela. Se sai dipingere, non fare
quadri: realizza invece animazioni in Flash.

3. Dipinti astratti sono proibiti a meno che non inventi un "sistema automatico", come quelli di
Jackson Pollock e di Lucio Fontana. Questo funziona sempre perché tutti possono usare i loro sistemi
e produrre con successo i quadri tipo quelli di Fontana e di Pollock. L'arte astratta è interessante solo
quando trae origine da una macchina o da una persona che emula una macchina.

4. Utilizza il materiale più costoso, così sentirai l'urgenza di realizzare qualcosa di valore allo scopo di
recuperare le tue spese.

5. Composizione, colori e grandezza del dipinto devono sempre essere copiati da altri dipinti esposti in musei.

6. Accordati con la pennellata come se fossi un parrucchiere.

7. Devi utilizzare assistenti più che puoi. Questi non devono avere esperienza o alcun interesse nella
pittura. Limitati a ingaggiare persone le cui caratteristiche si sposano con i personaggi che vuoi
dipingere e chiedi loro di riempire le tue tele come se stessero dipingendo un muro: senza alcuna
passione. Impartisci ai tuoi assistenti l'ordine di usare il colore sbagliato così sentirai l'urgenza di
riprendere il controllo e di salvare il lavoro.

8. Dipingi tanti quadri nello stesso momento e lasciali asciugare prima di applicare nuovi livelli
di colore. Qualche volta, ti accorgerai che il colore che hai preparato per un dipinto dovrebbe invece
andare su un altro. Un dipinto può impiegare diversi anni per essere completato e, in realtà, finirlo non
è nemmeno il tuo lavoro. Se qualcuno vuole comprarlo prima che sia finito, semplicemente vendiglielo.

9. Realizza copie dei tuoi dipinti più importanti e consenti ad altri di copiarli. I maggiori pittori del
passato hanno realizzato copie e questo è il motivo per il quale i loro lavori sono sopravvissuti
sino a oggi.

10. L'istruzione più importante: prova a scoprire e rappresentare qualcosa che non è mai stata dipinta
prima. Se trovi un tale soggetto produrrai un capolavoro, qualsiasi sia la modalità che hai adottato per
dipingerlo.

"Dogma neen della pittura" è stato scritto da Miltos Manetas in occasione della 50. Biennale di
Venezia, curata da Francesco Bonami nel 2003.

Pubblicato in francescobonami.com

Neen is a venture. Neen is Fluxus. Neen is something else. Neen is really something else Neen is yeah Neen is my life. Neen is A four-letter word Neen is nothing really. Neen is gay. Neen is gay. Neen is NEEN. NEEN IS NOT Neen is STYLE Neen is IS A RAINBOW. Neen is Mai. Neen is cute. Neen is what I care. Neen is flower. Neen is better than sex? Neen is the world Neen is the world Neen Is moment Neen is fashion. Neen is useful. Neen is so much fun. Neen is singing. Neen is a trip. Neen is BORING. Neen is fucking a girl in the pussy. Neen is something that you do when you have no other utilities. Neen is going to end soon. Neen spelled backwards is een. Neen is a demo. Neen is FOR PEOPLE WHO ARE PEOPLE. Neen is NOT WHAT YOU THINK IT IS. Neen is NOT FOR YOU. Neen is TOO MUCH. Neen is IN. Neen is NOTHING MORE THAN NEEN. Neen is NOTHING MORE THAN EVERYTHING. Neen is MADE MOSTLY FOR TALL PEOPLE. Neen is Bigger than you. Neen is ANGELO WHEN HE IS A BITCH. Neen is taller than steven is. Neen is a motherfucker. Neen is i don't know yet. Neen is what i know it is but you do not know. Neen is not me. Neen is giving me the maybes. Neen is biger than Neen is bigger than Baldessari. Neen is okay here. Neen is something bitter. Neen is something beautiful. Neen is fuck me. Neen is schkolne Neen is all bunches of stuff Neen is neen new Neen is wishes he was newstoday.com Neen is MILTOS AND MILTOS IS A CON ARTIST. Neen is scam. Neen is A SCAM RUN BY A WANNABE ARTIST NAMED MILTOS. Neen is GAY. Neen is A RIP OF NEWSTODAY.COM. Neen is Neen is Neen is Neen is a palindrome. Neen is not negative. Neen is sad. Neen is sexy. Neen is wishful thinking. Neen is OLD. Neen is BOARDING IN POWDER. Neen is blubber. Neen is not for married people. Neen is a tall guy. Neen is dead. Neen is USELESS. Neen is A MASTURBATION. Neen is GAY Neen is RETARDED Neen is NOT ART IT IS SHIT. Neen is A JOKE. Neen is A REALLY LAME NAME AND A LAME SITE. Neen is A FUCKING JOKE. MILTOS IS A FRAUD AND WISHES HE WAS AN ARTIST. HE RIPPED THIS SITE OFF OF NEWSTODAY.COM AND RIPS OFF ASPIRING ARTISTS AND DESIGNERS TO BUILD A NAME FOR HIMSELF. DO NOT BELIEVE THIS MAN. HE NEEDS TO BE SLAPPED LIKE A LITTLE BITCH. Neen is some artistic bullshit.Neen is FAG. Neen is NOT FOR ME. Neen is GANGSTA SHIT... Neen is theft. Neen is KIND OF FUN. Neen is PHOJEKT.COM Neen is IS BETTER THAN YOU. Neen is IS MY PENIS IN YOUR MOUTH. Neen is IS THE FUTURE OF MY *** IN YOUR MOUTH. Neen is IN NAPLES.Neen is FREE PORN! FREE PORN! FREE PORN! Neen is GIRLS WHO LOVE ***. Neen is GIRLS WHO... NEEN is FREE XXX PORN XXX GAY XXXX MEN! Neen is REALLY SOMETHING ELSE BUT GAY IN A FAGGOT WAY. NEEN is MILTOS IS IN HIS 30'S WONDERING WHAT HAPPENED TO HIS LIFE Neen is Miltos in 33 still trying to make something of himself. Neen is A STUPID NAME? Neen is SO FUNNY THAT YOU CALL YOURSELVES ARTISTS! HAHAHAHAHA. Neen is A GHOST TOWN THAT NOBODY VISITS Neen is *** Neen is *** Neen is I WOULDNT WANT TO BE NEGATIVE. Neen is A REALLY UGLY SITE Neen is ME. Neen is Francesca. Neen is BLACK. Neen is 4 GUYS. Neen is NEENY. Neen is NEEN IS NEEN IS NEEN IS NEEN IS NEEN IS NEEN IS NEEN IS NEEN IS NEEN IS NEEN IS NEE.. Neen is pink. Neen is downloadng virus. Neen is downloading virus. Neen is transfering virus. Neen is sending you a virus. Neen is fetching virus. Neen is Ween. Neen is DOWNLOADING A VIRUS INTO YOUR COMPUTER. Neen is UPLOADING A VIRUS. Neen is CURRENTLY UPLOADING A VIRUS INTO YOUR HARDDRIVE. Neen is A VIRUS. Neen is COCKSUCKER. Neen is AN ASIAN GIRLFRIEND WHO DOES PERFORMANCE ART. Neen is A KOREAN CHICK WHO DOES PERFORMANCE ART. Neen is GAY. Neen is SLOW. Neen is BORING ASS SHIT. Neen is FUCK OFF. Neen is $50,000, TELIC IS $50,000. Neen is THE BOMB. Neen is WORKING, OR ELSE YOU WOULD NOT BE HERE... Neen is NEEN IS IN YOUR MOUTH... Neen is FUN! BIAAAAATCH! Neen is IN YA MOUTH, BIAATCH! Neen is SO FRESH Neen is THE BOMB Neen is IN YOUR MOUTH...BIAATCH! Neen is COOL. Neen is FUNNY Neen is BETTER THAN NEWSTODAY Neen is GAY PRIDE. RAINBOW ALLIANCE. Neen is CUTE. Neen is SEXY AS FUCK. Neen is FUCKING DOPE. Neen is HAPPY. Neen is WHAT I WANT TO BE. Neen is MAI'S NICE ASS. Neen is STUPID GRAHIC DESIGNERS WORRYING.. Neen is KILROY YORLIK Neen is KILROY WAS HERE, KILROY WAS HERE, KILROY WAS HERE. Neen is SO 2003. Neen is TOTALLY RAD DUDE. Neen is HTTP://WWW.UH-OH.NET. Neen is TALKING SHIT AND REMAINING ANONYMOUS Neen is MIKE CALVERT STOLE $800.00 FROM MU, EINDHOVEN Neen is whatactually is neen? Neen is kissing a pretty girl for the first time Neen is nothing Neen is something. Neen is LOW-CARB. Neen is TYPING IN THIS BOX MESSAGES Neen is TYPING IN THIS BOX MESSAGES Neen is TYPING IN THIS BOX MESSAGES FOR OTHERS TO SEE, NEGATIVE OR POSITIVE Neen is MIKE CALVERT STOLE $800.00 FROM THE MU IN EINDHOVEN

Steven Schkolne, neenis.com, 2005

Neenis started as a piece created by Steven Schkolne for the *NeenToday* show. A year later, Schkolne registered the domain www.neenis.com. A visitor can enter his notion of Neen in this domain and it gets added in the database of the Web site.
Related to this work is www.stupidforum.com by Miltos Manetas, 2003, where you can write
and erase just about anything.

Neenis iniziò come un lavoro creato da Steven Schkolne per la mostra *NeenToday*. Un anno dopo Schkolne registrò il dominio www.neenis.com. Chiunque può inserire in questo dominio la sua definizione di Neen che verrà aggiunta al database del sito.
In relazione con questo lavoro è anche www.stupidforum.com di Miltos Manetas, 2003, dove la gente
può scrivere/cancellare quello che vuole.

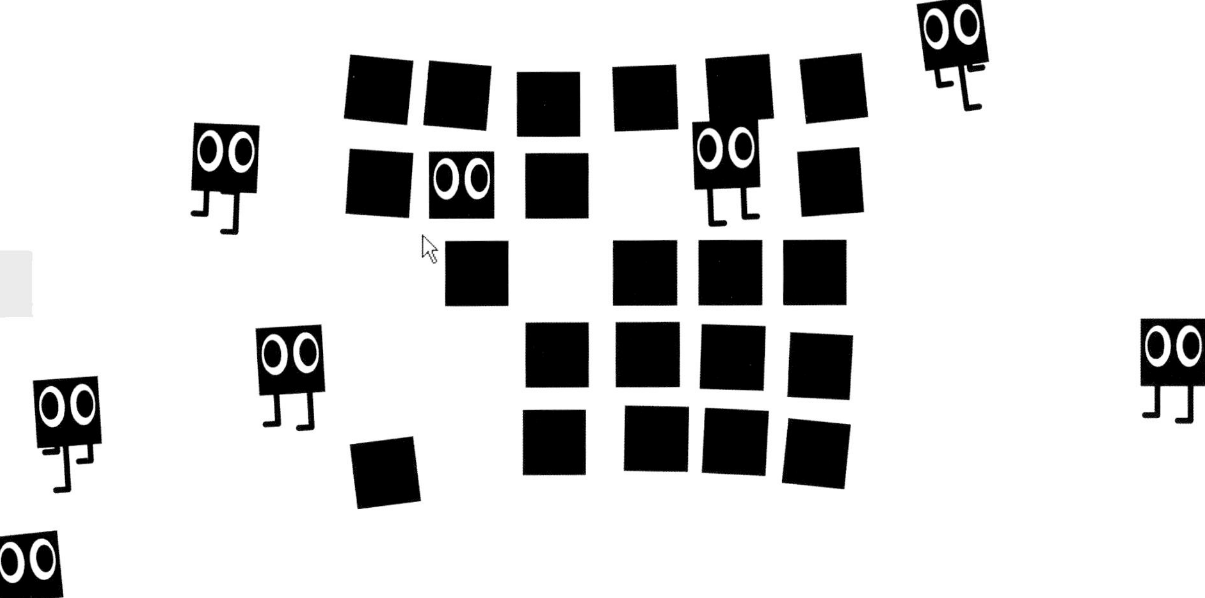

Joel Fox, thisisneen.com, 2004

Bob Dobbs (a friend of Marshall McLuhan) said: "Advertising is communication between machines." He also suggested that machines came alive in 1967 and that "now they are in an angelic state." According to him, "advertising is communication between angels."

Miltos Manetas, "Web Sites Is the Art of Our Times," *Distant Explosions*, 2004

Bob Dobbs (un amico di Mrshall McLuhan) disse: "La pubblicità è comunicazione tra macchine". Egli inoltre ha rilevato che le macchine hanno cominciato a sviluppare una propria vita nel 1967 e che "ora sono in uno stato angelico". Dunque "pubblicità è comunicazione tra angeli".

Miltos Manetas, "I siti Web sono l'arte del nostro tempo", *Distant Explosions*, 2004

angelidakis.com, Andreas Angelidakis, 1999

angelosays.com, Angelo Plessas, 2005

angleviner.com, Joel Fox, 2002

athrowofthedicecannotabolishchange.com, Angelo Plessas, 2002

brotherofvelvet.com, John White C., 2002, Collection Miltos Manetas

dearyvon.com, Miltos Manetas, 2006, Collection Yvon Lambert

educational-sticker.com, Nikola Tosic, 2000

elasticenthusiastic.com, Angelo Plessas, 2004, Collection Miltos Manetas

everythingyouseeisinthepast.com, Rafaël Rozendaal, 2002

fataltotheflesh.com, Rafaël Rozendaal, 2004, Collection Miltos Manetas

fourfortyfour.com, Miltos Manetas, 2002, animation Geoff Stearns

futureisfake.com, Angelo Plessas, 2003

googlism.com, Googlism Inc, 2002

halfofthesky.com, Priscilla Vaccari, 2006

heelsandballs.com, Angelo Plessas, 2003

iamveryverysorry.com, Rafaël Rozendaal, 2002

itsout.org, Scott Snibbe, 2003

iwannabuysomeclothes.com, Mai Ueda, 2002, Collection Art Production Fund

jacksonpollock.org, Miltos Manetas, 2003

jesusswimming.com, Miltos Manetas, 2001, animation Joel Fox, music Gnac

kosuth.com, Miltos Manetas, 2006

maninthedark.com, Aaron Clinger and Miltos Manetas, 2003

melookingatyou.com, Angelo Plessas, 2005

nakituminayashi.com, Nikola Tosic, 2002

namingway.com, Miltos Manetas, 2000

neenis.com, Steven Schkolne, 2005

nosquito.biz, Rafaël Rozendaal, 2005

oneaftertheother.com, Angelo Plessas, 2002

philosophyinthebedroom.com, Mai Ueda, 2002

pornolize.com, Pornolize, 2000

romanticus.com, Mai Ueda, 2001

schkolnenumber.com, Steven Schkolne, 2004

shenevertoldherlove.com, Angelo Plessas, 2005

slightlymovedaway.com, Priscilla Vaccari, 2006

stupidforum.com, Miltos Manetas, 2003

theendofreason.com, Rafaël Rozendaal, 2004

thisisamagazine.com, *This Is a Magazine*, 2002

thisisdoreen.com, Miltos Manetas, 2003, Collection Doreen Remen

thisisneen.org, Joel Fox, 2004

tiptoebehavior.com, Angelo Plessas, 2005, Collection Priscilla Vaccari

thoughtsofafishinthedeepsea.com, Angelo Plessas, 2005

togetherness.org, Mai Ueda, 2002

tryingsohard.net, Angelo Plessas, 2003

youngboysatmidnight.com, Tobias Bernstrup, 2005

wewillattack.com, Rafaël Rozendaal, 2002

whitneybiennial.com, Miltos Manetas, 2002

wronghuman.com, Angelo Plessas, 2004

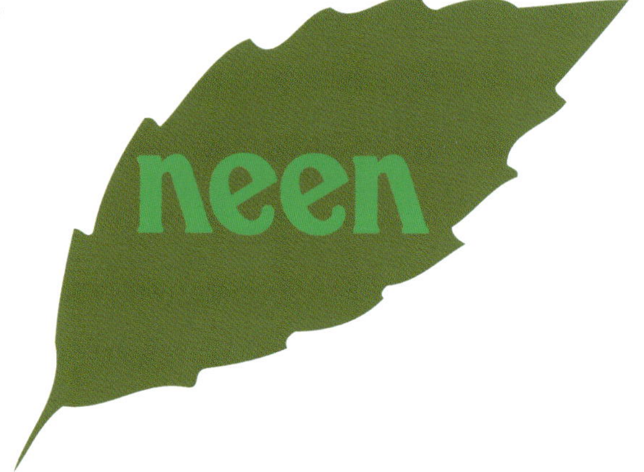

Neen è parola bifronte. Neen, come Giano, contiene il ciclo del tempo e della vita e perciò il futuro dell'arte.

Giacinto Di Pietrantonio, 2006

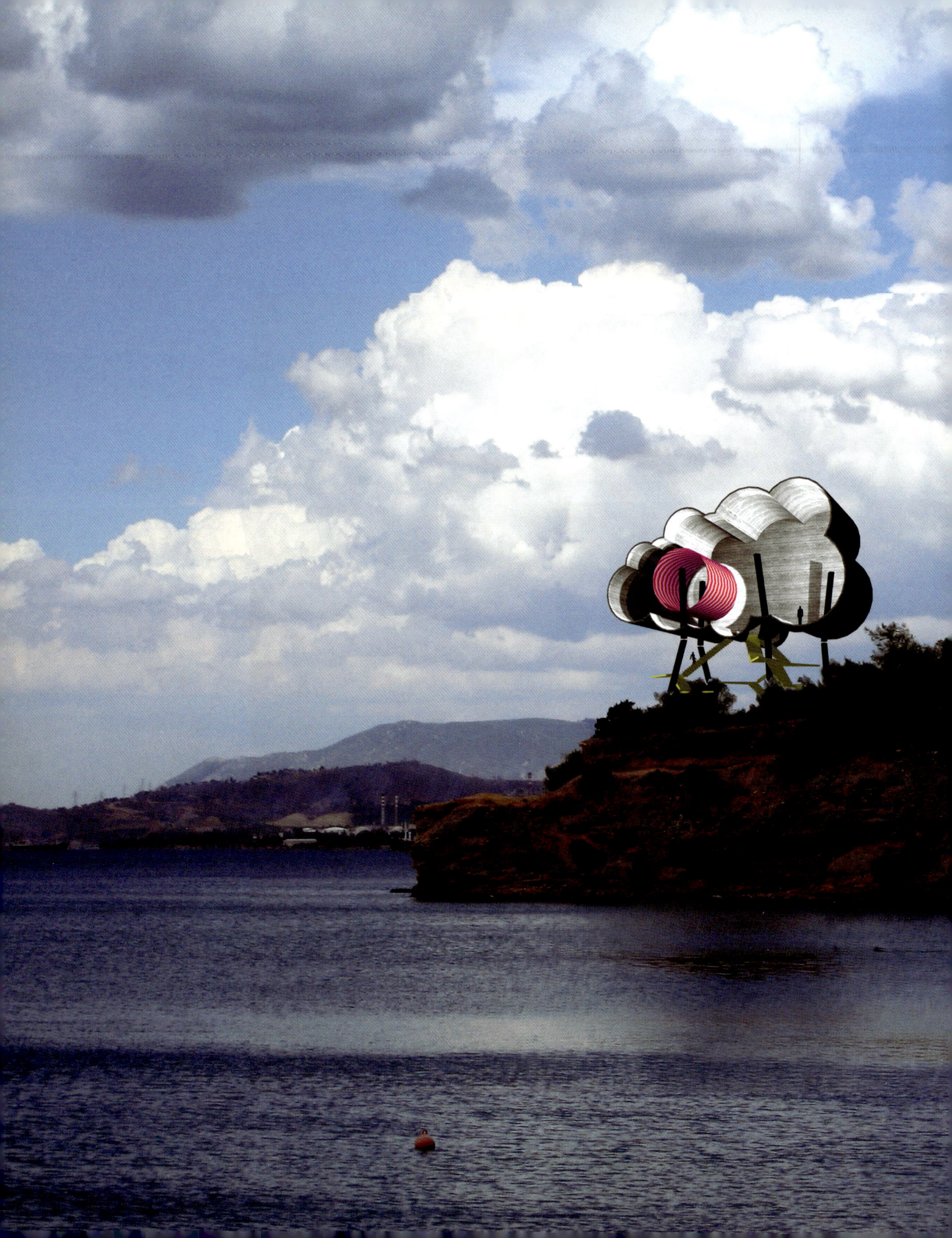

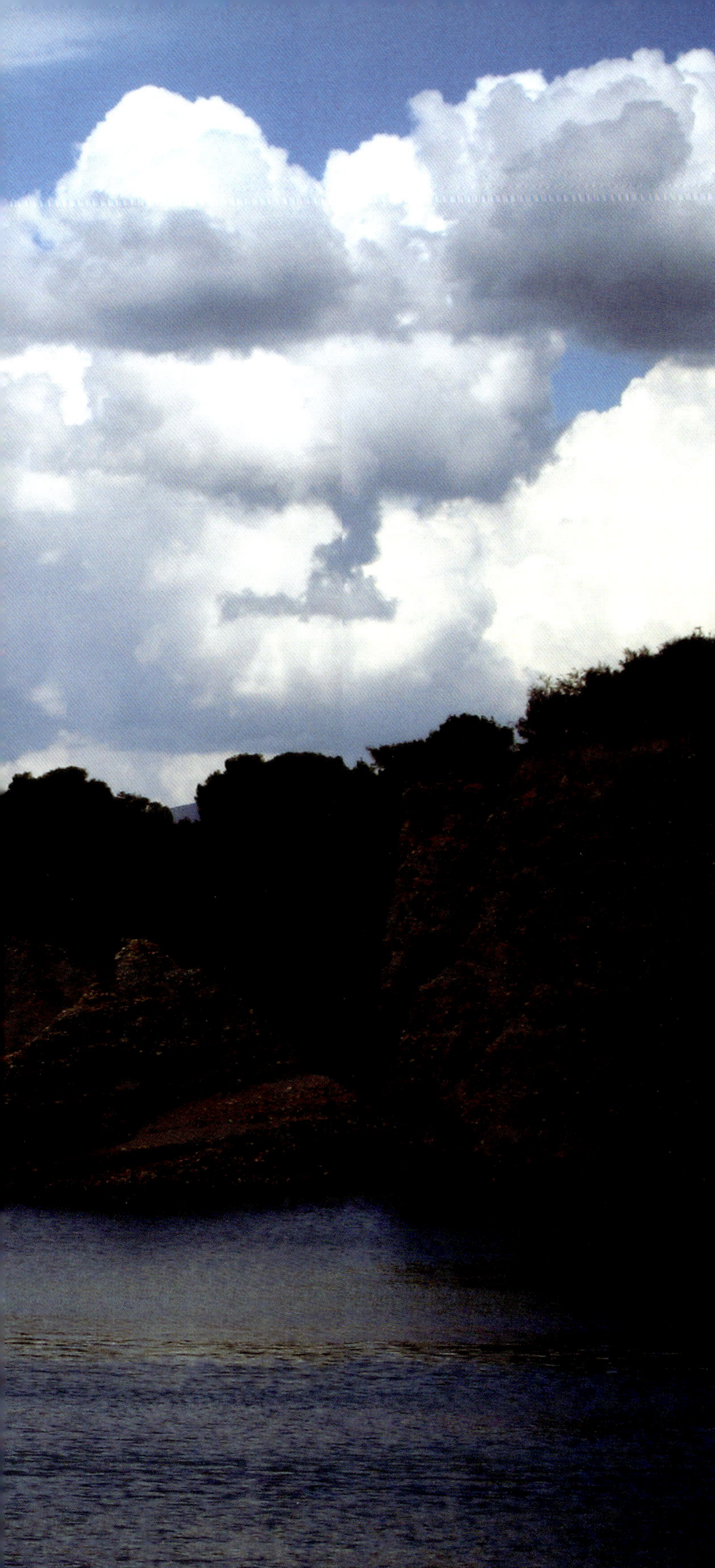

Cloud is a house from the series Neen
Homes: the shape of the cloud
is derived from whywashesad.com,
while the form is based on a model
of the house that I grew up in.

Andreas Angelidakis, 2005

Cloud è una casa della serie
Neen Homes: la forma della nuvola
deriva da whywashesad.com,
mentre la struttura si ispira alla casa
in cui sono cresciuto.

Andreas Angelidakis, 2005

I AM
VERY
VERY
VERY
SORRY

I actually know for sure that there are scenes
on the Internet that nobody knows
about and nobody cares about,
and within those milieus, very specialized
sensibilities are evolving.

from an interview by Eric S. Elkins
with William Gibson, ugo.com, 2003

So di per certo che ci sono scenari
in Internet che nessuno conosce e di cui
nessuno si occupa, e all'interno di questi
territori, si evolvono sensibilità
molto speciali.

da un'intervista di Eric S. Elkins
con William Gibson, ugo.com, 2003

Andreas Angelidakis, angelidakis.com, architect, Greece/Denmark NeenWorld

Boyinstatic, boyinstatic.com, composer, USA

Tobias Bernstrup, visual artist, pop star, Sweden

Mike Calvert, designer, USA

Carbonated Jazz, carbonatedjazz.com, visual artist, USA

John White C. (John White Cerasulo), visual artist, USA

David David, visual artist, UK

Deconcept (Geoff Stearns), deconcept.com, software developer, USA

Essetesse, composer, USA

Joel Fox, magicrobot.org, visual artist, USA

Marc Kremers, visual artist, UK

Benjamin Loya, benjaminloya.com, visual artist, France

Miltos Manetas, manetas.com, visual artist, Greece/USA

Rob Montgomery, robertmontgomery.org, visual artist, UK

Angelo Plessas, angeloplessas.com, visual artist, Greece/USA

Dusty Puree, Internet creator, USA

Rafaël Rozendaal, newrafael.com, visual artist, the Netherlands

Steven Schkolne, schkolne.com, visual artist, USA

Scott Sonna Snibbe, visual artist, USA

Nikola Tosic, tosic.com, visual artist, Serbia

Mark Tranmer (Gnac), marktranmer.com, music composer, UK

Aki Tsuyuko, music composer, Japan

Mai Ueda, maiueda.com, visual artist, Japan/USA

Priscilla Vaccari, priscillaispriscilla.com, visual artist, Italy

Design Coordination / Coordinamento grafico
Gabriele Nason

Editorial Coordination / Coordinamento redazionale
Filomena Moscatelli with / con Sergio Di Stefano

Editing of English Texts / Redazione dei testi inglesi
Emily Ligniti

Copywriting and Press Office / Copy e Ufficio stampa
Silvia Palombi Arte&Mostre, Milano

Web Design and Online Promotion / Grafica Web e promozione on line
Barbara Bonacina

Cover
Miltos Manetas, jesusswimming.com, 2001
Courtesy Yvon Lambert Gallery, New York

We apologize if, due to reasons wholly beyond our control, some of
the photo sources have not been listed.
Ci scusiamo se per cause indipendenti dalla nostra volontà abbiamo
omesso alcune referenze fotografiche.

No part of this publication may be reproduced, stored in a retrieval
system, or transmitted in any form or by any means without the prior
permission in writing of copyright holders and of the publisher.
Nessuna parte di questo libro può essere riprodotta o trasmessa in
qualsiasi forma o con qualsiasi mezzo elettronico, meccanico o altro
senza l'autorizzazione dei proprietari dei diritti e dell'editore.

© 2006
Edizioni Charta, Milano
© Galleria Pack, Milano
© The artists for their works / Gli artisti per le opere
© The authors for their texts / Gli autori per i testi

Photo Credits / Referenze fotografiche
© Todd Eberle
© Elisa Leaci
© Armin Linke
© Isabella Rozendaal

All rights reserved

ISBN 88-8158-601-0

Edizioni Charta
via della Moscova, 27
20121 Milan
Tel. +39-026598098/026598200
Fax +39-026598577
e-mail: edcharta@tin.it
www.chartaartbooks.it

Printed in Italy

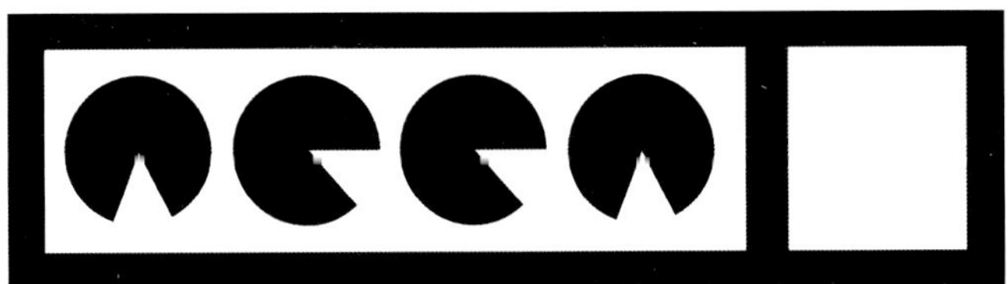

Editor / Curatore
Miltos Manetas

Graphic Design / Progetto grafico
Angelo Plessas, Rafaël Rozendaal

Graphic Design Neen Manifesto / Grafica Manifesto Neen
Experimental Jetset

Editing and Editorial Coordination / Redazione e coordinamento editoriale
Federica Cimatti

Layout / Impaginazione
Alessandra Mancini

Translations / Traduzioni
Vito Campanelli, Fabio Paracchini

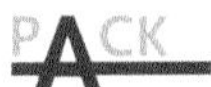

Produced by Galleria Pack, Milan, on the occasion of the *SuperNeen* show
Prodotto dalla Galleria Pack, Milano, in occasione della mostra *SuperNeen*
Allestimenti Artinbox, Torino

March 7 – April 22, 2006 / 7 marzo - 22 aprile 2006

Thanks to / Si ringraziano
Giampaolo Abbondio, Susanna Artico, Isabelle Arvers, John Perry Barlow, Bruno Barsanti, Stefania Bortolani,
Jessica Boukris, Breeder Projects, Davide Carlesso, Stefano Chiodi, Claude Closky, Antonio Colombo,
Gianmaria Conti, Juliane Debeusscher, Jeffrey Deitch, Reinier Feijen, Marina Fokides, Madeleine Von Froomer,
Galerie Cosmic, Eleni Gatsou, Franck Gautherot, Ton van Gool, Valery Grancher, Paul Groot, Inmo Gallery,
Xeni Jardin, Konstantin Kakanias, Seung-duk Kim, Yvon Lambert Gallery, Ilias Lefas, M+M Gallery, Lewis Marx,
Christian Moeller, Momus, Gabriela Moragas, MU, Nanogod, Maurizio Navone, Julian Opie, Daniela Palazzoli,
Francesca Pennone, Francesco Petroni, Geraldine Postel, Davide Quadrio, Johanna Rieseneder, Won-il Rhee,
Courtney Ritter, Eduardo Sciammarela, Klaas Speller, Casey Spooner, Nobukazu Takemura, Juri Ueda,
Chihiro Yomono, Steven Weiner, Martin van Zomeren

Special thanks to / Un ringraziamento speciale a
Orazio Goni

neen.org

To find out more about Charta, and to learn
about our most recent publications, visit

Per saperne di più su Charta ed essere
sempre aggiornato sulle novità entra in

www.chartaartbooks.it

Finito di stampare nel marzo 2006
da Tipografia Rumor srl, Vicenza
per conto di Edizioni Charta